SERVICE MANUAL

(2nd Edition)

CONTENTS

TILLER SERVICE SECTION

ENGINE SERVICE SECTION

Published by

TECHNICAL PUBLICATIONS DIV.

INTERTEC PUBLISHING CORPORATION
P.O. BOX 12901, OVERLAND PARK, KS 66212

©Copyright 1985 by Intertec Publishing Corp. Printed in the United States of America.

ARIENS

ARIENS COMPANY
655 West Ryan Street
Brillion, Wisconsin 54110

Model	Engine Make	Engine Series	Engine Horsepower	No. of Forward Speeds	Power Reverse?	Tilling Width (In.)	Drive Type
RT214	B&S	60000	2	1	No	14	Gear
RT320	B&S	80000	3	1	No	20	Gear
RT324	B&S	80000	3	1	No	24	Gear
RT424	B&S	110000	4	1	Yes	24	Gear
RT424X	B&S	110000	4	1	Yes	24	Gear
RT524	B&S	130000	5	2	Yes	24	Gear
RT524S	B&S	130000	5	2	Yes	24	Gear
RT524C	B&S	130000	5	1	No	24	Chain
RT5020	Tec.	H50	5	2	Yes	20	Gear
RT7020	Tec.	H70	7	4	Yes	20	Gear
RT8020	Kohler	K181	8	4	Yes	20	Gear
RT8028	Kohler	K181	8	4	Yes	28	Gear

LUBRICATION

ENGINE

All Models

Refer to appropriate Briggs and Stratton, Tecumseh or Kohler engine section for engine lubrication specifications.

Recommended oil grade is SAE 30 or equivalent. Recommended fuel is either regular or low-lead gasoline having an octane rating of 90 or higher. The use of non-leaded gasolines reduces cylinder head deposits, but could shorten engine valve life if carburetor is adjusted too lean.

WHEELS AND CONTROLS

All Models

Transport wheels on front tine models should be removed at least once a year and repacked with a multi-purpose grease. Pivot shaft on swing handle models should be greased at least once a year with Ariens Moly-Lithium grease or suitable equivalent.

CHAIN DRIVE

Model RT524C

Chain case oil should be checked at least every 25 hours of operation. Recommended lubricant is Ariens L-2 gear lube or suitable equivalent.

To check oil level in chain case place tiller on a level surface. Clean dirt from chain case housing and remove oil level plug (4 – Fig. AR7). Oil level should be at bottom of plug hole. If oil level is low remove fill plug and add oil slowly until it starts to run out of level plug hole, then reinstall plugs.

TINE GEAR CASE

All Models So Equipped

Gear case oil should be checked at least every 10 hours of operation. Recommended lubricant is Ariens L-2 gear lube or suitable equivalent.

To check gear case oil place tiller on a level surface. Clean dirt from around oil level plug (Fig. AR1) and remove plug. Oil level should be at bottom of plug hole. If oil level is low add oil through level hole until oil is flush with bottom of plug hole. Reinstall and tighten plug.

WHEEL DRIVE GEAR CASE

Models 5020, 7020, 8020 and 8028

Gear case oil should be checked at

beginning of every day and should be changed at least once a year. Recommended lubricant is Ariens L-2 gear lube or suitable equivalent.

To check gear case oil place tiller on a level surface. Clean dirt from top of gear case and remove oil level dipstick (1 – Fig. AR2). Oil level should be at full line (2) on dipstick. Add oil through hole if oil level is low. Reinstall dipstick and tighten.

MAINTENANCE

Inspect all fasteners for looseness and retighten as needed. Check control levers, linkage and cables for freedom of movement and excessive play. Inspect drive belt(s) for excessive stretching, wear, cracks or any other damage. Install new belt(s) if needed. Inspect all belt pulleys and renew if damaged or excessively worn.

Fig. AR1 – View of oil level plug for tine gear case. Oil level plug is shown at (1).

Fig. AR2 – View of oil level dipstick (1) for wheel drive gear case. Oil should be maintained at full mark (2).

ADJUSTMENT

CLUTCH CONTROL

Front Tine Models

Adjust clutch by repositioning clutch spring in clutch cable chain (Fig. AR3). Clutch spring should stretch slightly when clutch lever (1) is pulled up against handle bar. Chain should be shortened if spring does not stretch when clutch lever is pulled up.

Rear Tine Models

FORWARD CLUTCH SPRING. Place main clutch lever in forward position. Clutch spring (4–Fig. AR4) should stretch one inch. If spring does not stretch one inch, remove cotter pin (2) and pull adjustment link (3) out of idler bracket. Turn link on threaded rod, then reinstall link in idler bracket. Recheck spring stretch and continue adjustment procedure until one inch stretch is obtained. Install new cotter pin in adjustment link.

REVERSE IDLER. Adjust reverse clutch control by moving idler pulley (5) in or out in idler bracket slot. If tines do not disengage when main clutch lever is moved from reverse to neutral, idler pulley will need to be moved out away from belt. Loosen idler pulley retaining nut (6) and move pulley in slot until proper adjustment is obtained. Tighten nut and recheck for tine disengagement.

DRIVE BELT

Front Tine Models With Slotted Idler Brackets

If proper clutch adjustment cannot be obtained by lengthening or shortening clutch chain, loosen idler pulley retaining nut and slide pulley assembly in slotted bracket. Tighten idler pulley retaining nut and readjust clutch chain. Refer to **CLUTCH CONTROL ADJUSTMENT** section for adjusting procedure.

Rear Tine Models

To adjust belt center distance loosen four cap screws (2–Fig. AR5) securing frame to wheel drive gear case. Turn adjustment screw (1) to tighten or loosen drive belts, then retighten four cap screws. Refer to **CLUTCH CONTROL ADJUSTMENT** section to readjust forward clutch spring and reverse idler.

TINE GEAR CASE ADJUSTMENT

Rear Tine Models

Loosen adjustment cap (24–Fig. AR10) retaining set screw. Tighten cap until snug, then back off cap approximately 1/6 turn. Retighten set screw.

CHANGING FORWARD SPEEDS

Models RT524, RT524S, RT5020, RT7020, RT8020 and RT8028

PULLEY SPEED POSITIONS. Front tine models have one forward drive belt. Rear tine models have two forward drive belts. Inside pulley grooves are for low speed and outside grooves for high speed.

To change belt position disconnect spark plug lead from spark plug, then remove drive belt guard. Start belt out of pulley groove and pull starter rope to assist in removing belt. Reposition belt and pull starter rope to help roll belt in pulley groove. For rear tine models both drive belts must be removed and repositioned. Reinstall drive belt guard, then reconnect spark plug lead.

TRANSMISSION SPEED POSITIONS. Rear tine tiller Models RT7020, RT8020 and RT8028 have a high and low speed position in drive clutch assembly. Refer to Fig. AR6 for lever identification and speed positions. Disengage main clutch lever then select desired wheel drive speed. Engage tine lever, then engage main clutch lever.

OVERHAUL

ENGINE

All Models

Engine model no. is stamped on

Fig. AR3 – View of clutch control components for front tine tillers.

1. Clutch lever
2. Spring
3. Chain
4. Clutch cable

Fig. AR4 – View of clutch control components and drive belt(s) arrangement for Models RT5020, RT7020, RT8020 and RT8028.

1. Forward idler pulley assy.
2. Cotter pin
3. Adjustment link
4. Clutch spring
5. Reverse idler pulley assy.
6. Retaining nut
7. Reverse drive belt
8. Forward drive belts

Fig. AR5 – View of belt(s) center distance adjustment parts for Models RT5020, RT7020, RT8020 and RT8028.

1. Adjustment screw
2. Cap screws

Fig. AR6 – View of wheel drive and tine engagement levers and operating procedure.

1. Wheel drive engagement lever
2. Tine engagement lever

blower housing for Briggs and Stratton engines. Engine make and series no. is marked on data plate attached to engine for Kohler and Tecumseh engines. Refer to appropriate Briggs and Stratton, Kohler or Tecumseh engine section for overhaul procedures.

CHAIN CASE

Model RT524C

OIL SEAL INSTALLATION. Remove tines from tine shaft, then use seal puller to remove outer and inner seals from case hub. Clean tine shaft with emery cloth. Install inner seal with lip facing toward inside and outer seal with lip facing toward outside. Drive new seals in until outer seal is flush with case hub.

INSPECTION. Refer to Fig. AR7 for parts breakdown and identification. Inspect and renew all components that are worn or damaged. Install new gasket and seals. Lubricate chains, sprockets and bearings with a light film of gear lube during reassembly. Keep all dirt and foreign matter out of chain case during reassembly. Refer to LUBRICATION section for lubrication requirements after reassembly and installation.

TINE GEAR CASE

Models RT214, RT320, RT324 and RT424

OIL SEAL INSTALLATION. Remove tines from tine shaft. Using a screwdriver, pry seal out of case hub. Clean tine shaft with emery cloth. Drive new seal in until seal face is flush with case hub.

INSPECTION. Refer to Fig. AR8 for parts breakdown and identification. Remove bearing flange (9) securing bolts and remove flange (9) and gasket (8). Remove oil level plug (11), then turn adjustment plug (17) out of gear case. Remove Woodruff Key (21) from worm shaft (20) and push worm shaft assembly out of gear case. Remove tine shaft (5) and gear (4) from gear case. Be sure that gasket (16) is removed.

Inspect and renew all components that are worn or damaged. Install new gaskets and seals. Lubricate gears and bearings with a light film of gear lube during reassembly. Keep all dirt and foreign matter out of gear case during reassembly. Adjust worm shaft end play by turning adjustment plug (17) in until gasket (16) is compressed, then continue to tighten until plug indentation is aligned with hole for oil plug (11). Do not back off adjustment plug to obtain alignment.

Refer to LUBRICATION section after reassembly and installation.

Models RT424X, RT524 and RT524S

OIL SEAL INSTALLATION. Remove tines from tine shaft, then remove seal from case hub. Clean tine shaft with emery cloth. Drive new seal in until seal face is flush with case hub.

INSPECTION. Refer to Fig. AR9 for parts breakdown and identification. Remove bearing flange (9) securing bolts and remove flange (9) and gasket (8). Remove tine shaft (2) assembly. Pry dust cap (21) out of gear case, then remove snap ring (20). Tap input end of worm shaft and remove bearing cup (13) and worm shaft assembly from gear case. Caution should be used during disassembly, excessive effort applied on internal case parts could result in damage and renewal of part(s).

Inspect and renew all components that are worn or damaged. Install new gaskets and seals. Lubricate gears and bearings with a light film of gear lube during reassembly. Keep all dirt and foreign matter out of gear case during reassembly. Use a press to remove and install shaft bearings. To adjust end play clearance between bearing cones and cups on input worm shaft, thickness of snap ring (20 – Fig. AR9) is changed. Install thickest snap ring possible to provide shaft with recommended zero end play. Refer to LUBRICATION section after reassembly and installation.

Models 5020, 7020, 8020 and 8028

OIL SEAL INSTALLATION. Remove tines from tine shaft, then remove seals from case hub. Clean tine shaft

Fig. AR7—Exploded view of chain case components for tiller Model RT524C.

1. Chain case, L.H.
2. Oil seal
3. Oil fill plug
4. Check plug and gasket
5. Oil seals
6. Chain
7. Gasket
8. Needle bearing
9. Spacer
10. Tine shaft assy.
11. Idler sprocket
12. Bearing race
13. Needle bearings
14. Bushing
15. Input shaft
16. Sprocket
17. Roll pin
18. Chain
19. Chain case, R.H.
20. Expansion plug

Fig. AR8—Exploded view of gear case components for tiller Models RT214, RT320, RT324 and RT424.

1. Gear case (Aluminum)
2. Bushing
3. Washer
4. Bronze gear
5. Tine shaft
6. Woodruff key
7. Bushing
8. Gasket
9. Bearing flange
10. Seal
11. Oil level plug
12. Seal
13. Bushing
14. Washers
15. Worm gear
16. Gasket
17. Adjustment plug
18. Cap screw
19. Woodruff key
20. Worm shaft
21. Woodruff key
22. Needle bearing
23. Seal

with emery cloth. Install inner seal with lip facing toward inside and outer seal with lip facing toward outside. Drive new seals in until outer seal is flush with case hub.

INSPECTION. Refer to Fig. AR10 for parts breakdown and identification. Remove bolts and lockwashers securing bearing flange (9) to gear case. Remove flange and gasket(s) noting number of gasket(s) removed. Withdraw tine shaft (6), worm gear (7) and bearing cones (2) from housing. Loosen Allen head set screw (15) and turn adjusting cap out of housing. Remove bearing cup (17) by tapping it out with worm shaft, then remove worm shaft assembly from gear case housing. Caution should be used during disassembly, excessive effort applied on internal case parts could result in damage and renewal of part(s).

Inspect and renew all components that are worn or damaged. Install new gaskets and seals. Lubricate gears and bearings with a light film of gear lube during reassembly. Preload between bearing flange cover (9) and bearings (2) should be 0.001-0.005 inch (0.03-0.13 mm). Obtain correct preload by installing flange cover on gear case without gaskets. Tighten screws which retain cover (9) evenly until cover is snug, then measure distance between cover and gear case with a feeler gage. Remove cover and install gaskets less than measured gap to provide correct preload on bearings. Refer to **TINE GEAR CASE ADJUSTMENT** section for worm shaft end play adjusting procedure. Refer to **LUBRICATION** section for lubrication requirements after reassembly and installation.

WHEEL DRIVE GEAR CASE

Models 5020, 7020, 8020 and 8028

INSPECTION. Refer to Fig. AR11 for parts breakdown and identification. Inspect and renew all components that are worn or damaged. Install new gaskets and seals. Lubricate gears and bearings with a light film of gear lube during reassembly.

End play in worm shaft (2) should be 0.002 inch (0.05 mm). Thickness of snap ring (8) determines amount of end play in worm shaft.

End play in pinion shaft (45) should be 0.001-0.005 inch (0.03-0.13 mm). To measure for correct end play install flange cover (47) without gaskets and tighten retaining screws evenly until cover is snug, then measure distance between cover and gear case with a feeler gage. Remove cover and install gaskets which provide correct end play.

Preload between bearing flange cover (15) and bearings (6) should be

Fig. AR9—Exploded view of gear case components for tiller Models RT424X, RT524 and RT524S.

1. Gear case (Cast iron)
2. Tine shaft
3. Woodruff key
4. Bronze gear
5. Bearing cone
6. Bearing cup
7. Snap ring
8. Gasket
9. Bearing flange
10. Seal
11. Dust cover
12. Snap ring
13. Bearing cup
14. Bearing cone
15. Bearing spacer
16. Worm gear
17. Worm shaft
18. Woodruff key
19. Straight key
20. Snap ring (various thicknesses)
21. Dust cap
22. Needle bearing
23. Seal
24. Breather
25. Oil level plug

Fig. AR10—Exploded view of tine gear case for Models RT5020, RT7020, RT8020 and RT8028.

1. Gear housing
2. Bearing cone
3. Bearing cup
4. Snap ring
5. Oil seals
6. Tine shaft
7. Worm gear
8. Gasket
9. Bearing flange cover
10. Needle bearing
11. Oil seal
12. Flat washer
13. Spring
14. Oil level plug
15. Set screw
16. Snap ring
17. Bearing cup
18. Bearing cone
19. Spacer
20. Worm shaft
21. Roll pin
22. Woodruff key
23. Worm gear
24. Bearing adjusting cap

Fig. AR11—Exploded view of wheel drive gear case assembly for Models RT5020, RT7020, RT8020 and RT8028.

1. Transmission housing
2. Worm shaft
3. Woodruff key
4. Worm gear
5. Spacer
6. Bearing cone
7. Bearing cup
8. Snap ring
9. Spacer
10. Sliding hub
11. Axle shaft
12. Check ball
13. Spring
14. Woodruff key
15. Bearing flange cover
16. Gasket
17. Oil seal
18. Snap ring
19. Spacer
20. Low gear assy.
21. Spacer
22. Snap ring
23. Plug
24. Roll pin
25. Clutch yoke
26. Sliding hub
27. High gear assy.
28. Oil drain plug
29. Seal
30. Snap ring
31. Spacer
32. Bushing
33. Yoke shaft & lever
34. Dipstick
35. Snap ring
36. Seal
37. Lower pinion gear
38. Snap ring
39. Worm gear
40. High pinion gear
41. Spacer
42. Roll pin
43. Woodruff key
44. Woodruff key
45. Pinion shaft
46. Gasket
47. Pinion flange

0.001-0.005 inch (0.03-0.13 mm). To measure for correct preload, install flange cover (15) on gear case without gaskets. Snug down cover with securing screws and measure distance between cover and gear case with a feeler gage. Remove cover and install correct number of gaskets to apply a 0.001-0.005 inch (0.03-0.13 mm) preload on bearings.

Refer to **LUBRICATION** section for lubrication requirements after reassembly and installation.

DRIVE BELTS

Model RT524C

Remove drive belt cover. Remove belt from pulleys and install new belt. Drive belt size is ½-inch x 32 inches long. Refer to Fig. AR12 for belt routing and parts identification. Refer to **CLUTCH CONTROL ADJUSTMENT** section for adjusting procedure. Reinstall drive belt cover.

Models RT214 and RT320

Refer to Fig. AR13 for belt routing and parts identification. Disconnect wire from spark plug, then remove drive belt guard. Remove cap screw (3) and swing belt finger (1) clear of belt. Unhook clutch chain from lever. Loosen idler pulley retaining nut and slide pulley clear of belt. Remove belt from pulleys and install new belt. Drive belt size is ½-inch x 32 inches long. Refer to **DRIVE BELT AND CLUTCH CONTROL ADJUSTMENT** sections for belt adjusting procedures. Reinstall cap screw and adjust belt finger to provide 1/16-1/8 inch (1.6-3.2 mm) clearance between belt and finger when clutch is engaged. Reinstall belt cover, then reconnect spark plug wire.

Model RT324

Refer to Fig. AR14 for belt routing and parts identification. Disconnect wire from spark plug, then remove drive belt guard. Remove cap screw (5) and swing

belt finger (6) clear of belt. Unhook clutch chain from lever. Loosen idler bracket cap screw (4) enough to allow belt to slide clear of pulley. Remove belt from pulleys and install new belt. Drive belt size is ½-inch x 32 inches long. Retighten cap screw (4). Refer to **CLUTCH CONTROL ADJUSTMENT** section for adjusting procedure. Reinstall cap screw (5) and adjust belt finger to provide 1/16-1/8 inch (1.6-3.2 mm) clearance between drive belt and finger when clutch is engaged. Reinstall belt cover, then reconnect spark plug wire.

Models RT424, RT424X, RT524 and RT524S

Refer to Fig. AR15 for routing belts and parts identification. Disconnect wire from spark plug, then remove drive belt guard. Remove forward drive belt wire finger and securing bolt. Unhook clutch chain from lever. Tip forward idler away from belt and remove belt from pulleys. Forward drive belt size is ½-inch x 32 inches long. To replace reverse belt, loosen forward engine pulley (2) set screws and remove pulley from shaft. Unhook reverse clutch chain from lever. Remove reverse belt finger securing nuts and washers and swing belt finger clear of belt. Loosen idler arm cap screw (6) enough to allow belt to slide clear of pulley. Remove belt from pulleys and install new belt. Reverse drive belt size is ⅜-inch x 32 inches long. Reassemble in reverse order of disassembly. Refer to **CLUTCH CONTROL ADJUSTMENT** section for adjusting procedure. Adjust belt fingers to provide 1/16-1/8 inch (1.6-3.2 mm) clearance between drive belt and fingers when clutch is engaged. Reinstall belt cover, then reconnect spark plug wire.

Models RT5020, RT7020, RT8020 and RT8028

Refer to Fig. AR4 for routing belts and parts identification. Disconnect wire from spark plug, then remove drive belt

guard. Unbolt and remove forward drive belt wire finger. Remove cotter pin (2) from adjustment link (3) and

Fig. AR13 — View of drive belt and components for Models RT214 and RT320.

1. Belt finger
2. Idler pulley assy.
3. Cap screw
4. Engine pulley
5. Drive belt

Fig. AR14 — View of drive belt and components for Model RT324.

1. Engine pulley
2. Gear case pulley
3. Idler pulley assy.
4. Idler bracket cap screw
5. Belt finger cap screw
6. Belt finger
7. Drive belt

Fig. AR15 — View of belt arrangement and components for tiller Models RT424, RT424X, RT524 and RT524S.

1. Reverse engine pulley
2. Forward engine pulley
3. Reverse idler assy.
4. Forward idler assy.
5. Gear case pulley
6. Idler arm cap screw
7. Reverse drive belt
8. Forward drive belt

Fig. AR12 — View of drive belt and components for tiller Model RT524C.

1. Chain case drive pulley
2. Engine pulley
3. Idler pulley assy.
4. Cable lever
5. Drive belt

remove link from idler bracket. Swing idler assembly clear of drive belts and remove belts. Forward drive belt(s) size is ½-inch x 32 inches long. To replace reverse belt, remove reverse belt finger securing nuts and washers and swing belt finger clear of belt. Remove cotter pin from reverse idler linkage rod, then remove linkage rod from idler bracket. Swing idler assembly clear of belt and remove belt from pulleys. Reverse drive belt size is ⅜-inch x 31 inches long. Replace belts and reassemble in reverse order of disassembly. Refer to **CLUTCH CONTROL ADJUSTMENT** section for adjusting forward clutch spring and reverse idler. Adjust belt fingers to provide 1/16-1/8 inch (1.6-3.2 mm) clearance between drive belt and fingers when clutch is engaged. Reinstall belt cover, then reconnect spark plug wire.

ATLAS

ATLAS POWER EQUIPMENT CO.
P.O. Box 70
Harvard, IL 60033

Model	Engine Make	Engine Series	Engine Horsepower	No. of Forward Speeds	Power Reverse?	Tilling Width (In.)	Drive Type
12-2100	B&S	60000	2	1	No	10.5-18.5	Chain
12-3010	B&S	80000	3	1	No	14-24	Gear
12-3011	B&S	80000	3	1	No	14-24	Gear
12-3100	B&S	80000	3	1	No	14-24	Chain
12-3150	B&S	80000	3	1	No	10.5-18.5	Chain
12-5012	B&S	130000	5	1	No	9.75-26	Gear
12-5012	Tec.	H50	5	1	No	9.75-26	Gear
12-5013	B&S	130000	5	1	No	9.75-26	Gear
12-5013	Tec.	H50	5	1	No	9.75-26	Gear
12-5015	B&S	130000	5	1	Yes	9.75-26	Gear
12-5016	B&S	130000	5	1	Yes	9.75-26	Gear
12-5021	B&S	130000	5	2	Yes	9.75-26	Gear
12-5022	B&S	130000	5	2	Yes	9.75-26	Gear
12-5100	B&S	130000	5	1	Yes	14-26	Chain
12-5300	B&S	130000	5	1	No	14-26	Chain

LUBRICATION

ENGINE

All Models

Refer to appropriate engine section for engine lubrication requirements. Recommended fuel is regular or unleaded.

WHEELS AND CONTROLS

All Models

A few drops of oil should be placed oc-

Fig. AT1 — View of gear box oil fill plug (21) location on models so equipped.

Fig. AT2 — Typical exploded view of tiller gear box and frame assemblies used on all gear-drive models. Refer to Figs. AT7, AT8 and AT9 for drive belt arrangement.

1. Belt guide
2. Belt retainer
3. Frame
4. Worm shaft
5. Roll pin
6. Belt guard
7. Axle
8. Washer
9. Oil seal
10. Sleeve bearing
11. Gear housing
12. Key
13. Output shaft
14. Retainer ring
15. Bronze gear
16. "O" ring
17. Needle bearing
18. Gear housing cover
19. Oil seal
20. Dust shield
21. Oil level plug
22. Tine assy.
23. Worm gear
24. Center worm spacer
25. Ball bearing
26. End worm spacer
27. Snap ring
28. End cover

casionally on all movable parts such as wheel bearings and idler roller arms. Caution should be used in not getting oil on drive belts.

GEAR DRIVE

All Models So Equipped

Manufacturer recommends AMOCO worm gear oil, however, SAE 140 EP oil, may be used if AMOCO oil is unavailable. Proper gear housing oil level is approximately ½-inch (12.7 mm) below bottom of filler plug opening (21–Fig. AT1 or AT2) with gear housing in level position. Oil level should be checked after every 5 hours of operation. Renew oil after every 50 hours of operation.

CHAIN DRIVE

All Models So Equipped

Models 12-2100 and 12-3150 are lubricated during assembly and do not require periodic lubrication. All other chain drive models are lubricated by SAE 50 oil poured through oil fill plug (15–Fig. AT3) opening. With tiller setting in normal position, oil level should be approximately ½-¾ inch (12.7-19.1 mm) below bottom of filler plug hole. Oil level should be checked every 5 hours and added as necessary.

MAINTENANCE

Check condition of control levers, linkage and cables and renew if excessive play or binding prohibits easy, complete engagement of drive mechanism. Inspect drive belt(s) and renew if frayed, cracked, burnt or otherwise damaged. Inspect belt pulley(s) and renew if damaged or worn excessively. Output shaft dust shields should be checked and renewed if cracked, split or otherwise damaged.

ADJUSTMENT

DRIVE BELTS

Models 12-3100, 12-5100, 12-5300

With engagement lever (5–Fig. AT4) in drive position adjust turnbuckle (13) until spring (10) has slight tension and

Fig. AT4—Exploded view of Models 12-3100, 12-5100 and 12-5300 handle assembly.

1. Handle frame
2. Throttle cable
3. Throttle lever
4. Knob
5. Drive lever
6. Stud
7. Pin
8. Spring
9. Spacer
10. Spring
11. Bolt
12. Upper control rod
13. Turnbuckle
14. Lower control rod
15. Bushing
16. Bellcrank
17. Idler control rod
18. Idler pulley plate
19. Idler pulley
20. Forward idler arm
21. Reverse arm
22. Idler bracket
23. Spacer

gap between pin (7) and stud washer (24–Fig. AT5) is approximately 1/16-inch (1.6 mm).

Models 12-2100, 12-3150

Adjust bolt (B–Fig. AT6) on engagement lever (L) until cable (C) is tight and there is slight tension on spring (S) with lever in off position.

All Other Models

To adjust engagement lever on Models 12-5012, 12-5013, 12-5015, 12-5016, 12-5021 and 12-5022, rotate turnbuckle on engagement rod. For initial setting pull back on engagement lever until lever is approximately 3/16 inch (4.8 mm) from top end of slot when pulled on with moderate hand pressure. Tighten both locknuts at turnbuckle. If rod bends excessively the turnbuckle is adjusted too tight.

If belt slack is excessive on gear-drive models, install washers between engine and tiller hood on each engine mounting bolt. Total thickness of washers at each bolt should be equal so engine is level. Repeat adjustment procedure on Models 12-5012, 12-5013, 12-5015, 12-5016, 12-5021 and 12-5022.

OVERHAUL

ENGINE

All Models

Engine model no. is stamped on blower housing for Briggs and Stratton

Fig. AT5—Drawing of turnbuckle adjustment on Models 12-3100, 12-5100 and 12-5300. Refer to Fig. AT4 for parts identification except for: 24. Stud washer.

Fig. AT3—Exploded view of chain drive components on Models 12-3100, 12-5100 and 12-5300.

1. Pulley
2. Roll pin
3. Oil seal
4. Bushing
5. Chain case
6. Input shaft & sprocket
7. Bushing
8. Sleeve
9. Output shaft & sprocket
10. Spacer
11. Bushing
12. Seal
13. Dust seal
14. Upper intermediate sprocket
14A. Lower intermediate sprocket
15. Oil fill plug
16. Plate
17. Gasket
18. Inner tine & hub assy.
19. Outer tine & hub assy.
20. Chain (no. 35)
21. Chain (no. 420)
22. Chain (no. 50)

engines. Engine make and series no. is marked on data plate attached to engine for Tecumseh engines. Refer to appropriate Briggs and Stratton or Tecumseh engine section for overhaul procedures.

DRIVE BELTS

Models 12-3010, 12-3011, 12-5012, 12-5013

To renew belt, remove lower belt

Fig. AT6—Adjust drive belt on Models 12-2100 and 12-3150 by turning bolt (B) as outlined in text.

guard (6–Fig. AT2) then remove belt from lower and upper pulleys (1 and 3–Fig. AT7). Install belt by reversing removal procedure. Drive belt size is ½-inch x 31 inches long. After belt installation be sure belt guide (1–Fig. AT2) is properly installed and idler pulley is on outside of belt. Refer to **ADJUSTMENT** section for belt adjustment. It may be necessary to remove washers between engine and tiller hood to permit proper adjustment.

Models 12-5015, 12-5016

To renew belts remove lower belt guard (6–Fig. AT2) then remove forward drive belt (2–Fig. AT8) from upper and lower pulleys. To remove reverse belt (2A) both engine drive pulleys (3 and 12) must be removed. Unscrew set screws (5) and slide or pull the forward drive pulley off the shaft, then remove the reverse drive pulley and belt. Install belts by reversing removal procedure. Drive belt(s) size is ½-inch x 31 inches long. After belt installation be sure belt guide (1–Fig. AT2) is properly installed and idler pulley is on outside of belt. Refer to **ADJUSTMENT** section for belt adjustment. It may be necessary to remove washers between engine and tiller hood to permit proper adjustment.

Models 12-5021, 12-5022

To renew belts remove lower belt guard (6–Fig. AT2), then remove high speed drive belt (2B–Fig. AT9) from lower and upper pulleys (1 and 3). If

Fig. AT9—Exploded view of belt and pulley arrangement for Models 12-5021 and 12-5022.

1. Gear box pulley
2A. Reverse drive belt
2B. High-speed belt
2C. Low-speed belt
3. Forward engine pulley
4. Idler arm plate
5. Set screw
6. Key
7. Idler arm spring
8. Washer
9. Idler pulley
10. Forward idler arm
11. Spring
12. Reverse engine pulley
13. Woodruff key
14. Nut
15. Low-speed arm
16. Reverse idler arm
17. Idler arm spacer

Fig. AT7—Exploded view of belt and pulley arrangement for Models 12-3010, 12-3011, 12-5012 and 12-5013. Refer to Fig. AT9 for parts identification except for: 2. Drive belt; 19. Spacer.

Fig. AT8—Exploded view of belt and pulley arrangement for Models 12-5015 and 12-5016. Refer to Fig. AT9 for parts identification except for: 2. Forward drive belt; 18. Link.

Fig. AT10—Exploded view of frame assembly used on Models 12-2100, 12-3150. Refer to Fig. AT11 for parts identification except for: 35. Idler pulley; 36. Bracket; 37. Idler arm; 38. Control cable.

other belts are to be removed then engine pulleys (3 and 12) must be removed. Loosen set screws, then slide pulleys with belts from shafts. Install belts by reversing removal procedure. Drive belt(s) size is ½-inch x 31 inches long. Refer to **ADJUSTMENT** section for belt adjustment. It may be necessary to remove washers between engine and tiller hood to permit proper adjustment.

Models 12-2100, 12-3100, 12-3150, 12-5100 and 12-5300

To renew belts remove belt guard assembly (11 – Fig. AT10 or AT11). Relieve idler pulley tension then slip belts off pulleys. To install belts reverse removal procedure. Models 12-2100, 12-3100, 12-3150 and 12-5300 drive belt size is ½-inch x 36 inches long. For Model 12-5100 forward drive belt size is ½-inch x 36 inches long. Reverse drive belt size is ½-inch x 32 inches long.

CHAIN CASE

All Models

INSPECTION. For Models 12-2100 and 12-3150 refer to Fig. AT12 for parts breakdown and identification. For Models 12-3100, 12-5100 and 12-5300 refer to Fig. AT3 for parts breakdown and identification. A ½-inch x 13 thread per inch screw is used as a jackscrew for removal of input shaft pulley on Models 12-2100 and 12-3150. Drive cross pin (2 – Fig. AT12) out of drive pulley (1) and input shaft, then thread screw into

pulley hub until it bottoms against end of input shaft. Continue to turn screw until pulley is removed from shaft.

Inspect and renew all components that are worn or damaged. Install new gasket and seals. Lubricate chains, sprockets and bearings with a light film of oil during reassembly. Keep all dirt and foreign matter out of chain case during reassembly. Models 12-2100 and 12-3150 do not require any lubrication other than the light film of oil. For Models 12-3100, 12-5100 and 12-5300 refer to **LUBRICATION** section for lubrication requirements after reassembly and installation.

GEAR CASE

All Models

INSPECTION. Refer to Fig. AT2 for parts breakdown and identification. Inspect and renew all components that are worn or damaged. Install new seals. Lubricate gears and bearings with a light film of oil during reassembly. Keep all dirt and foreign matter out of gear case during reassembly. Refer to **LUBRICATION** section for lubricating requirements after reassembly and installation.

Fig. AT11 – Exploded view of frame assembly used on 12-5100. Models 12-3100 and 12-5300 are similar except for absence of reverse drive parts.

1. Deflector
2. Reverse drive belt
3. Set screw
4. Reverse engine pulley
5. Woodruff key
6. Forward engine pulley
7. Key
8. Forward drive belt
9. Handle brace cover
10. Belt guide
11. Belt guard
12. Hood
13. Handle support
14. Drag bracket pivot pin
15. Drag bar depth pin
16. Spring
17. Spacer
18. Washer
19. Drag bracket pivot
20. Drag bar
21. Plate
22. Spring
23. Spacer
24. Washer
25. Wheel height pin
26. Spring
27. Spacer
28. Bracket
29. Frame rail, right
30. Frame rail, left
31. Spacer
32. Wheel bracket
33. Spacer
34. Washer

Fig. AT12 – Exploded view of chain drive components for Models 12-2100 and 12-3150.

1. Pulley
2. Roll pin
3. Oil seal
4. Bushing
5. Chain case
6. Input shaft & sprocket
7. Bushing
8. Sleeve
9. Output shaft & sprocket
10. Spacer
11. Bushing
12. Seal
14. Intermediate sprocket
19. Gasket
21. Chain (no. 420)
23. Chain (no. 42)

CLINTON

CLINTON ENGINE CORPORATION
Maquoketa, Iowa 52060

Model	Engine Make	Engine Series	Engine Horsepower	No. of Forward Speeds	Power Reverse?	Tilling Width (In.)	Drive Type
500-T-14	Clinton	500	3	1	No	14	Chain

LUBRICATION

ENGINE

Mix ¾ pint of SAE 30 two stroke (or high quality outboard) oil with each gallon of gasoline (approximately 10:1 ratio).

CHAIN DRIVE

Chain case contains approximately ¼ pint of 140 EP gear lube. To check oil level clean dirt from case housing, then remove plug (15 – Fig. CL2). Oil should come to the bottom of the level plug hole. If oil level is low remove fill plug (16). Add oil through fill plug hole (16) until it begins to run out of level check hole. Reinstall and tighten plugs.

MAINTENANCE

Inspect all bolts and nuts for looseness and retighten as necessary. Inspect drive belt for excessive stretching, wear, cracks or any other damages. Install new belt if needed. Inspect wheel bearings for excessive wear, lubricate wheel bearings occasionally with SAE 30W oil to prevent premature bearing failure.

Inspect all pulleys for damage and excessive wear. Renew as needed. Inspect operation of clutch cable, tension adjustment on spring and freedom of movement of all linkage.

CLUTCH CONTROL ADJUSTMENT

If tines do not disengage when clutch lever is released, adjust by inserting spring (2 – Fig. CL1) in a higher chain link (3), so that there is no tension on spring when clutch lever (1) is released. If belt slippage occurs, adjust by attaching spring (2) to a lower link of chain (3) until there is tension on spring when clutch lever (1) is engaged. Clutch cable adjustment is necessary after installing a new drive belt or to compensate for normal belt stretching.

OVERHAUL

ENGINE

Engine make and series no. is marked on data plate attached to engine. Refer to appropriate Clinton engine section for overhaul procedures.

CHAIN CASE

INSPECTION. Refer to Fig. CL2 for parts breakdown and identification. Inspect and renew all components that are worn or damaged. Install new gaskets and seals. Lubricate gears, chains and bearings with a light film of oil during reassembly. Keep all dirt and foreign matter out of chain case during reassembly. Refer to **LUBRICATION** section for lubrication requirements after reassembly and installation.

DRIVE BELT

Remove drive belt guard. Remove belt from input shaft pulley and engine pulley. Install new belt on pulleys. Drive belt size is ⅜-inch x 27 inches long. Manufacturer recommends using a notched belt. Refer to **CLUTCH CONTROL ADJUSTMENT** section for adjusting procedure. Reinstall belt guard cover.

Fig. CL1 – Drawing of clutch control components.

1. Clutch lever
2. Spring
3. Clutch cable and chain assy.

Fig. CL2 – Exploded view of chain drive components for Model 500-T-14.

1. Right hand chain case cover
2. Left hand chain case cover
3. Tine shaft with sprocket
4. Cover bearings (2)
5. Cover oil seals (2)
6. Lower chain
7. Upper chain
8. Sprocket assy.
9. Idler sleeve
10. Bearings (2)
11. Cap screw
12. Nut
13. Cap screw
14. Nut
15. Oil check plug
16. Oil plug
17. Input shaft bearings (2)
18. Gasket
19. Input shaft
20. Input shaft sprocket
21. Roll pin

JOHN DEERE

DEERE & COMPANY
John Deere Road
Moline, Illinois 61265

Model	Engine Make	Engine Series	Engine Horsepower	No. of Forward Speeds	Power Reverse?	Tilling Width (In.)	Drive Type
216	B&S	60000	2	1	No	16	Chain
324	Tec.	H35	3.5	1	Yes	13-24	Gear
524	Tec.	H50	5	1	Yes	13-24	Gear
624	Tec.	H60	6	1	Yes	13-34	Gear

LUBRICATION

ENGINE

All Models

Refer to appropriate Briggs and Stratton or Tecumseh engine section for engine lubrication specifications. Recommended oil grade is SAE 30 or equivalent. Recommended fuel is either regular or low-lead gasoline having an octane rating of 90 or higher. The use of non-leaded gasolines reduces cylinder head deposits, but could shorten engine

Fig. JD1 — View of oil level plug for Model 216.

Fig. JD2 — View of oil fill plug for Model 216.

valve life if carburetor is adjusted too lean.

WHEELS AND CONTROLS

All Models

Wheel bolts (Fig. JD3) should be removed and lubricated with SAE multi-purpose grease at least once a year. All moveable parts should be lubricated occasionally with a few drops of oil. Caution should be taken in not getting oil on drive belts.

CHAIN DRIVE

All Models So Equipped

Chain case oil should be checked weekly or every 25 hours depending upon the amount of operation. Recommended oil for chain case is SAE 30 engine oil.

To check oil level in chain case place tiller on a level surface. Clean dirt from chain case housing and remove oil level plug (Fig. JD1). Oil level should be at bottom of plug hole. If oil level is low remove rubber fill plug from side of chain case (Fig. JD2). Add oil slowly until it starts to run out of level plug hole. Reinstall plugs.

GEAR DRIVE

All Models So Equipped

Oil level in gear case should be

Fig. JD3 — View of oil level plug for Models 324, 524 and 624.

checked at the beginning of each season or after every 25 hours of operation. Recommended gear case oil is SAE 90 gear lubricant or equivalent SCL multi-purpose type gear oil. Gear case capacity is 8 ozs. or 0.237 liter.

To check oil level in gear case, place tiller on a level surface. Clean surface around oil level plug (Fig. JD3) and remove plug. Oil level should be at bottom of plug hole. If oil level is low add oil through plug hole until it begins to run out, then reinstall plug.

BENT SIDEWALL   SIDEWALLS DISHED OUT

CHIPPED SIDEWALL

Fig. JD4 — Check pulleys for damages indicated above.

WHEEL BOLT   GEAR CASE OIL LEVEL PLUG

Fig. JD5 — View of clutch control components for Model 216.
1. Control cable hook
2. Drive control rod
3. Control handle

CHAIN CASE

Model 216

OIL SEAL INSTALLATION. Installation of tine shaft oil seals (19 – Fig. JD7) may be done without removing chain case from tiller. Remove tines from shaft. Use seal puller or use a sharp punch to split oil seal, then pry seal from chain case hub. Clean tine shaft with emery cloth. Drive new seal in until it bottoms out in case hub.

REMOVE AND DISASSEMBLE. Drain fuel from tank and engine oil from crankcase. Unhook clutch cable chain. Remove lower handle bar "U" bolts, handle bars, drive belt cover, drive belt, transport wheel assembly and tines. Remove four engine attaching bolts, then remove engine. Remove one remaining bolt which attaches tine shield to frame, then remove shield. Remove two bolts which attach chain case to frame, then withdraw chain case toward front.

Refer to Fig. JD7 for parts breakdown and identification. Loosen the two drive pulley set screws and slide pulley from input shaft. Clean surfaces of tine shaft with emery cloth. Remove chain case bolts and center chain case hex nut. Split chain case, then remove input shaft and sprocket assembly. Withdraw chain and sprocket assemblies from case for inspection. Completion of disassembly may be done with referral to Fig. JD7. Thoroughly clean all parts with suitable cleaning solvent. Inspect sprockets for

MAINTENANCE

Inspect all fasteners for looseness and retighten as needed. Check control levers, linkage and cables for freedom of movement and excessive play. Inspect drive belt(s) for excessive stretching, wear, cracks or any other damage. Install new belt(s) if needed. Inspect all pulleys and renew if damaged or excessively worn (Fig. JD4).

ADJUSTMENT

CLUTCH CONTROL

Model 216

Adjust by lengthening or shortening chain on control cable hook (1 – Fig. JD5). Clearance between drive control rod (2) and bottom of tiller control handle (3) should be approximately two inches when idler pulley begins to tighten drive belt. Drive belt should slip on all pulleys when drive control is released. To check, disconnect wire from spark plug and pull recoil starter. If tiller creeps, provide more slack in cable by lengthening chain at hook.

Models 324, 524 and 624

Adjust by turning clutch spring (Fig. JD6) up or down on clutch rod to change belt tension. If forward drive belt slips on pulleys when clutch handle is raised, increase spring tension by disconnecting

spring from clutch control handle. Turn spring down on control rod one or two turns, then reconnect spring to handle. Spring should stretch ½-inch (12.7 mm) when handle is raised. Continue procedure until ½-inch (12.7 mm) stretch is obtained.

OVERHAUL

ENGINE

All Models

Engine model no. is stamped on blower housing for Briggs and Stratton engines. Engine make and series no. is marked on data plate attached to engine for Tecumseh engines. Refer to appropriate Briggs and Stratton or Tecumseh engine section for overhaul procedures.

Fig. JD6 — View and identification of clutch control components for Models 324, 524 and 624.

Fig. JD7 — Exploded view of chain drive components for Model 216.

1. Right hand tube	7. Spacer	14. Woodruff key
2. Gasket (2 used)	8. Washer	15. Set screws
3. Oil plug	9. Bushings	16. Drive pulley
4. Right hand chain case half	10. Flange tube	17. Spacer
5. Chain	11. Oil seal	18. Spacer (4 used)
6. Input shaft and sprocket	12. Gasket	19. Oil seal (2 used)
	13. Left hand chain case half	20. Bearing (2 used)
		21. Washer
22. Threaded shaft		
23. Bushing (2 used)		
24. Sprocket		
25. Tine shaft		
26. Chain		
27. Spacer		
28. Self-tapping screw		
29. Cork washer		

Fig. JD8—Exploded view of gear case for Models 324, 524 and 624.

1. Oil seal	6. Bronze gear
2. Needle bearing	7. Woodruff key
3. Gear case cover	8. Tine shaft
4. Gasket	9. Dust cap
5. Thrust washer (2	10. Cotter pin
used)	11. Slotted nut
12. Washer	18. Gear case
13. Tapered roller bearing	19. Bearing cup
14. Bearing cup	20. Input shaft
15. Groove pin	21. Tapered roller bearing
16. Worm gear	22. Snap ring
17. Oil level plug	23. Seal

excessive wear or broken teeth. Inspect chains for loose or binding links. Inspect sprocket shafts for excessive wear. Clearance between bearings and shaft should be 0.005-inch (0.13 mm). Reassemble in reverse order of disassembly. Install new oil seals and gaskets. Refer to **LUBRICATION** section for lubrication requirements after reassembly and installation.

GEAR CASE

Models 324, 524 and 624

OIL SEAL INSTALLATION. Installation of tine shaft oil seals (1 – Fig. JD8) may be done without removing gear case from tiller. Remove tines from shaft. Use a seal puller or use a sharp punch to split oil seals and pry seals from side cover and case. Clean tine shaft with emery cloth. Press new seals in cover and case hub until seal face is flush with outside of castings. Reassemble in reverse order of disassembly. Refer to **LUBRICATION** section for lubrication requirements.

REMOVE AND DISASSEMBLE. Remove engine and tines. Remove idler pivot bolt (Fig. JD9) and lift out idler assemblies and belts. Loosen drive pulley set screw. Remove four bolts securing gear case to frame. Slide gear case forward sharply to knock drive pulley from shaft. Remove gear case from frame.

Refer to Fig. JD8 for parts breakdown and identification. Remove dust cap (9), oil level plug (17) and drain oil. Remove cotter pin (10), nut (11), washer (12) and bearing (13) from input shaft. Tap input shaft rearward to remove oil seal from case (Fig. JD10). Remove snap ring (22 – Fig. JD8) from input shaft. Remove bolts securing tine shaft cover (3). Remove cover and tine shaft (8) from gear case. Align worm gear (16) with outer race (14) and press input shaft and race out of gear case (Fig. JD11). Drive groove pin (15 – Fig. JD8) out of input shaft assembly. Remove worm gear from shaft. Clean all parts with suitable cleaning solvent and inspect closely. Inspect bearings and races for excessive wear. Renew both bearing and race if either is found to be bad. Inspect gears

for worn, broken or damaged teeth. Bronze gear may be pressed off of tine shaft if replacement is necessary.

REASSEMBLE AND REINSTALL. Press rear roller bearing back on input shaft past snap ring groove. Reinstall snap ring and press bearing back up in contact with snap ring. Install new tine shaft oil seals. Install outer race in case. Install Woodruff key on input shaft and slide shaft in case through worm gear. Drive groove pin through worm gear and shaft. Install thrust washer on each side of bronze gear and install tine shaft assembly in case. Install side cover (3 – Fig. JD8) with new gasket. Install input shaft lower bearing (13), washer (12) and nut (11). Tighten nut until snug, then back off until shaft has 0.002-0.012 inch (0.05-0.31 mm) end play. Install cotter pin and dust cap. Install upper seal (23) being careful not to cut seal on input shaft keyway. Drive seal in until flush with casting.

Install gear case in frame reversing order of removal. Clearance between drive pulley and ½-inch bolt heads should be 1/16-inch (1.6 mm). Tighten drive pulley set screw. Install drive

Fig. JD11—Remove input shaft and race by pressing out toward front as shown.

Fig. JD9—View of idler assemblies for Models 324, 524 and 624.

Fig. JD10—Remove rear oil seal as described in text.

belts, idler assemblies and idler pivot
bolt. Install belts on pulleys and check
adjustment. Refer to **CLUTCH CON-
TROL ADJUSTMENT** section for adjusting procedure. Refer to **LUBRICA-
TION** section for lubrication requirements.

DRIVE BELT

Model 216

Remove drive belt cover. Remove belt
from pulleys and install new belt. Drive
belt size is 17/32-inch x 49 inches long.
Loosen engine mounting bolts, slide
engine until distance between shafts
Fig. JD12) is 15¼ inches (38.7 cm), then
retighten engine mounting bolts.
Reinstall belt cover and check clutch adjustment. Refer to **CLUTCH CON-
TROL ADJUSTMENT** section for adjusting procedure.

Model 324

FORWARD DRIVE BELT. Remove
belt guard from rear of engine. Loosen
belt guides (Fig. JD13) and swing clear
of belts. Remove belt from pulleys and
install new belt. Drive belt size is ½-inch
x 33 inches long. Reposition belt guides.
Clearance between belts and guides
should be ⅛-inch (3.2 mm) when belt is
engaged. Reinstall belt guard. Refer to
CLUTCH CONTROL ADJUSTMENT
section for adjusting procedure.

REVERSE DRIVE BELT. Remove
and reinstall forward drive belt as outlined in **FORWARD DRIVE BELT** section. Loosen engine crankshaft pulley
set screws, then use a suitable puller to
partially remove pulley. Install new
reverse belt. Drive belt size is ½-inch x
33 inches long. Reinstall pulley back in
original position, then tighten pulley set
screws.

Models 524 and 624

Remove belt guard from rear of
engine. Loosen belt guides (Fig. JD14)
and swing clear of belts. Remove belts
from pulleys and install new belts. Forward drive belt size is ½-inch x 33 inches
long. Reverse drive belt size is ½-inch x
32 inches long. Reposition belt guides so
that clearance between belts and guides
is ⅛-inch (3.2 mm) when belt is engaged.
Reinstall belt guard. Refer to **CLUTCH
CONTROL ADJUSTMENT** section for
adjusting procedures.

Fig. JD12—Drive belt ar-
rangement and adjustment
setting for Model 216.

Fig. JD13—Drive belt ar-
rangement and attaching
parts for Model 324.

Fig. JD14—Drive belt ar-
rangement and attaching
parts for Models 524 and
624. Belt guides are located
as called out in Fig. JD13.

FELDMANN

FELDMANN ENGINEERING AND MANUFACTURING CO., INC.
Box 153
Sheboygan Falls, WI 53085

Model	Engine Make	Engine Series	Engine Horsepower	No. of Forward Speeds	Power Reverse?	Tilling Width (In.)	Drive Type
73335	B&S	60000	2	1	No	6-18	Chain
83335	B&S	80000	3	1	No	6-18	Chain

LUBRICATION

ENGINE

All Models

Refer to Briggs and Stratton engine section for engine lubrication requirements. Recommended oil grade is SAE 30 or equivalent. Recommended fuel is either regular or low-lead gasoline having an octane rating of 90 or higher.

WHEELS AND CONTROLS

All Models

Lubricate transport wheels, idler pulley and pivot points at least every 10 hours of operation with SAE 30 oil. Do not allow oil on drive belts.

CHAIN DRIVE

Check oil in chain case every 10 hours of operation or at lease once a year. Recommended lubricant is SAE 90 gear oil.

To check oil level in chain case, place tiller on a level surface. Clean dirt from chain case housing and remove oil level plug at bottom of housing on left side. Oil level should be at bottom of plug hole. If oil level is low, add oil slowly until it starts to run out of plug hole, then reinstall plug.

MAINTENANCE

Inspect all fasteners for looseness and retighten as needed. Check control levers, linkage and cables for freedom of movement and excessive play. Inspect drive belt(s) for excessive stretching, wear, cracks and any other damage. Install new belt(s) if needed. Inspect all

belt pulleys and renew if damaged or excessively worn.

ADJUSTMENT

CLUTCH CONTROL CABLE

All Models

For initial adjustment, allow 24 inches of cable between spring and handle, then lengthen or shorten cable to provide proper tension of idler pulley on belt.

Fig. FE2 — View of drive belt routing for all models.

1. Engine pulley
2. Control cord
3. Belt
4. Transmission pulley
5. Spring
6. Idler pulley

Fig. FE1 — Exploded view of chain drive for all models.

1. Washer
2. Felt washer
3. Seal
4. Chain case
5. Gasket
6. Chain
7. Bronze bearings
8. Washers
9. Input shaft & sprocket assy.
10. Intermediate sprocket
11. Tine shaft & sprocket assy.
12. Spacers

FORD

FORD TRACTOR OPERATIONS
Troy, Michigan 48084

Model	Engine Make	Engine Series	Engine Horsepower	No. of Forward Speeds	Power Reverse?	Tilling Width (In.)	Drive Type
1005	B&S	190000	8	2	Yes	12-26	Gear
1013	B&S	130000	5	1	No	12-26	Chain
1023	B&S	130000	5	1	Yes	12-26	Gear
1094	B&S	90000	3.5	1	No	12-26	Gear
1105	B&S	90000	3.5	1	Yes	7-22	Gear
1114A	B&S	130000	5	1	Yes	1	Chain
1134	B&S	13000	5	1	Yes	18	Chain
1183	B&S	13000	.5	1	Yes	18	Chain
1200	B&S	8000	3	1	No	7-22	Gear

LUBRICATION

ENGINE

All Models

Refer to appropriate Briggs and Stratton engine section for engine lubrication specifications. Recommended oil grade is SAE 30 or equivalent. Recommended fuel is either regular or low-lead gasoline having an octane rating of 90 or higher. The use of non-leaded gasolines reduces cylinder head deposits, but could shorten engine valve life if carburetor is adjusted too lean.

WHEELS AND CONTROLS

All Models

Transport wheels on models so equipped should be lubricated occasionally with SAE 30 oil. Drive belt idler pulley shafts and all other pivot joints should be lubricated at least every 8-10 operating hours with SAE 30 oil. Caution should be taken in not getting oil on drive belts.

CHAIN DRIVE

Model 1013

Chain case oil should be checked at least every 10 hours of operation. Recommended oil is lead base (EP) SAE 140 heavy duty gear oil.

To check oil level, clean case and remove oil level plug (18–Fig. F17). Tilt rear of tiller up so that center gear bolt (27) and oil fill plug (28) are parallel with ground. Oil level should be at bottom of plug hole (18). Add oil if level is low, then reinstall plugs.

Models 1114A, 1134 and 1183

Wheel drive case and tine drive case should be checked at least every 25 hours of operation. Recommended oil is lead base (EP) SAE 140 heavy duty gear oil.

Fig. F2—Tine drive oil level plug for Models 1114A, 1134 and 1183.

To check oil level of wheel drive case, clean case and remove level and fill plug (Fig. F1). Set depth control lever at shallowest setting. Oil level should be at

Fig. F1—Wheel drive oil level plug for Models 1114A, 1134 and 1183.

OIL LEVEL PLUG

bottom of plug hole. If necessary, add oil until flush with bottom of plug hole, then reinstall oil level plug.

To check oil level of tine drive case, clean case and remove level plug (Fig. F2). Set depth control lever at deepest setting. If oil level is below bottom of plug hole, remove fill plug (Fig. F3). Add oil until oil begins to run out oil level hole (Fig. F2), then reinstall and tighten plugs.

GEAR CASE

Models 1105 and 1200

Recommended oil is lead base (EP) SAE 140 heavy duty oil.

To check gear case oil level tip tiller on its left side. Clean case and remove oil fill screw (Fig. F4). Case should be completely full of oil. If case is low add oil, then reinstall oil fill screw.

Model 1094

Recommended oil is lead base (EP) SAE 140 heavy duty oil. Oil level should be checked at least every 25 hours of operation. Gear case bushing (Fig. F5) should be greased with #2 wheel bearing grease at least every 10 operating hours.

To check gear case oil place tiller on a level surface, clean dirt from around oil level plug (Fig. F5) and remove plug. Oil level should be at bottom of plug hole. If oil level is low add oil through level hole until oil begins to run out, then reinstall and tighten plug.

Model 1023

Recommended oil is lead base (EP) SAE 140 heavy duty oil. Oil level should be checked at least every 25 hours of operation.

To check gear case oil place tiller on a level surface. Clean dirt from front of gear case and remove oil level plug (Fig. F6). Oil level should be at bottom of plug hole. If oil level is low remove oil fill plug (Fig. F6), add oil until oil begins to run out level hole, then reinstall and tighten plugs.

Model 1005

Recommended oil is lead base (EP) SAE 140 heavy duty oil. Oil level should be checked at least every 25 hours of operation.

To check gear case oil, block up tiller wheels until center line of level plug is parallel to ground (Fig. F7). Clean dirt from front of gear case and remove oil level plug. Oil level should be at bottom of plug hole. If oil level is low, remove oil fill plug (Fig. F7). Add oil until oil begins to run out level hole, then reinstall and tighten plugs.

MAINTENANCE

Inspect all fasteners for looseness and retighten as needed. Check control levers, linkage and cables for freedom of movement and excessive play. Inspect drive belt(s) for excessive stretching, wear, cracks, or any other damage. Install new belt(s) if needed. Inspect all pulleys and renew if damaged or excessively worn.

Fig. F5 — Gear case oil level plug for Model 1094.

Fig. F6 — Gear case oil level and fill plug for Model 1023.

Fig. F7 — Gear case oil level and fill plug for Model 1005.

Fig. F4 — Gear case oil fill screw for Models 1105 and 1200.

Fig. F3 — Tine drive oil fill plug for Models 1114A, 1134 and 1183.

Fig. F8 — Clutch adjusting parts for Model 1013.

ADJUSTMENT

CLUTCH CONTROL

Model 1013

Loosen hex nut at end of lever bracket (Fig. F8). Move idler arm until there is a clearance of ¼-inch (6.4 mm) between belt and pulley, move lever bracket (Fig. F8) forward until clutch cable is tight, then retighten hex nut.

Models 1114A, 1134 and 1183

Adjust handle bar to lowest position. Loosen adjustment nut (Fig. F9), move clutch control lever on handle bar until it is centered in neutral position, then retighten adjustment nut.

Models 1105 and 1200

Push the clutch control handle to the forward position. Loosen set screw (Fig. F10), move cam (Fig. F10) until clearance between cam and pad is 3/16-inch (4.8 mm), then retighten set screw.

Model 1094

Adjustment is made by raising or lowering clevis pin position in control rod (Fig. F11). If tines turn when control rod is in neutral position, install clevis pin in a higher hole of control rod. Continue this procedure until tines do not turn in neutral position.

Models 1005 and 1023

Adjustment is made by raising or lowering stop collar on control rod (Fig. F12). With clutch control lever in forward position, clearance between pivot bushing and stop collar should be ¼-inch (6.4 mm). If clearance is incorrect loosen set screw (Fig. F12), move stop collar, then retighten set screw.

BELT ADJUSTMENT

Model 1013

Loosen engine bolts and slide engine forward. Refer to **CLUTCH CONTROL ADJUSTMENT** section for readjustment of clutch lever.

Models 1114A, 1134 and 1183

TINE DRIVE BELT. To adjust, loosen clamp cap screws (Fig. F13), then rotate chain case assembly. Clearance between inside surfaces of belt (Fig. F14) should be ¾-inch (19 mm) when clutch control lever is in forward position. Retighten clamp cap screws, then check to see if tines turn in neutral position. If tines do not turn in neutral position, adjustment is complete. If tines rotate, readjust belt to increase slack slightly.

WHEEL DRIVE BELT. Clearance between upper idler and belt should be ¼-inch (6.4 mm) with clutch control lever in neutral position (Fig. F15). If adjustment is incorrect, idler (Fig. F15) must be repositioned by removing machine screw and reinstalling in

another of the four adjustment locations. Install new belt if correct adjustment is not possible.

Models 1005 and 1023

Adjustment is accomplished by installing shims between engine and tine shield. Install shims until 1/16-1/8-inch (1.6-3.2 mm) clearance is obtained between input pulley belt finger (Fig. F16) and belt when belt is fully engaged.

ADJUSTMENT HOLES
COTTER PIN
CLEVIS PIN

Fig. F11—Clutch adjusting parts for Model 1094.

CAM
3/16"
PAD
¼ x ¼ SQUARE HD. SET SCREW

Fig. F10—Clutch adjusting parts for Models 1105 and 1200.

Control Rod
Pivot Bushing
Stop Collar
1/4"
Set Screw

Fig. F12—Clutch adjusting parts for Models 1023 and 1005.

ADJUSTMENT NUT

Fig. F9—Clutch adjustment for Models 1114A and 1134.

TINE CHAIN CASE
ROTATE
CLAMP CAP SCREWS

Fig. F13—Tine drive belt adjusting capscrews for Models 1114A and 1134.

Fig. F14—Tine drive belt clearance when clutch lever is in forward position.

3/4"

CHANGING FORWARD SPEEDS

Model 1005

The engine drive pulley and input pulley have 3 V-belt grooves. The inside 2 grooves are for forward speed adjustment. Groove closest to engine will provide fastest tine speed. If belt is new or tight, it may be necessary to loosen engine bolts, then tilt engine back to change pulley grooves.

OVERHAUL

ENGINE

All Models

Engine model number is stamped on blower housing. Refer to appropriate Briggs and Stratton engine section for overhaul procedures.

CHAIN CASE

Model 1013

OIL SEAL INSTALLATION. Remove tines from tine shaft. Use a suitable tool to remove oil seal from chain case hub. Clean tine shaft with emery cloth. Drive new seal in until bottomed in case hub.

UPPER IDLER

1/4"

ADJUSTMENT IDLER

MACHINE SCREW

Fig. F15—Wheel drive belt clearance when clutch lever is in neutral position.

GEAR CASE ADJUSTMENT

Models 1005, 1023 and 1094

Remove cotter pin (15–Fig. F19 or 4–Fig. F20) and tighten worm shaft adjustment plug (16–Fig. F19 or 21–Fig. F20) until snug, then back off one notch and reinstall cotter pin.

Input Pulley Belt Finger

Fig. F16—Drive belt(s) arrangement for Models 1023 and 1005.

Fig. F17—Exploded view of chain case for Model 1013.

1. Shaft sleeve plug	8. Spacer	15. Washer	22. Chain
2. Right chain case	9. Seal	16. Tine shaft	23. Gasket
3. Bearing	10. Bearing	17. Woodruff key	24. Left chain case
4. Idler gear	11. Seal	18. Oil level plug	25. Center gear axle
5. Drive gear	12. Washer	19. Sprocket assy.	26. Center gear
6. Pin	13. Bearing	20. Snap ring	27. Center gear bolt
7. Input shaft	14. Inner race	21. Washer	28. Oil fill plug

INSPECTION. Refer to Fig. F17 for parts breakdown and identification. Inspect all components and renew all that are worn or damaged. Install new gaskets and seals. Lubricate gears, chains and bearings with a light film of oil during reassembly. Keep all dirt and foreign matter out of chain case during reassembly. Refer to LUBRICATION section for lubrication requirements.

Models 1114A, 1134 and 1183

Tine Drive and Wheel Traction Chain Cases

OIL SEAL INSTALLATION. Remove tines or wheels from output shaft. Use a suitable tool to remove oil seal from chain case hub. Clean shaft with emery cloth. Drive new seal in until bottomed in case hub.

INSPECTION. Wheel traction chain case is factory sealed and must be renewed as a complete unit. Refer to Fig. F18 for tine chain case parts breakdown and identification. Inspect all components and renew all that are worn or damaged. Install new gaskets and seals. Lubricate gears, chains and bearings with a light film of oil during reassembly. Keep all dirt and foreign matter out of chain case during reassembly. Refer to LUBRICATION section for lubricating requirements after reassembly and installation.

GEAR CASE

Models 1105 and 1200

OIL SEAL INSTALLATION. Remove tines from output shaft. Use a suitable tool to remove oil seal from gear case hub. Clean shaft with emery cloth. Drive new seal in until bottomed in case hub. Refer to LUBRICATION section for lubricating requirements.

Gear case is factory sealed and must be replaced as a complete unit if service is required.

Model 1094

OIL SEAL INSTALLATION. Remove tines from output shaft. Remove bolts securing side cover (17 – Fig. F19) to gear case and remove cover. Remove old seal (20), install new oil seal, then reinstall side cover and bolts. On opposite side of gear case hub (5), pry seal from hub and drive new seal in until bottomed in bore of case hub.

INSPECTION. Refer to Fig. F19 for gear case parts breakdown and identification. Inspect all components and renew all that are worn or damaged. In-

stall new gaskets and seals. Lubricate gears and bearings with a light film of oil during reassembly. Refer to GEAR CASE ADJUSTMENT section for end play adjusting procedure. Refer to LUBRICATION section for lubrication requirements.

Models 1005 and 1023

OIL SEAL INSTALLATION. Remove tines from output shaft. On Model 1005 remove bolts securing cover (31 – Fig. F20) to gear case and remove cover. On Model 1023 remove cotter pin (36) and lock cover (35), then withdraw

cover (33) from gear case. Remove and replace oil seal. Reinstall cover and securing parts. On opposite side, pry oil seal out of hub, then drive new seal in until bottomed in bore of case hub.

INSPECTION. Refer to Fig. F20 for gear case parts breakdown and identification. Inspect all components and renew all that are worn or damaged. Install new gaskets and seals. Lubricate gears and bearings with a light film of oil during reassembly. Keep all dirt and foreign matter out of gear case during reassembly. Refer to GEAR CASE AD-

Fig. F18 – Exploded view of tine chain case for Models 1114A and 1134.

1. Fill plug
2. Seal
3. Right chain case
4. Needle bearing
5. Idler sleeve
6. Shim
7. Spacer cup
8. Tine shaft assy.
9. Gasket
10. Upper chain
11. Bearing
12. Sprocket assy.
13. Lower chain
14. Input shaft assy.
15. Snap ring
16. Washer
17. Bearing
18. Left chain case
19. Seal
20. Oil level plug

Fig. F19 – Exploded view of gear box for Model 1094.

1. Alignment bushing
2. Felt wick
3. Worm shaft bushing
4. Grease fitting
5. Gear case
6. Oil level plug
7. Worm shaft bearing cup
8. Bearing cone
9. Worm spacer
10. Worm
11. Snap ring
12. Worm shaft
13. Hypro key
14. "O" ring
15. Cotter pin
16. Adjustment plug
17. Gear case cover
18. Cover gasket
19. Cover gasket
20. Tine shaft seal
21. Bushing
22. Washer
23. Snap ring
24. Tine shaft
25. Woodruff key
26. Worm wheel
27. Intermediate felt seal
28. Inner felt seal
29. Washer
30. Inner tine hub assy.
31. Outer tine hub assy.
32. Tine

JUSTMENT section for end play adjusting procedure. Refer to **LUBRICATION** section for lubrication requirements.

CLUTCH CONE ASSEMBLY

Model 1094

To renew clutch assembly, engine must be removed from engine base (2 – Fig. F21) and bell housing (8). Disconnect throttle control (11), remove the three 5/16 x 1⅞ inch bolts securing engine to base and bell housing, then remove engine. Inspect upper cone (4) and clutch cone assembly (5) for excessive wear, renew as necessary. Inspect condition of spring (6) and renew if stretched or broken. Clutch yoke (13), rollers (16), clutch cone and worm shaft splines should be cleaned and lubricated with SAE 30 oil. Reassemble in reverse order of disassembly.

DRIVE BELTS

Model 1013

Remove drive belt cover. Remove belt from pulleys and install new belt. Drive belt size is ½-inch x 29 inches long. Loosen engine mounting bolts and slide engine. Belt should slip on pulleys when idler pulley is not engaged. Reinstall belt cover and check clutch adjustment.

Fig. F21 — Exploded view of upper body for Model 1094.

1. Hypro key
2. Engine base
3. Cone clutch hub
4. Upper cone
5. Clutch cone assy.
6. Clutch spring
7. Reinforcement plate
8. Bell housing assy.
9. Spring
10. Clutch rod
11. Throttle control
12. Handle assy.
13. Clutch yoke
14. Retaining ring
15. Pivot pin spacer
16. Clutch roller
17. Clevis pin
18. Pivot pin

Refer to **CLUTCH CONTROL ADJUSTMENT** section for adjusting procedure.

Models 1114A, 1134 and 1183

TINE DRIVE BELT. Refer to Fig. F22 for correct belt routing. Place clutch lever in neutral position. Remove drive belt cover and belt guide (7). Slip belt (13) from pulleys and install new belt. Drive belt size is ⅜-inch x 38 inches long. Reinstall belt guide. Refer to **BELT ADJUSTMENT** section for belt adjusting procedure. Reinstall drive belt cover.

WHEEL DRIVE BELT. Remove tine drive belt as outlined in previous paragraph. Remove retaining ring (4 – Fig. F22) from idler arm shaft. Remove belt from wheel drive case pulley (12). Remove retaining ring (10) from wheel drive case pulley shaft, then remove pulley taking care not to lose Woodruff key. Remove cotter pin (6) from link (5). Slide idler arm assemblies (3) out until spacer (2) can be withdrawn from between idler arms, then remove belt (14). Reverse removal procedure to install belt. Drive belt size is ⅜-inch x 46 inches long. Reinstall tine drive belt. Refer to **BELT ADJUSTMENT** section for adjusting procedure.

Models 1105 and 1200

Place control lever in neutral, remove bolts securing engine to tiller, then remove engine. Remove belt by slipping it over input pulley (I – Fig. F23). Install

Fig. F20 — Exploded view of gear box used on Models 1023 and 1005. Parts 29 through 32 are used on 1005 models and parts 33 through 36 are used on 1023 models.

1. Bushing	10. Tine, R.H.	19. Snap ring	28. Hypro key
2. Gear box housing	11. Outer hub	20. Seal	29. Gasket
3. Oil fill plug	12. Tine, L.H.	21. Adjustment plug	30. Gasket
4. Cotter pin	13. Worm shaft	22. Seal	31. Cover
5. Oil level plug	14. Hypro key	23. Cup	32. Lock plate
6. Inner felt seal	15. Cup	24. Cone	33. Cover
7. Washer	16. Cone	25. Bronze worm wheel	34. Seal
8. Intermediate felt seal	17. Spacer	26. Snap ring	35. Lock cover
9. Inner hub	18. Worm gear	27. Tine shaft	36. Cotter pin

belt by reversing removal procedure making certain belt is installed inside pins (P). Drive belt size is ⅜-inch x 20 inches long. Reinstall engine.

Models 1023 and 1005

Remove belt guard and unhook spring (6 – Fig. F24) from idler arm assembly. Remove input pulley belt guide (7) and idler roller belt guide (4). Remove

reverse drive belt (2) noting its position. Remove forward drive belt (1). Install new belts by reversing removal procedure. Model 1023 forward drive belt size is ½-inch x 35 inches long and reverse drive belt size is ⅜-inch x 37 inches long. Model 1005 forward drive belt size is ½-inch x 37 inches long and reverse drive belt size is ⅜-inch x 39 inches long. Refer to **BELT ADJUSTMENT** section for adjusting procedure.

Fig. F23 – View of proper belt arrangement for Models 1105 and 1200.

P. Belt guide pins
I. Input pulley
B. Drive belt

Fig. F24 – View of belt and pulley system for Models 1023 and 1005. High speed pulleys (8 and 10) are only used on Model 1005.

1. Forward drive belt
2. Reverse drive belt
3. Idler roller
4. Idler roller belt guide
5. Idler arm assy.
6. Idler spring
7. Input pulley belt guide
8. High speed pulley groove
9. Engine pulley
10. High speed pulley groove
11. Input pulley

Fig. F22 – View of proper belt arrangement and attaching parts for Models 1114A and 1134.

1. Engine pulley
2. Spacer
3. Idler arm assemblies
4. Retaining ring
5. Idler arm link
6. Cotter pin
7. Belt guide
8. Tine drive idler pulley
9. Belt guide pin
10. Retaining ring
11. Tine drive case pulley
12. Wheel drive case pulley
13. Tine drive belt
14. Wheel drive belt

GILSON

GILSON BROTHERS CO.
Box 152
Plymouth, Wisconsin 53073

Model	Engine Make	Engine Series	Engine Horsepower	No. of Forward Speeds	Power Reverse?	Tilling Width (In.)	Drive Type
51081	B&S	130000	5	1	Yes	12-26	Gear
51088	Tec.	H60	6	1	Yes	12-26	Gear
51097	B&S	130000	5	1	Yes	12-26	Gear
51174	B&S	13000	5	1	Yes	12-26	Gear

LUBRICATION

ENGINE

All Models

Refer to Briggs and Stratton or Tecumseh engine section for engine lubrication requirements. Recommended fuel is regular or low lead gasoline.

Fig. G1 — View of gear box oil fill plug (F) and oil level plug (L) location.

Fig. G2 — View of belt and pulley system.
1. Forward drive belt
2. Reverse drive belt
3. Idler roller
4. Idler roller belt guide
5. Idler arm assy.
6. Idler spring
7. Input pulley belt guide
8. Input pulley
9. Engine pulley

GEAR DRIVE

Oil level in gear housing should be

Fig. G3 — Drawing of clutch control lever adjustment. Refer to text for procedures.
1. Control rod
2. Pivot bushing
3. Stop collar
4. Set screw

checked at least every 25 hours of operation. Gear housing oil level should be even with oil level plug hole (L–Fig. G1) with tiller in level position. If oil level is low, then add oil through fill plug hole (F) until oil runs out level hole. Recommended oil is SAE 140EP.

MAINTENANCE

Inspect belt pulleys and renew if damaged or worn excessively. Check condition of control levers and linkage and renew if excessive play or binding prohibits easy, complete engagement of drive mechanism. After every 8 to 10 hours of operation the idler roller (3–Fig. G2) should be removed and bearing wick saturated with SAE 30 oil. Periodically lubricate wheel bushings with SAE 30 oil.

ADJUSTMENT

CLUTCH CONTROL LEVER. Move clutch control lever forward (in the drive

Fig. G4 — Exploded view of gear box assembly.
1. Seal
2. Bushing
3. Gear box housing
4. Oil fill plug
5. Cotter pin
6. Tine shaft
7. Pipe plug
8. Worm shaft
9. Hypro key
10. Bearing cup
11. Bearing cone
12. Spacer
13. Worm
14. Snap ring
15. "O" ring
16. Adjustment plug
17. Woodruff key
18. Seal
19. Bushing
20. Washer
21. Worm wheel
22. Snap ring
23. Gasket
24. Cover
25. Lock tab

position), slide stop collar (3–Fig. G3) up to ¼ inch (6.4 mm) from pivot bushing (2), then tighten set screw (4). Place control lever in neutral then pull on engine recoil starter with spark plug wire disconnected to check that belts slip on all pulleys and tiller does not creep. If tiller moves forward in the neutral position loosen set screw and move stop collar upward slightly. If tiller moves backward slide stop collar downward slightly. Retighten set screw.

Repeat procedure until tiller does not creep in neutral.

GEAR CASE BEARING ADJUSTMENT. After many hours of operation, end play may develop in worm shaft bearings (11–Fig. G4). To adjust, remove cotter pin (5) from gear housing and turn adjustment plug (16) in as far as possible then back off one notch and install cotter pin.

BELT ADJUSTMENT. Engine shims (20–Fig. G5) or washers may be used to compensate for belt stretch. Add shims or washers between engine and tine shield (23) until proper belt tension is attained.

OVERHAUL

ENGINE

All Models

Engine model no. is stamped on blower housing for Briggs and Stratton engines. Engine make and series no. is marked on data plate attached to engine for Tecumseh engines. Refer to appropriate Briggs and Stratton or Tecumseh engine section for overhaul procedures.

DRIVE BELTS

To renew belts, remove belt guard (9–Fig. G5) and unhook spring (6–Fig. G2) from the idler arm assembly. Remove input pulley belt guide (7) and idler roller belt guide (4). Remove reverse drive belt, noting its position. Remove forward drive belt, then install new belts by reversing removal procedure. Manufacturer recommends Gilson No. 6163 for reverse drive belt and Gilson No. 1110 for forward drive belt. After installation belt guides (4 and 7) should be adjusted 1/16/1/8 inch (1.6-3.2 mm) from pulleys.

GEAR BOX

Overhaul of gear box assembly is evident after inspection of unit and referral to Fig. G4. Clean gear box housing thoroughly before disassembling to prevent dirt from entering unit. Examine bronze gear and renew if teeth are broken, chipped or excessively worn. Inspect bearings and cones and renew if chipped, pitted or discolored. Always install complete new bearing assembly if either cone or cup is damaged. Remove rust and burrs from areas of shaft where seals contact using #400 emery cloth. Do not damage shaft by over-polishing because leakage may result. Inspect shaft especially around seal contact surfaces and around hypro key for cracking, galling or other damage. Renew or repair shaft if necessary. Center bronze gear over key to maintain proper alignment with worm gear. Always renew gaskets and seals when overhauling unit.

Fig. G5 – Exploded view showing drive components.

1. Throttle control
2. Handle assy.
3. Control lever
4. Control rod
5. Pivot bushing
6. Stop collar
7. Set screw
8. Spring
9. Belt guard
10. Reverse idler assy.
11. Idler assy.
12. Belt guide
13. Idler arm assy.
14. Engine pulley
15. Depth control stake
16. Frame
17. Belt guide
18. Reverse belt
19. Forward belt
20. Engine spacer shims
21. Input pulley
22. Engine base
23. Tine shield
24. Intermediate felt seal
25. Inner felt seal
26. Washer
27. Inner tine hub assy.
28. Tine
29. Outer tine hub assy.

GILSON

Model	Engine Make	Engine Series	Engine Horsepower	No. of Forward Speeds	Power Reverse?	Tilling Width (In.)	Drive Type
51082	B&S	130000	5	2	Yes	12-26	Gear
51085	B&S	190000	8	2	Yes	12-26	Gear

LUBRICATION

ENGINE

All Models

Refer to Briggs and Stratton engine section for engine lubrication requirements. Recommended fuel is regular or low lead gasoline.

GEAR DRIVE

Oil level in gear housing should be checked at least every 25 hours of operation. Gear housing oil level should be even with oil level plug hole (L–Fig. G10) with tiller in level position. It may be necessary to place boards under tiller wheels to level unit. If oil level is low, add SAE 140 EP oil through fill plug hole (F) until oil runs out level hole.

MAINTENANCE

Inspect belt pulleys and renew if damaged or worn excessively. Check condition of control levers and linkage and renew if excessive play or binding prohibits easy, complete engagement of drive mechanism. Each year the idler roller (3–Fig. G11) should be removed and the bearing wick saturated with SAE 30 oil. Periodically lubricate the wheel bushings with SAE 30 oil.

ADJUSTMENT

CLUTCH CONTROL LEVER

Move clutch control lever forward (in the drive position), slide stop collar (3–Fig. G12) up to ¼ inch (6.4 mm) from

Fig. G10 — View of gear box oil fill plug (F) and oil level plug (L) location.

Fig. G12 — Drawing of clutch control lever adjustment. Refer to text for procedures.
1. Control rod
2. Pivot bushing
3. Stop collar
4. Set screw

Fig. G11 — View of belt and pulley system.
1. Forward drive belt
2. Reverse drive belt
3. Idler roller
4. Idler roller belt guide
5. Idler arm assy.
6. Idler spring
7. Input pulley belt guide
8. High speed pulley groove
9. Engine pulley
10. High speed pulley groove
11. Input pulley

Fig. G13 — Exploded view of gear box assembly. Parts 33-36 are substituted for 29-32 on Model 51082.
1. Bushing
2. Gear box housing
3. Oil fill plug
4. Cotter pin
5. Oil level plug
6. Inner felt seal
7. Washer
8. Intermediate felt seal
9. Inner hub
10. Tine, R.H.
11. Outer hub
12. Tine, L.H.
13. Worm shaft
14. Hypro key
15. Cup
16. Cone
17. Spacer
18. Worm gear
19. Snap ring
20. Seal
21. Adjustment plug
22. Seal
23. Cup
24. Cone
25. Bronze worm wheel
26. Snap ring
27. Tine shaft
28. Hypro key
29. Gasket
30. Gasket
31. Cover
32. Lock tab
33. Cover
34. Seal
35. Lock cover
36. Cotter pin

pivot bushing (2), then tighten set screw (4). Place control lever in neutral and disconnect wire from spark plug, then pull recoil starter to check that belts slip on all pulleys and tiller does not creep. If tiller moves forward in neutral position, then loosen set screw and move stop collar upward slightly. If tiller moves backward slide stop collar downward slightly. Retighten set screw. Repeat procedure until tiller does not creep in neutral.

CHANGING SPEEDS

Forward speed ranges are low and high. The forward drive belt (1–Fig. G11) must be relocated on pulleys to shift forward speed from low to high or vice versa. To change belt from low to high move belt (1) to pulleys (8 and 10). If belt is too tight to change pulley positions, loosen engine to base bolts and tilt engine back, then relocate belt.

DRIVE BELT

Engine shims (11–Fig. G14) or washers may be used to compensate for belt stretch. Add shims or washers between engine and tine shield until proper belt tension is attained.

GEAR CASE BEARING

After many hours of operation, end play may develop in the worm shaft bearings. To adjust, remove cotter pin (4–Fig. G13) from gear housing and turn adjustment plug (21) in as far as possible then back off one notch and install cotter pin.

OVERHAUL

ENGINE

All Models

Engine model no. is stamped on blower housing. Refer to appropriate Briggs and Stratton engine section for overhaul procedures.

DRIVE BELTS

To renew belts, remove belt guard (50–Fig. G14) and unhook spring (6–Fig. G11) from the idler arm assembly. Remove input pulley belt guide (7) and idler roller belt guide (4). Remove reverse drive belt (2), noting its

position. Remove forward drive belt, then install new belts by reversing removal procedure. Manufacturer recommends Gilson No. 6163 for reverse drive belt and Gilson No. 1110 for forward drive belt. After installation, belt guides (4 and 7) should be adjusted 1/16-1/8 inch from pulleys.

GEAR BOX

Overhaul of gear box assembly is evident after inspection of unit and referral to Fig. G13. Clean gear box housing thoroughly before disassembling to prevent dirt from entering unit. Examine bronze gear and renew if teeth are

broken, chipped or excessively worn. Inspect bearings and cones and renew if chipped, pitted or discolored. Always install complete new bearing assembly if either cone or cup is damaged. Remove rust and burrs from areas of shaft where seals contact using #400 emery cloth. Do not damage shaft by over-polishing because leakage may result. Inspect shaft especially around seal contact surfaces and around hypro key for cracking, galling or other damage. Renew or repair shaft if necessary. Center bronze gear over key to maintain proper alignment with worm gear. Always renew gaskets and seals when overhauling unit.

Fig. G14—Exploded view of typical drive components.

1. Idler arm shaft	13A. Reverse idler assy.	25. Knob	38. Belt guide
2. Bushing	14. Idler shaft	26. Control rod	39. Belt guide
3. Idler arm	14A. Reverse idler shaft	27. Stop collar	40. Reverse belt
4. Washer	15. Washer	28. Set screw	41. Forward belt
5. Idler spring	16. Belt guide	29. Link	42. Set screw
6. Belt guide	17. Bushing	30. Pivot bushing	43. Main frame
7. Lock washers	18. Washer	31. Pivot arm	44. Wheel bushing
8. Key	19. Throttle control	32. Clevis pin	45. Axle
9. Engine pulley	20. Handle assy.	33. Depth control	46. Input pulley
10. Set screw	21. Lever spring	34. Tailpiece assy.	47. Hypro key
11. Engine shim	22. Control pin	35. Handle bracket	48. Engine base
12. Washer	23. Control tube	36. Hanger pin	49. Tine shield
13. Idler roller	24. Control lever	37. Bolt	50. Belt guard

GILSON

Model	Engine Make	Engine Series	Engine Horsepower	No. of Forward Speeds	Power Reverse?	Tilling Width (In.)	Drive Type
51083	B&S	190000	8	4	Yes	12-26	Gear

LUBRICATION

ENGINE

Refer to Briggs and Stratton engine section for engine lubrication requirements. Recommended fuel is regular or low lead gasoline.

GEAR DRIVE

Oil level in gear housing should be checked at least every 25 hours of operation. Gear housing oil level should be even with oil level plug hole (L – Fig. G20) with tiller in level position. It may be necessary to place boards under the tiller wheels to level unit. If oil level is low, add oil through fill plug hole (F) until oil runs out level hole. Recommended oil is SAE 140 EP.

MAINTENANCE

Inspect belt pulleys and renew if damaged or worn excessively. Check condition of control levers and linkage and renew if excessive play or binding prohibits easy, complete engagement of drive mechanism. After each 8-10 hours of operation the idler roller (31 – Fig. G21) should be removed and the bearing wick saturated with SAE 30 oil. Periodically lubricate wheel bushings with SAE 30 oil.

ADJUSTMENT

CLUTCH CONTROL ROD

With clutch control lever in neutral position, tiller should not creep to reverse or forward. Check by disconnecting spark plug wire and pulling recoil

starter. If tiller moves forward in the neutral position, loosen jam nut (7 – Fig. G23) remove spring clip (5A) and rotate control rod (6) clockwise one or two turns into ball joint assembly (8). If tiller moves backward turn control rod (6) counter-clockwise one or two turns out of ball joint assembly (8). Recheck for improper engagement in neutral, then retighten jam nut (7) against ball joint assembly (8) when proper adjustment is attained.

BELT

To compensate for belt stretch loosen jam nut (7 – Fig. G23), remove spring clip (5A) and rotate control rod (6) counter-clockwise out of ball joint assembly (8) two turns then retighten jam nut (7). Check for correct neutral

adjustment as outlined in previous section.

GEAR CASE BEARING

After many hours of operation end play may develop in worm shaft bearings (8 – Fig. G22). To adjust, remove cotter pin (6) from gear housing and turn adjustment plug (14) in as far as possible then back off one notch and reinstall cotter pin.

OVERHAUL

ENGINE

Engine model no. is stamped on

Fig. G20 – View of gear box oil fill plug (F) and oil level plug (L) location.

Fig. G21 – Exploded view of belt, pulley and drive system.

1. Belt guide
2. Pivot shaft
3. Pivot bracket
4. Engine pulley
5. Set screw
6. Engine block
7. Drive support bracket
8. Friction wheel roller
9. Lockwasher
10. Spacer
11. Bearing
12. Snap ring
13. Reverse pulley half
14. Drive shaft
15. Bushing
16. Pulley center
17. Pulley half
18. Washer
19. Drive support plate
20. Spacer
21. Lockwasher
22. Washer
23. Lockwasher
24. Hypro key
25. Input pulley
26. Upper drive belt
27. Lower drive belt
28. Spring
29. Spring bracket
30. Washer
31. Idler roller
32. Idler shaft
33. Idler arm assy.
34. Washer
35. Bushing
36. Spacer
37. Lockwasher

blower housing. Refer to appropriate Briggs and Stratton engine section for overhaul procedures.

DRIVE BELTS

To renew belts remove belt guard (2–Fig. G23) and unhook spring (28–Fig. G21) from idler roller assembly. Remove two bolts securing drive support plate (19–Fig. G21) to drive support bracket (7) and rotate support plate (19) 90-degrees from secured position. Remove lower drive belt (27) from input pulley (25). Remove upper drive belt after removing belt guide (1). Install new belts by reversing removal procedure. Manufacturer recommends Gilson No. 26345 for lower drive belt and Gilson No. 26344 for upper drive belt. After installation, belt guide (1) should be adjusted 1/16-1/8 inch (1.6-3.2 mm) from pulleys.

GEAR BOX

Overhaul of gear box assembly is evident after inspection of unit and referral to Fig. G22. Clean gear box housing thoroughly before disassembling to prevent dirt from entering unit. Examine bronze gear and renew if teeth are broken, chipped or excessively worn. Inspect bearings and cones and renew if chipped, pitted or discolored. Always install complete new bearing assembly if either cone or cup is damaged. Remove rust and burrs from areas of shaft where seals contact using #400 emery cloth. Do not damage shaft by over-polishing because leakage may result. Inspect shaft especially around seal contact surfaces and around hypro key for cracking, galling or other damage. Renew or repair shaft if necessary. Center bronze gear over key to maintain proper alignment with worm gear. Always renew gaskets and seals when overhauling unit.

Fig. 22 – Exploded view of gear box assembly.

1. Worm shaft
2. Ball bearing
3. Gasket
4. Gear box housing
5. Vent plug assy.
6. Cotter pin
7. Cups
8. Cones
9. Spacers
10. Worm gear
11. Snap ring
12. Hypro key
13. "O" ring
14. Adjusting plug
15. Oil level plug
16. Seals
17. Cups
18. Cones
19. Bronze worm wheel
20. Snap ring
21. Key
22. Tine shaft
23. Gasket
24. Gasket
25. Cover
26. Washer
27. Lockwasher

Fig. G23 – Exploded view of Model 51083 tiller assembly.

1. Handle assy.
2. Belt guard
3. Spacer
4. Rubber disc
5. Control lever assy.
5A. Spring clip
6. Control rod
7. Jam nut
8. Ball joint
9. Lockwasher
10. Tine shield
11. Depth control
12. Tail piece assy.
13. Hanger pin
14. Handle bracket
15. Main frame assy.
16. Washer
17. Bearing
18. Spacer
19. Axle
20. Engine base
21. Support strap
22. Gear case
23. Intermediate felt seal
24. Inner felt seal
25. Washer
26. Inner tine hub assy.
27. Outer tine hub assy.
28. Tine

GILSON

Model	Engine Make	Engine Series	Engine Horsepower	No. of Forward Speeds	Power Reverse?	Tilling Width (In.)	Drive Type
51094	B&S	90000	3.5	1	No	12-26	Gear
51096	B&S	130000	5	1	No	12-26	Gear
51106	B&S	130000	5	1	No	12-24	Gear

LUBRICATION

ENGINE

All Models

Refer to Briggs and Stratton engine section for engine lubrication requirements. Recommended fuel is regular or low lead gasoline.

GEAR DRIVE

Oil level in gear housing should be checked at least every 25 hours of operation. Gear housing oil level should be even with oil level plug hole (L–Fig. G31) with tiller in level position. Recommended oil is SAE 140 EP.

The worm shaft bushing (4–Fig. G32) is lubricated through a grease fitting (F–Fig. G31) with number 2 wheel bearing grease. A small amount of grease should be added after every 10 hours of operation.

MAINTENANCE

Inspect nuts and bolts periodically for looseness and retighten as necessary. Check condition of control linkage and shift yoke (13–Fig. G33) and repair or renew if excessive play or binding pro-

hibits easy, complete engagement of drive mechanism. The pivot pin (18–Fig. G33) should be lubricated annually to avoid binding and lessen wear of clutch linkage. Remove pivot pin (18) by first removing retaining ring (14) and pushing pivot pin out of the bell housing (8) with a wooden dowel rod the same size or slightly smaller in diameter than the pivot pin. Once the pivot pin is removed clean thoroughly and lubricate with SAE 30 oil. To install pivot pin, push dowel through bell housing with pivot pin (18), then reinstall retaining ring. Periodically lubricate wheel bushings with SAE 30 oil.

ADJUSTMENT

CLUTCH CONTROL ROD ADJUSTMENT-NEUTRAL. Clutch control rod may be adjusted to compensate for normal wear of clutch cone assembly. With clutch control rod (1–Fig. G34) in neutral position, tines should not turn. Check by disconnecting

spark plug wire and pulling recoil starter. If tines turn, move control rod out of neutral, then remove cotter pin (3) and clevis pin (4) making note of previous holes used. Relocate clutch yoke (2) to next higher set of holes in control rod (1). Reinstall clevis pin (4) and cotter pin (3), then recheck adjustment.

GEAR CASE BEARING ADJUSTMENT. After many hours of operation, end play may develop in the worm shaft bearings (10–Fig. G32). To adjust, remove cotter pin (7) from gear housing and turn adjustment plug (17) in as far as possible, then back off one notch and reinstall cotter pin.

OVERHAUL

ENGINE

All Models

Engine model no. is stamped on

Fig. G31 – Drawing of gear box oil level plug (L) and worm shaft bushing grease fitting (F).

Fig. G32 – Exploded view of gear box assembly. Shaft 23 is substituted for 21 on Models 51094 and 51096.

1. Snap ring
2. Alignment bushing
3. Felt wick
4. Bushing
5. Grease fitting
6. Gear case
7. Cotter pin
8. Oil level plug
9. Bearing cup
10. Bearing cone
11. Spacer
12. Worm shaft
13. Hypro key
14. Worm gear
15. Snap ring
16. "O" Ring
17. Adjustment plug
18. Seal
19. Bushing
20. Washer
21. Tine shaft
22. Hypro key
23. Tine shaft
24. Worm wheel
25. Snap ring
26. Gasket
27. Gasket
28. Cover
29. Lock tab

Fig. G33 — Exploded view of Model 51106 tiller. Parts 33, 34, 35 and 36 are substituted for parts 23, 27, 28, 29, 30, 31 and 32 on Models 51094 and 51096.

1. Hypro key	19. Depth control
2. Engine base	20. Spring clip
3. Cone clutch hub	21. Clevis pin
4. Upper cone	22. Tailpiece assy.
5. Clutch cone assy.	23. Gear case assy.
6. Clutch spring	24. Felt seal
7. Reinforcement plate	25. Washer
8. Bell housing assy.	26. Seal
9. Spring	27. Seal collar
10. Clutch rod	28. Tine washer
11. Throttle control	29. Tine
12. Handle assy.	30. Tine extension
13. Clutch yoke	31. Bushing
14. Retaining ring	32. Lockwasher
15. Pivot pin spacer	33. Gear case assy.
16. Clutch roller	34. Inner tine hub assy.
17. Clevis pin	35. Tine
18. Pivot pin	36. Outer tine hub assy.

blower housing. Refer to appropriate Briggs and Stratton engine section for overhaul procedures.

CLUTCH CONE ASSEMBLY

To renew clutch assembly, engine must be removed from engine base (2–Fig. G33) and bell housing assembly (8). Disconnect throttle control (11) and three 5/16 x 1⅞ bolts securing the engine to base and bell housing, then remove engine. Inspect upper cone (4) and clutch cone assembly (5) for gouging and excessive wear, renew as necessary. The upper cone (4) and clutch assembly (5) should be renewed as a set. Check condition of spring (6) and renew if stretched or broken. Clean and lubricate splines of worm shaft and clutch cone assembly (5) with SAE 30 oil. Check condition of clutch yoke assembly (13) including rollers (16) and renew if worn or damaged. Clean and lubricate clutch yoke and rollers with SAE 30 oil before assembling.

GEAR CASE

All Models

OIL SEAL INSTALLATION. Remove tines from output shaft. Remove bolts securing side cover (28–Fig. G32) to gear case and remove cover. Remove old seal (18), install new oil seal, then reinstall side cover and bolts. On opposite side of gear case hub, pry seal from hub and drive new seal in until bottomed in bore of case hub.

INSPECTION. Refer to Fig. G32 for gear case parts breakdown and identification. Inspect all components and renew all that are worn or damaged. Install new gaskets and seals. Lubricate gears and bearings with a light film of oil during reassembly. Refer to **GEAR CASE ADJUSTMENT** section for end play adjusting procedure. Refer to **LUBRICATION** section for lubrication requirements.

Fig. G34 — Drawing of clutch control. Refer to text for adjustment procedures.

1. Clutch rod	3. Cotter pin
2. Clutch yoke	4. Clevis pin

GILSON

Model	Engine Make	Engine Series	Engine Horsepower	No. of Forward Speeds	Power Reverse?	Tilling Width (In.)	Drive Type
51080	B&S	90000	3.5	1	No	12-26	Gear
51084	B&S	90000	3.5	1	Yes	12-26	Gear

LUBRICATION

ENGINE

All Models

Refer to Briggs and Stratton engine section for engine lubrication requirements. Recommended fuel is regular or low lead gasoline.

GEAR DRIVE

Oil level in gear housing should be checked at least every 25 hours of operation. Gear housing oil level should be even with oil level plug hole (L–Fig. G41) with tiller in level position. It may be necessary to place boards under the tiller wheels to level the unit. Recommended oil is SAE 140 EP.

The worm shaft bushing (3–Fig. G42) is lubricated through a grease fitting (F–Fig. G41) with number 2 wheel bearing grease. A small amount of grease should be added at least every 10 hours of operation.

MAINTENANCE

Inspect belt pulleys and reverse disc (if so equipped) and renew if damaged or worn excessively. Check condition of control levers and linkage and renew if

excessive play or binding prohibits easy, complete engagement of drive mechanism. The success of the slide type pulley engagement system is dependent upon the ability of the engine base slides (33 and 35–Fig. G44) to move freely over the slide blocks (32) thus allowing the pulleys and belt to engage and disengage properly. Periodically clean and lubricate the slide blocks (32) with a lithium type grease. Periodically lubricate wheel bushings with SAE 30 oil.

ADJUSTMENT

CLUTCH CONTROL

With the clutch control lever in neutral position, tiller should not creep either forward or reverse (if so equipped). Check by disconnecting spark plug wire and pulling recoil starter. If tiller moves backward (Model 51084 only) loosen lock nut (2–Fig. G43) remove

Fig. G43–Drawing of clutch control rod adjustment. Refer to text for procedures.

1. Control rod	
2. Lock nut	5. Clevis pin
3. Clevis	6. Bell crank
4. Spring clip	7. Clutch link

Fig. G41–Drawing of gear box oil level plug (L) and worm shaft bushing grease fitting (F).

Fig. G42–Exploded view of gear box assembly.

1. Alignment bushing	9. Spacer	17. Gear case cover	25. Woodruff key
2. Felt wick	10. Worm gear	18. Cover gasket	26. Worm wheel
3. Worm shaft bushing	11. Snap ring	19. Cover gasket	27. Intermediate felt seal
4. Grease fitting	12. Worm shaft	20. Tine shaft seal	28. Inner felt seal
5. Gear case	13. Hypro key	21. Bushing	29. Washer
6. Oil level plug	14. "O" ring	22. Washer	30. Inner tine hub assy.
7. Worm shaft bearing cup	15. Cotter pin	23. Snap ring	31. Outer tine hub assy.
8. Bearing cone	16. Adjustment plug	24. Tine shaft	32. Tine

spring clip (4) and clevis pin (5). Turn clevis (3) counter-clockwise off of the control rod (1) one to two turns. If the tiller moves forward follow above procedures except turn the clevis (3) clockwise one to two turns. Recheck for improper engagement in neutral, then retighten jam nut (2) against clevis (3) when proper adjustment is attained.

GEAR CASE BEARING

After many hours of operation end play may develop in the worm shaft bearings (8 – Fig. G42). To adjust, remove cotter pin (15) from gear housing and turn adjustment plug (16) in as far as possible then back off one notch and reinstall cotter pin.

OVERHAUL

ENGINE

All Models

Engine model no. is stamped on blower housing. Refer to appropriate Briggs and Stratton engine section for overhaul procedures.

GEAR CASE

All Models

OIL SEAL INSTALLATION. Remove tines from output shaft. Remove bolts securing side cover (17 – Fig. G42) to gear case and remove cover. Remove old seal (20), install new seal, then reinstall side cover and bolts. On opposite side of gear case hub, pry seal from hub and drive new seal in until bottomed in bore of case hub.

INSPECTION. Refer to Fig. G42 for gear case parts breakdown and identification. Inspect all components and renew all that are worn or damaged. Install new gaskets and seals. Lubricate gears and bearings with a light film of oil

Fig. G44 — Exploded view of typical tiller assembly. Parts 16A and 29A are used only on Model 51084.

1.	Spring	13.	Handle assy.	22.	Washer
2.	Control tube	14.	Washer	23.	Input pulley
3.	Cotter pin	15.	Control bushing	24.	Drive belt
4.	Control pin	16.	Bellcrank, Model	25.	Hypro key
5.	Roll pin		51080	26.	Engine
6.	Control rod	16A.	Bellcrank, Model	27.	Hypro key
7.	Throttle control		51084	28.	Set screw
8.	Throttle clamp	17.	Connecting link	29.	Engine pulley
9.	Jam nut	18.	Spring	29A.	Reverse disc
10.	Clevis	19.	Washer	30.	Engine base
11.	Clevis pin	20.	Cotter pin	31.	Belt guide
12.	Spring clip	21.	Spring retainer pin	32.	Slide block
33.	Engine base slide, L.H.
34.	Frame
35.	Engine base slide, R.H.
36.	Wheel frame assy.
37.	Tailpiece pin
38.	Spring clip
39.	Tailpiece lock
40.	Tailpiece assy.
41.	Depth control

during reassembly. Refer to **GEAR CASE ADJUSTMENT** section for end play adjusting procedure. Refer to **LUBRICATION** section for lubrication requirements.

DRIVE BELT

All Models

Refer to Fig. G44 for parts breakdown and identification. Remove cotter pin from connecting link (17), then remove

link from bell crank (16 or 16A). Remove engine securing bolts, then lift engine assembly from tiller frame. Slip drive belt off engine pulley and install new belt. Manufacturer recommends Gilson drive belt No. 28673. Reinstall engine assembly on tiller frame. Reach under front of tiller frame and slip belt on gear case drive pulley. Complete reassembly in reverse order of disassembly. Refer to **CLUTCH CONTROL** section for adjusting procedure.

GILSON

Model	Engine Make	Engine Series	Engine Horsepower	No. of Forward Speeds	Power Reverse?	Tilling Width (In.)	Drive Type
51095	B&S	60000	2	1	No	12-26	Gear
51170	B&S	60000	2	1	No	6-18	Gear
51105	B&S	90000	3.5	1	Yes	12-26	Gear

LUBRICATION

ENGINE

All Models

Refer to Briggs and Stratton engine section for engine lubrication requirements. Recommended fuel is regular or low lead gasoline.

WHEELS AND CONTROLS

All Models

Periodically lubricate wheel bushings and check for loose bolts. Idler pulley shaft (14–Fig. G53) on Models 51095 and 51170 should be lubricated with SAE 30 oil after each 10 hours of opera-

Fig. G51– View showing oil fill screw of Model 51105. Refer to text for lubrication procedures.

Fig. G52– View of belt and pulley system on Models 51095 and 51170.

1. Engine pulley
2. Engine bolt
3. Drive belt
4. Idler pulley
5. Input pulley

Fig. G53– Exploded view of tiller Models 51095 and 51170.

1. Control rod
2. Handle assy.
3. Clutch arm assy.
4. Belt guard
5. Square key
6. Set screw
7. Drive belt
8. Depth bar
9. Tine shield
10. Support assy.
11. Snap ring
12. Washer
13. Idler pulley
14. Idler shaft
15. Input pulley
16. Gear case assy.
17. Seal
18. Felt seal
19. Felt seal
20. Washer
21. Seal collar
22. Tine washer
23. Tine
24. Tine extension
25. Bushing

35

Fig. G54—Drawing of clutch control rod and cam adjustment. Refer to text for adjusting procedures.

1. Cam
2. Pad
3. Set screw
4. Pivot pin
5. Control rod

tion. Caution should be taken in not getting oil on drive belt.

The success of the slide type pulley engagement system on Model 51105 is de-

pendent upon the ability of the engine base (7–Fig. G55) to move freely over the slides (8), thus allowing the pulleys and belt to engage and disengage properly. Periodically clean and lubricate slide points with a lithium type grease.

GEAR DRIVE

The gear box on Models 51095 and 51170 is lubricated for the life of the unit and there is no plug for adding oil. Model 51105 is also lubricated for the life of the unit; however, oil may be added should leakage occur. To add oil, turn tiller on side as shown in Fig. G51, remove oil fill screw and completely fill unit with SAE 140 EP oil. When no air bubbles are evident, reinstall screw.

MAINTENANCE

Check condition of control levers and linkage and renew if excessive play or binding prohibits easy, complete en-

Fig. G56—Drawing showing belt guard tab (T) properly secured against side of engine.

gagement of drive mechanism. Inspect drive belt and renew if frayed, cracked, burnt or otherwise damaged. Inspect belt pulleys and renew if damaged or worn excessively.

ADJUSTMENT

CLUTCH CONTROL ROD

Model 51105

With clutch control lever in forward position initial adjustment should be 3/16-inch (4.8 mm) gap between cam (1–Fig. G54) and pad (2). Adjustment is made by loosening set screw (3) and sliding pivot pin (4) over rod (5) until proper gap is attained, then retighten set screw. With control rod in neutral, tiller should not creep either forward or reverse. Check by disconnecting spark plug wire and pulling recoil starter. If tiller moves backward, gap between the cam (1) and pad (2) will have to be increased slightly with control rod in forward position. If tiller moves forward in neutral, gap between cam (1) and pad (2)

Fig. G55—Exploded view of tiller Model 51105.

1. Control handle
2. Woodruff key
3. Shroud
4. Control rod
5. Throttle control
6. Handle assy.
7. Engine base assy.
8. Slide
9. Spring
10. Engine pulley
11. Screw
12. Pin
13. Input pulley
14. Drive belt
15. Frame assy.
16. Depth bar
17. Cam
18. Washer
19. Set screw
20. Pivot pin
21. Gear case assy.
22. Seal
23. Felt seal
24. Felt seal
25. Washer
26. Seal collar assy.
27. Tine washer
28. Tine
29. Tine extension
30. Bushing

Fig. G57—Drawing of proper belt arrangement.

P. Belt guide pin
I. Input pulley
B. Drive belt

Fig. G58 — Exploded view of gearcase used on Models 51095 and 51170.

1. Left gearcase	6. Idler arm	11. Ball	16. Bearing
2. Gasket	7. Right gearcase	12. Pin	17. Race
3. Snap ring	8. Seal	13. Worm shaft	18. Flange bearing
4. Gear	9. Tine shaft	14. Thrust washer	19. Flange bearing
5. Thrust washer	10. Key	15. Race	20. "O" ring

GEAR BOX

Models 51095 and 51170

Overhaul of gear box assembly is evident after inspection of unit and referral to Fig. G58. Note that gear box housing is riveted together and will require special tools to overhaul.

Model 51105

Gear box assemblies on these models cannot be serviced and individual repair parts are not available. Gear box is renewed as a unit.

DRIVE BELT

Models 51095 and 51170

To renew belt, remove belt guard (4 – Fig. G53) from engine and pull up on belt (3 – Fig. G52) sliding it off engine pulley (1). If belt will not come off engine pulley, then loosen engine-to-gear case assembly bolts and tilt engine back until belt slides off. Install belt by reversing removal procedure. Manufacturer recommends Gilson drive belt 33622. Belt guard tab (T – Fig. G56) must be pushed down securely against side of engine.

Model 51105

To remove belt, place control lever (1 – Fig. G55) in neutral position and remove bolts securing engine to tiller. Detach throttle control cable (5) from engine and remove engine from tiller. Remove belt by slipping over input pulley (I – Fig. G57). Install belt by reversing removal procedure. Manufacturer recommends the use of Gilson drive belt 36019. Be certain belt is installed inside pins (P) as shown in Fig. G57.

will have to be decreased slightly with control rod in forward position.

Models 51095 and 51170

There is no clutch adjustment provided. If drive belt slippage is encountered, drive belt and/or other worn parts will need to be renewed. Refer to **DRIVE BELT** section for belt removal procedures.

OVERHAUL

ENGINE

All Models

Engine model number is stamped on blower housing. Refer to appropriate Briggs and Stratton engine section for overhaul procedures.

GILSON

Model	Engine Make	Engine Series	Engine Horsepower	No. of Forward Speeds	Power Reverse?	Tilling Width (In.)	Drive Type
51114	B&S	130000	5	1	Yes	18	Chain
51134	B&S	130000	5	1	Yes	18	Chain
51159	B&S	130000	5	1	Yes	18	Chain
51175	B&S	130000	5	1	Yes	18	Chain
51175A	B&S	130000	5	1	Yes	18	Chain
51176A	B&S	130000	5	1	Yes	18	Chain
51135	B&S	190000	8	5	Yes	26	Chain
51179	B&S	190000	8	5	Yes	26	Chain
51179A	B&S	190000	8	5	Yes	26	Chain

LUBRICATION

ENGINE

All Models

Refer to Briggs and Stratton engine section for engine lubrication requirements. Recommended fuel is regular or low lead gasoline.

DRIVE CONTROLS

All Models

Clean and lubricate friction points with SAE 30 oil after each eight hours of operation. Caution should be taken in not getting oil on belts.

Inner flange of variable speed pulley mounted on engine must slide freely in and out. Clutch control lever may be difficult to move into forward drive position if pulley flange does not move free-

ly. To clean, drive roll pin (2–Fig. G73) from outer pulley half (22) and engine pulley (1), then remove ouer pulley half. While removing roll pin hold pulley securely because internal spring (19)

should force pulley apart. Remove inner pulley half (20), then clean pulley half and shaft portion of engine pulley (1). Reassemble cleaned parts dry. Do not apply oil or grease to pulley parts.

Fig. G62—Oil level and fill plug location on wheel drive case. Note depth control lever is on shallowest setting.

Fig. G61—Drawing showing depth control lever.

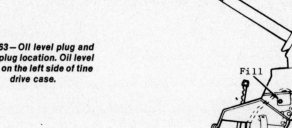

Fig. G63—Oil level plug and oil fill plug location. Oil level plug is on the left side of tine drive case.

WHEEL DRIVE CASE

To check oil level, place tiller depth control lever at shallowest setting as shown in Fig. G61. Unbolt and remove right wheel from output shaft. Clean dirt from around oil level and fill plug (Fig. G62), then remove plug. Oil level should be at bottom of plug hole. Recommended oil is SAE 140 EP and capacity is 16 ounces. Oil level should be checked at least every 25 hours of operation and added as needed.

TINE DRIVE CASE

All Models Except 51114

To check oil level, locate tiller on level ground, then set tilling depth control lever at shallowest setting (Fig. G61). Clean dirt from around oil level plug (Fig. G63) and remove plug. Oil level should be at bottom of plug hole. If oil level is low, clean dirt from around fill plug and remove plug. Add oil slowly until it runs out level plug hole, then reinstall both plugs.

Model 51114

To check oil level, set tilling depth control lever Fig. G61 to deepest setting and raise front drive wheels six inches off ground by placing boards under wheels. Clean dirt from around oil level and fill plug Fig. G64, then remove plug. Oil level should be at bottom of plug hole. Recommended oil is SAE 140 EP gear lube and capacity is one pound. Check gear oil at least every 25 hours and add as needed.

Fig. G64 — Tiller Model 51114 must have its tires raised six inches before oil level may be accurately checked. Note depth control lever set on deepest setting.

Fig. G65 — Drawing highlighting points of handle control lever adjustment nut on Models 51114 and 51134.

1. Adjustment nut
2. Plunger assy.
3. Wheel drive pulley
4. Tine drive pulley
5. Tine drive belt
6. Belt guide pin
7. Belt guide
8. Retaining ring
9. Spacer
10. Idler arm assys.
11. Engine pulley
12. Idler pulley
13. Adjustment idler
14. Machine screw

MAINTENANCE

Inspect nuts and bolts for looseness and retighten as needed. Check condition of control linkage and idler arm assemblies (10 – Fig. G65). Renew if excessive play or binding prohibits easy, complete engagement of drive mechanism. Inspect drive belts and renew if frayed, cracked, burnt or otherwise damaged. Inspect pulleys and renew if damaged or worn excessively.

ADJUSTMENT

CLUTCH CONTROL LEVER

Models 51114, 51134 and 51135

Adjustment is provided to center clutch control lever in slot at handle, if necessary, due to wear. To adjust, locate

Fig. G66 — Adjustment nut is provided to center the clutch control lever in the slot on the handle.

Fig. G67 — Clutch control lever shown in neutral position.

Fig. G67A — View showing correct adjustment of clutch lever (1) in forward position on Models 51159, 51175 and 51175A.

DRIVE BELTS

Models 51114, 51134, 51159, 51175, 51175A, and 51176A

TINE DRIVE BELT. With clutch control lever in forward drive position, distance between inside of belt (A – Fig. G69) should be ⅞-inch (22.2 mm) on Model 51114 and ¾-inch (19 mm) on Models 51134, 51159, 51175, 51175A and 51176A. Adjustment is accomplished by loosening bolts securing tine chain case (11 – Fig. G71) to frame slots (9). Rotate case forward to loosen belt and back to tighten belt. Tighten clamp bolts securely after adjustment. Move

Fig. G69 — Drawing showing adjustment distance (A) on Models 51114, 51134, 51159, 51175, 51175A, and 51176A. Refer to text for specific model requirement on the tine drive belt adjustment.

handle bar straight to rear and in lowest position. Loosen adjustment nut shown in Fig. G66, center clutch lever in neutral area (Fig. G67), then retighten adjustment nut.

Models 51159, 51175 and 51175A

Refer to Fig. G67B and position stop collar (5) 2¾ inches (69.9 mm) from end of tine drive link (4). To check adjustment, refer to Fig. G67A. With clutch lever (1) in forward gear position and all slack taken up in linkage, specified clearance between lever and bottom of slot is ¼-inch (6.4 mm).

Fig. G67B — View showing control linkage adjustment on Models 51159, 51175 and 51175A.

1. Control link	4. Tine drive link
2. Pivot	5. Stop collar
3. Wheel drive link	6. Lower trunnion

Fig. G68 — Exploded view typical of Models 51114, 51134, 51159, 51175, 51175A, and 51176A.

1. Set screw	10. Square key	20. Hinge rod	30. Felt seal
2. Woodruff key	11. Set screw	21. Spring	31. Felt seal
3. Camshaft pulley	12. Belt guide	22. Skid assy.	32. Washer
4. Engine crankshaft pulley	13. Wheel drive pulley	23. Snap ring	33. Felt seal
5. Washer	14. Snap ring	24. Tine drive pulley	34. Left tine assy.
6. Right frame assy.	15. Belt guard	25. Tine case assy.	35. Left frame assy.
7. Adjusting slot	16. Right tine assy.	26. Wheel case assy.	36. Oil seal
8. Idler pulley	17. Tine shield	27. "O" ring	37. Counterweight
9. Spacer	18. Depth control assy.	28. Cup	38. Counterweight
	19. Hinge	29. Washer	39. Snap ring

40. Washer	
41. Tine idler brackets	
42. Spacer	
43. Wheel idler bracket	
44. Bellcrank	
45. Link	
46. Cotter pin ⅛-inch	
47. Cotton pin 3/32-inch	
48. Control rod	
49. Tine drive spring	
50. Washer	
51. Swivel	
52. Wheel drive spring	
53. Control rod	
54. Tire drive belt	
55. Tine drive belt	

depth control lever to shallowest setting Fig. G61 and start engine. With clutch control lever in neutral position, tines should not rotate. If tines rotate, readjust to increase belt slack until tines do not drive in neutral.

WHEEL DRIVE BELT. Traction belt should have approximately ¼-inch (6.4 mm) clearance between upper idler and belt (Fig. G70), with control lever in neutral position. Adjustment is accomplished by removing screw (14–Fig. G65), then moving pulley (13) to another of four locations.

Fig. G70—Drawing showing proper belt adjustment of wheel drive belt on Models 51114, 51134, 51175, 51175A and 51176A. Refer to text for adjustment procedures.

Fig. G71—Exploded view of frame assembly parts on Models 51135, 51179 and 51179A.

1. Belt cover	6. Spring	11. Tine case assy.	16. Felt seal
2. Right tine assy.	7. Right frame assy.	12. Washer	17. Left tine assy.
3. Tine shield	8. Left frame assy.	13. Felt seal	18. Wheel case assy.
4. Depth control assy.	9. Adjusting slot	14. Felt seal	19. Counterweight
5. Hinge rod	10. Skid assy.	15. Washer	20. Counterweight

Fig. G70A — View showing location of pivot bolt (1) and clamp bolt (2) on Models 51179 and 51179A. Refer to text for tine drive belt adjustment.

Fig. G70B — View showing tine drive belt pulley spring compressed to proper length when tine clutch is in forward position on Models 51179 and 51179A.

½ - Inch (12.7mm)
to ¾ - Inch (19 mm)

Fig. G72 — View of belt and pulley system on Model 51135.

1. Engine pulley
2. Roll pin
3. Wheel drive belt
4. Tine drive belt
5. Reverse belt
6. Reverse drive pulley
7. Wheel drive pulley
8. Tine drive pulley
9. Tine idler pulley
10. Forward idler pulley
11. Reverse idler pulley
12. Flat idler
13. Forward idler arm
14. Reverse idler arm

Fig. G72A — View of belt and pulley system used on Models 51179 and 51179A.

1. Ground speed lever
2. Tine drive belt
3. Reverse drive belt
4. Primary drive belt
5. Secondary drive belt
6. Wheel drive pulley
7. Pivot bracket cap screw
8. Secondary idler pulley
9. Middle pulley
10. Engine pulley
11. Shoulder bolt

Fig. G73 — Exploded view of drive assembly belt and pulley system used on Model 51135.

1. Engine pulley	9. Tine idler pulley	16. Spacer cup	23. Reverse arm assy.
2. Roll pin	10. Forward idler pulley	17. Adjuster	24. Bearing
3. Wheel drive belt	11. Reverse idler pulley	18. Clutch rod	25. Drive ring
4. Tine drive belt	12. Flat idler	19. Compression spring	26. Spring
5. Reverse belt	13. Forward idler arm	20. Inner pulley half	27. Swivel
6. Reverse drive pulley	14. Reverse idler arm	21. Bushing	28. Compression spring
7. Wheel drive pulley	15. Spacer	22. Outer pulley half	29. Idler arm assy.
8. Tine drive pulley			30. Reverse rod

Model 51135

TINE DRIVE BELT. With clutch lever in drive, idler arm compression spring (28 – Fig. G73) should be compressed ½ to ¾-inch (12.7-19 mm) from roll pin (C – Fig. G75).

Adjustment is accomplished by loosening bolts securing tine chain case (11 – Fig. G71) to frame assembly, then rotating entire chain case in slots (9). Rotate chain case up and forward to slacken belt and down and back to tighten. With clutch control lever in neutral (Fig. G67) drive belt should slip on drive pulleys. Check for proper adjustment by disconnecting plug wire and pulling recoil starter with control lever in neutral. If tines turn, then drive belt tension will need to be lowered.

WHEEL DRIVE BELT. With handle bar clutch control in neutral, drive belt should be loose enough to keep tines from rotating. With clutch control lever in forward drive and ground speed lever in fast or up position, drive belt should be tight enough to propel tiller.

The forward wheel drive belt (3 – Fig. G72) is adjusted by relocating adjustment end of traction and tine control rod (16 – Fig. G73) in one of the various holes in adjustment lever (17). Insert rod in hole closer to rear of lever (17) to increase belt tension.

Models 51179 and 51179A

TINE DRIVE BELT. Adjustment is made by pivoting entire chain case and tine assembly. Refer to Fig. 70A and loosen pivot bolt (1) and clamp bolt (2). Rotate case forward to loosen belt and back to tighten belt. Tighten pivot and clamp bolts securely after adjustment. With clutch control lever in neutral position, tines should not rotate. If tines rotate, readjust to increase belt slack until tines do not drive in neutral. When adjustment is correct, tine belt idler spring should be compressed ½-inch (12.7 mm) to ¾-inch (19 mm) as shown in Fig. 70B.

PRIMARY FORWARD DRIVE BELT. Belt is self-adjusted by spring-loaded idler pulley.

SECONDARY FORWARD DRIVE BELT. Place ground speed lever in lowest forward speed, then slide middle pulley (9 – Fig. G72A) towards outside as far as it will go. Move clutch control lever all the way forward. If belt slips after moving middle pulley, slide secondary idler pulley (8) down until belt is tight.

Fig. G75 — Distance (C) is the amount idler arm spring is compressed from roll pin on 51135 model only. Refer to text for adjustment procedures.

Fig. G74 — Exploded view of handle and control parts typical of Models 51114, 51134, 51135, 51176A, 51179 and 51179A.

1. Clutch control lever
2. Link assy.
3. Handle control lever
4. Handle shroud
5. Throttle control assy.
6. Handle control rod
7. Clutch control rod
8. Handle assy.
9. Lever
10. Bellcrank assy.
11. Pin
12. Spacer
13. Washers
14. Clevis pin
15. Pivot assy.
16. Clamp spacer
17. Clamp
18. Pin
19. Pawl
20. Spring
21. Detent spring
22. Ball
23. Tunnel assy.
24. Plunger assy.
25. Cam assy.
26. Retainer assy.

1. Throttle control assy.
2. Handle assy.
3. Rubber spacer
4. Clutch handle assy.
5. Control link
6. Handle support assy.
7. Wheel drive link
8. Wheel drive spring
9. Pivot bracket
10. Tine drive link
11. Stop collar
12. Pivot bracket

Fig. G74A — Exploded view of handle and control parts typical of Models 51159, 51175 and 51175A.

REVERSE DRIVE BELT. Belt is self-adjusted by spring-loaded idler pulley.

OVERHAUL

ENGINE

All Models

Engine model number is stamped on blower housing. Refer to appropriate Briggs and Stratton engine section for overhaul procedures.

CHAIN CASE

All Models

INSPECTION. Refer to Figs. G76, G77 and G78 for parts breakdown and identification for all models.

Inspect and renew all parts that are worn or damaged. Install new gasket and seals. Lubricate chains, sprockets and bearings with a light film of oil during reassembly. Keep all dirt and foreign matter out of chain case during reassembly. Refer to **LUBRICATION** section for lubrication requirements after reassembly and installation.

DRIVE BELTS

Models 51114, 51134, 51159, 51175, 51175A and 51176A

TINE DRIVE BELT. To remove belt, place clutch control lever in neutral position. Remove belt guard (15–Fig. G68) and belt guide (7–Fig. G65). Slide belt (5) off tine drive case pulley (4). Remove belt from engine pulley (11) and slip from between pulley and idler arm (10). Reverse removal procedure to install belt. Gilson recommends using Gilson drive belt 200554. Be sure belt is installed over guide pin (6). Check tine

Fig. G76 – Exploded view of tine drive chain case parts on Models 51134, 51135, 51159, 51175, 51175A, 51176A, 51179 and 51179A.

1. Fill plug
2. Seals
3. Right chain case
4. Needle bearings
5. Idler sleeve
6. Shim
7. Spacer cup
8. Tine shaft assy.
9. Gasket
10. Upper chain
11. Bearing
12. Sprocket assy.
13. Lower chain
14. Input shaft assy.
15. Snap ring
16. Washer
17. Bearing
18. Left chain case
19. Seal
20. Oil level plug

drive belt adjustment as previously outlined.

WHEEL DRIVE BELT. Remove tine drive belt as previously outlined. Remove snap ring (14–Fig. G68) securing wheel drive pulley (13) to case shaft, then remove pulley taking care not to lose Woodruff key (2). Remove cotter pin (46) from link (45). Slide idler arm assemblies (10–Fig. G65) out until spacer (9) can be slid out from between idler arms. Remove belt (12). To reinstall, reverse removal procedure. Gilson recommends using Gilson belt 200555. Be sure belt is installed with flat side against engine drive pulley. Check for proper belt adjustment as previously outlined.

Model 51135

FORWARD WHEEL DRIVE BELT. Place clutch control lever in neutral position as shown in Fig. G67. Remove belt guard and slide belt off engine pulley (1–Fig. G72), then remove belt from wheel drive pulley (7). Belt may now be removed from tiller after slipping between forward pulley (7) and reverse pulley (6). Reverse removal procedure to install belt. Gilson recommends using Gilson drive belt 208526. Be sure belt is installed under upper belt guide pin and on top of tractor arm guide pin. Check drive belt adjustment as previously outlined.

REVERSE WHEEL DRIVE BELT. Remove forward wheel drive belt as outlined in previous paragraph. Move clutch control lever to forward position. Raise reverse idler arm (14–Fig. G73) and remove belt (5–Fig. G72) from reverse idler pulley (11). Belt may be removed from between wheel drive pulley and rubber reverse drive wheel. Reverse removal procedure to install belt. Gilson recommends using Gilson belt 208525. Be sure belt is under upper

belt guide pin. Reinstall forward drive belt. Check drive belt adjustment as previously outlined.

TINE DRIVE BELT. Remove forward drive belt and reverse drive belt as outlined in previous paragraphs. Move clutch control lever to neutral position as shown in Fig. G67. Slide belt (4–Fig. G72) off tine drive pulley (8). Remove snap ring from tine driver idler pulley shaft, then slide tine drive idler pulley (9) so belt can be removed. Remove snap ring from idler pivot pin. Slide idler arm outward so belt can be removed. Unhook clutch rod (18–Fig. G73) from adjustment lever after removing cotter pin securing them together. Remove retaining

ring from idler arm shaft, then slide both reverse idler arm (14–Fig. G72) and traction idler arm outward until belt can be removed from engine pulley. Remove belt.

To reinstall belt, reverse removal procedure. Gilson recommends using Gilson belt 208527. Be sure belt is on top of flat idler (12–Fig. G72), under upper guide pin and above belt guide pin at tine drive pulley. Reinstall reverse wheel drive belt and forward wheel drive belt. Check drive belt adjustments as previously outlined.

Models 51179 and 51179A

PRIMARY FORWARD DRIVE BELT. Place clutch lever in neutral position. Remove belt guard and unscrew cap screw (7–Fig. G72A) on left side of pivot bracket approximately ¾-inch (19 mm). Remove bolt (11) from inside of pivot bracket and remove screws from top of pivot bracket. Place ground speed lever (1) in low speed position, then remove pulleys from inside of pivot bracket. Remove outside shoulder bolt, outside section of bracket and speed lever as an assembly. Move clutch control lever to forward position and slip secondary drive belt (5) off secondary idler pulley (8). Slide primary drive belt (4) off engine pulley (10) and forward idler pulley, then slide belt through space between forward idler and left

Fig. G77 – Exploded view of wheel chain case parts on Models 51135, 51179 and 51179A.

1. Seals	7. Bearings	13. Washers	18. Axle shaft assy.
2. Right chain case	8. Chain	14. Bearings	19. Spacer cup
3. Gear assy.	9. Gasket	15. Left chain case	20. Shim
4. Bearings	10. Roll pin	16. Seal	21. Oil level plug
5. Idler sleeves	11. Input gear	17. Snap ring	22. Gear & sprocket assy.
6. Bearings	12. Input shaft		23. Oil fill plug

frame assembly. Remove belt by sliding between secondary idler pulley and rubber reverse drive wheel.

Reverse removal procedure to install belt. Gilson recommends using Gilson drive belt 213926. When reassembling, be sure ground speed lever is ahead of stop tab and in lowest position. Belt is self-adjusted by spring-loaded idler pulley.

SECONDARY FORWARD DRIVE BELT. Remove primary forward drive belt (4–Fig. G72A) as outlined in previous section. Slide secondary belt (5) off wheel drive pulley (6) and secondary idler pulley (8). Reinstall by reversing removal procedure. Gilson recommends using Gilson drive belt 208525. Check adjustment as previously outlined.

REVERSE DRIVE BELT. Remove primary forward drive belt and secondary forward drive belt as previously outlined. Unhook spring from idler arm assembly and remove cotter pin holding trunnion to idler arm assembly. Remove retaining ring from idler arm pivot and move clutch lever to neutral position. Lift up reverse idler and slide off belt (3–Fig. G72A). Slide idler arm assembly off pivot pin and slide belt off engine pulley (10). Remove belt by rolling between rubber drive wheel and drive wheel pulley. Reinstall by reversing removal procedure. Gilson recommends using Gilson belt 208525. Belt is self-adjusted by spring-loaded idler pulley.

TINE DRIVE BELT. Remove forward drive belts and reverse drive belt as outlined in previous paragraphs. Move clutch control lever to neutral position. Remove retaining ring from tine drive idler pulley shaft and slide belt (2–Fig. G72A) off tine drive pulley. Remove retaining ring from reverse drive wheel. Remove pulley hanger pivot pin. Slide hanger outward until belt can be removed and remove belt. Reinstall by reversing removal procedure. Gilson recommends using Gilson belt 208527. Check adjustment as previously outlined.

1. Seal cup
2. "O" ring
3. Left chain case
4. Chain
5. Sprocket
6. Input shaft & sprocket
7. Sprocket shaft
8. "U" clip
9. Idler sprocket
10. Right chain case
11. Seal
12. Wheel shaft
13. Drive pin
14. Thrust washer
15. Sprocket
16. Washer
17. Chain
18. Sprocket
19. Washer

Fig. G78—Exploded view of wheel drive chain case used on Models 51159, 51175, 51175A and 51176A.

GILSON

Model	Engine Make	Engine Series	Engine Horsepower	No. of Forward Speeds	Power Reverse?	Tilling Width (In.)	Drive Type
51104	B&S	60000	2	1	No	7-22	Chain
51171	B&S	80000	3	1	No	7-22	Chain
51171A	B&S	8000	3	1	No	7-22	Chain
51181	B&S	130000	5	1	No	7-22	Chain
51116	B&S	130000	5	1	No	12-26	Chain
51158	B&S	130000	5	1	No	12-26	Chain
51142	B&S	130000	5	1	No	12-26	Chain
51143	B&S	130000	5	1	Yes	12-26	Chain
51172	B&S	130000	5	1	No	12-26	Chain
51173	B&S	130000	5	1	Yes	12-26	Chain

LUBRICATION

ENGINE

All Models

Refer to Briggs and Stratton engine section for engine lubrication requirements. Recommended fuel is regular or low lead gasoline.

WHEELS AND CONTROLS

All Models

Transport wheel bushings should be lubricated occasionally with SAE 30 oil. **DO NOT** oil idler rollers as this will attract dirt and cause premature bearing failure.

CHAIN DRIVE

Oil level in chain case should be checked at least every 25 hours or more frequently if there are signs of continuous leakage. Recommended oil for all models is SAE 140 EP.

Models 51104, 51171, 51171A and 51181

To check oil level wipe dirt from around oil level and fill screw, then remove screw. Raise tiller handle to vertical position as shown in Fig. G80. Oil should be level with bottom of oil fill screw hole with tiller in raised position.

Models 51116 and 51158

To check oil level, place tiller on level surface and place the wheel hanger (17– Fig. G83) in center hole. Clean dirt from around slotted level plug (Fig. G81) and remove. Oil should be level with bottom of level plug hole. If oil level is low clean dirt from around fill plug and remove plug. Add oil slowly until it runs out level plug hole, then reinstall plugs.

Models 51142, 51143, 51172 and 51173

To check oil level place tiller on level surface. Clean dirt from around oil level plug (Fig. G82) and remove plug. Oil should be level with bottom of level plug hole. If oil level is low, clean dirt from around fill plug and remove. Add oil slowly until it runs out level plug hole, then reinstall plugs.

MAINTENANCE

Inspect nuts and bolts for looseness and retighten as necessary. Check condition of control linkage and idler arm assemblies. Renew if excessive play or binding prohibits easy, complete engagement of drive mechanism. Inspect drive belt(s) and renew if frayed, cracked, burnt or otherwise damaged. Inspect belt pulleys and renew if damaged or worn excessively.

BELT

ADJUSTMENT

Models 51116 and 51158

Adjustment is provided to compensate for belt wear. To adjust, loosen outside

Fig. G80—Drawing showing proper position of tiller when checking chain case oil level on Models 51104, 51171, 51171A and 51181.

Fig. G81—Oil level plug and oil fill plug location on Models 51116 and 51158.

Fig. G82—Oil level plug and oil fill plug location on Models 51142, 51143, 51172 and 51173. Oil level plug is found on the left side of tine drive case.

Fig. G84—Drawing showing lever bracket and hex nut on Models 51116 and 51158. Refer to text for proper belt adjusting procedure.

Fig. G83—Exploded view of tiller Models 51116 and 51158.

<table>
</table>

1. Handle bar assy.
2. Clutch handle
3. Clutch spring
4. Throttle control
5. Clutch cable
6. Drive belt
7. Set screw
8. Engine pulley
9. Belt guide
10. Square key
11. Belt guard bracket
12. Tine shield
13. Belt guard
14. Rear hitch casting
15. Rear hitch
16. Depth control bar
17. Wheel hangar
18. Spade
19. Chain case
20. Set screw
21. Woodruff key
22. Input pulley
23. Lever bracket
24. Clutch lever assy.
25. Idler pulley
26. Felt seal
27. Washer
28. Felt seal
29. Washer
30. Felt seal
31. Inner tine hub
32. Outer tine hub
33. Tine
34. Engine mount

Fig. G85—Adjuster spring and stud used for proper tensioning of clutch cable. It is important to temporarily remove cable from adjustment stud when turning stud.

Fig. G87—Exploded view of tine drive chain case parts on Models 51142, 51143, 51172 and 51173.

1. Oil fill plug
2. Seals
3. Needle bearings
4. Right chain case
5. Gasket
6. Shim
7. Spacer cup
8. Bearings
9. Upper chain
10. Input shaft assy.
11. Snap rings
12. Washers
13. Bearings
14. Left chain case
15. Seal
16. Sprocket assy.
17. Idler sleeve
18. Lower chain
19. Tine shaft assy.
20. Oil level plug

Fig. G86—Drawing showing parts used in adjusting clutch on Models 51143, 51172 and 51173. Refer to text for procedure.

21. Washer
22. Chain
23. Gasket
24. Left chain case
25. Center gear axle
26. Center gear
27. Center gear bolt
28. Oil fill plug

Fig. G88—Exploded view of the tine drive chain case parts on Models 51116 and 51158.

1. Shaft sleeve plugs
2. Right chain case
3. Bearings
4. Idler gear
5. Drive gear
6. Pin
7. Input shaft
8. Spacer
9. Seal
10. Bearings
11. Seals
12. Washer
13. Bearings
14. Inner races
15. Washer
16. Tine shaft
17. Woodruff key
18. Oil level plug
19. Sprocket assy.
20. Snap ring

Fig. G88A—Exploded view of tine drive chain case used on Models 51104, 51171, 51171A and 51181.

1. Idler arm assy.
2. "O" ring
3. Left chain case
4. Washer
5. Snap ring
6. Chain
7. Input shaft & sprocket
8. Sprocket
9. "U" clip
10. Idler sprocket
11. Spacer
12. Right chain case
13. Seal
14. Tine shaft
15. Pop rivet
16. Thrust washer
17. Shaft
18. Chain
19. Sprocket
20. Washer
21. "O" ring
22. Cup

hex nut securing lever bracket to clutch lever (Fig. G84). Move idler arm up until idler pulley tightens belt. With idler arm held in this position move lever bracket forward until clutch cable is tight. Retighten outside hex nut. Check adjustment by disconnecting plug wire and pulling recoil starter. Belt should slip on pulleys. If belt does not slip on pulleys when clutch lever is released, follow preceding procedure to move idler further away from belt.

Model 51142

Adjustment is provided to compensate for belt wear. Adjustment is accomplished by overtightening control cable slightly, then loosening clutch control cable to just provide complete disengagement. To determine if adjustment is necessary, disconnect spark plug wire, push down on handle to raise tines off ground, then pull on recoil starter. If tines rotate, loosen clutch cable by turning nylon adjustment stud (Fig. G85) counterclockwise just enough so that tines do not rotate when recoil starter is pulled. Be certain cable still runs through "U" shaped bracket on lower left corner of handle. **NOTE:** Remove

Fig. G89—View showing where belt guard is secured to tiller.

Fig. G90—Drawing showing belt and pulley system typical of Models 51104, 51171, 51171A and 51181.

1. Spring
2. Drive belt
3. Input pulley
4. Idler pulley
5. Engine pulley

Fig. G94 — View of belt and pulley assembly on Models 51143 and 51173.

1. Camshaft pulley
2. Reverse idler pulley
3. Forward drive belt
4. Reverse drive belt
5. Forward idler pulley
6. Spring
7. Input pulley

Briggs and Stratton engine section for overhaul procedures.

Fig. G91 — Exploded view of tiller Models 511142 and 51172.

1. Clutch lever
2. Clutch cable
3. Handle assy.
4. Throttle control
5. Drive belt
6. Set screw
7. Engine pulley
8. Square key
9. Guard bracket
10. Handle support
11. Belt guard
12. Chain case
13. Right frame
14. Hitch plate
15. Snap rings
16. Input pulley
17. Square key
18. Washer
19. Felt seal
20. Felt seal
21. Washer
22. Felt seal
23. Inner tine hub
24. Tine shield
25. Spring
26. Spacer
27. Idler pulley

CHAIN CASE

All Models

INSPECTION. Refer to Fig. G88A for an exploded view of the chain case used on Models 51116 and 51158. Refer to Fig. G87 for an exploded view of the chain case used on Models 51142, 51143, 51172 and 51173.

Inspect and renew all parts that are worn or damaged. Install new gasket

cable from nylon adjustment stud temporarily when turning adjustment stud.

If tines do not rotate with clutch lever engaged, tighten cable by turning nylon adjustment stud (Fig. G85) clockwise in increments of one full turn until tines just begin to rotate when engine is turned with recoil starter.

OVERHAUL

ENGINE

All Models

Engine model number is stamped on blower housing. Refer to appropriate

Models 51143, 51172 and 51173

To check adjustment, place clutch control lever in neutral position, disconnect spark plug wire, then pull recoil starter. Belt should slip on all pulleys. If tiller moves forward, loosen jam nut (Fig. G86) and top hex nut. Move bottom hex nut up slightly by turning, then retighten top hex nut and jam nut. If tiller moves backward, when clutch lever is in neutral position, then move bottom hex nut down slightly and retighten top hex nut and jam nut.

Fig. G93 — Exploded view of tiller Models 51143 and 51173.

1. Clutch lever
2. Control bracket
3. Lever spring
4. Control rod
5. Handle assy.
6. Swivel
7. Handle support
8. Set screw
9. Reverse drive belt
10. Forward drive belt
11. Woodruff key
12. Camshaft pulley
13. Engine pulley
14. Square keys
15. Guard bracket
16. Belt guard
17. Chain case
18. Hitch plate
19. Left frame
20. Clevis pin
21. Wheel hanger
22. Washer
23. Felt seal
24. Felt seal
25. Washer
26. Felt seal
27. Inner tine hub
28. Tine shield
29. Idler pulley
30. Spacers
31. Snap rings
32. Input pulleys
33. Snap ring
34. Tine
35. Idler bracket

Fig. G92 — Belt and pulley assembly on Models 51142 and 51172.

1. Belt guide
2. Drive belt
3. Engine pulley
4. Idler pulley
5. Input pulley

Fig. G95 – Exploded view of tiller Model 51104.

1. Upper control rod
2. Lower control rod
3. Spring
4. Handle control rod
5. Handle assy.
6. Wing screw
7. Throttle control
8. Grip
9. Belt guard
10. Square key
11. Set screws
12. Engine pulley
13. Frame assy.
14. Wheel hanger
15. Depth stick
16. Pulley assy.
17. Drive belt
18. Washer
19. Idler pulley
20. Snap ring
21. Tine shield
22. Chain case
23. Seal
24. Felt seal
25. Felt seal
26. Washer
27. Seal collar
28. Tine washers
29. Tine extension
30. Tine
31. Bushing

install belt, reverse removal procedure. Gilson recommends the use of Gilson drive belt 280301 for Model 51142 and drive belt 207159 for Model 51172. Be sure belt is installed between belt guides. Check drive belt adjustment as outlined in **ADJUSTMENT** section.

Models 51143 and 51173

FORWARD DRIVE BELT. Remove belt guard (16 – Fig. G93) and unhook spring (6 – Fig. G94) from engine mounting frame (19 – Fig. G93), then remove belt. To install, reverse removal procedure. Gilson recommends the use of Gilson drive belt 208301 for Model 51143 and drive belt 207159 for Model 51173. Be sure belt is installed between belt guides. Check drive belt adjustment as outlined in **ADJUSTMENT** section.

REVERSE DRIVE BELT. Remove forward drive belt as previously outlined, then remove reverse belt. Gilson recommends the use of Gilson drive belt 208626 for both models. Be sure belt is installed between belt guides and under reverse idler.

and seals. Lubricate chains, sprockets and bearings with a light film of oil during reassembly. Keep all dirt and foreign matter out of chain case during reassembly. Refer to **LUBRICATION** section for lubrication requirements after reassembly and installation.

DRIVE BELTS

Models 51104, 51116, 51171, 51171A, 51116 and 51158

To renew belt, remove two screws and belt guard (Fig. G89). Slip belt over edge of engine pulley (5 – Fig. G90) and turn pulley until belt slides off, then remove belt from input pulley (3). Install new belt by reversing removal procedure. Gilson recommends the use of Gilson drive belts as follows: Drive belt 35900 for Model 51104, drive belt 35901 for Models 51171 and 51171A, drive belt 237985 for Model 51181 and drive belt 9304 for Models 51116 and 51158. Check drive belt adjustment as outlined in **ADJUSTMENT** section.

Models 51142 and 51172

To renew belt, remove belt guard (11 – Fig. G91) and unhook clutch cable from nylon adjustment stud (Fig. G85). Remove belt (2 – Fig. 92) from around engine pulley (3) and input pulley (5). To

Fig. G96 – Exploded view of tiller typical of Models 51171, 51171A and 51181.

1. Clutch cable
2. Belt guard bracket
3. Handle support assy.
4. Belt guard
5. Engine spacer
6. Wheel hanger assy.
7. Frame
8. Depth stick
9. Washers
10. Pulley
11. Washers
12. Idler pulley
13. Belt
14. Tine shield
15. Chain case
16. Seal
17. Felt seal
18. Felt seal
19. Washer
20. Seal collar
21. Right tine
22. Left tine
23. Tine washer
24. Tine extension
25. Bushing

HABAN

HABAN MANUFACTURING CO.
2100 Northwestern Avenue
Racine, Wisconsin 53404

Model	Engine Make	Engine Series	Engine Horsepower	No. of Forward Speeds	Power Reverse?	Tilling Width (In.)	Drive Type
861-002	B&S	130000	5	2	Yes	12-26	Chain

LUBRICATION

ENGINE

Refer to Briggs and Stratton section for engine lubrication requirements.

CHAIN CASE

Oil level in chain case should be checked at least every 10 hours of operation. Oil level with tiller in level position should be even with oil level plug hole (6A – Fig. HB1) on lower right side of chain case. Recommended oil is SAE 140 EP. Chain case oil capacity is four ounces.

MAINTENANCE

Inspect belt pulleys and renew if damaged or worn excessively. Check condition of control levers and linkage. Renew or repair parts if excessive play or binding prohibits easy, complete engagement of drive mechanism. A few drops of oil should be placed periodically on all movable parts such as wheel bearings and idler roller arms.

ADJUSTMENT

CLUTCH

Clutch lever adjustment is accomplished by loosening locknut (N – Fig. HB2), then turning rod (R) clockwise to decrease belt tension after removing pin (P). Clutch rod should return to neutral when released.

If clutch lever does not automatically seek a neutral position the drive lever spring (S – Fig. HB3) may be stretched

Fig. HB2 – Drawing of clutch control components. Refer to text and adjust as outlined.

or otherwise incorrectly adjusted. Spring length (T) should be adjusted to approximately 2⅝ inches (66.7 mm) measured between spring loop ends. This length should not be less than 2½ inches (63.5 mm) nor more than 2¾ inches (69.8 mm). The spring may be adjusted by turning nuts (N) until proper length (T) is attained.

DRIVE BELTS

REVERSE DRIVE BELT. To check

Fig. HB1 – View of transmission oil fill plug (6) and oil level plug (6A) location.

Fig. HB3 – View of clutch lever spring (S). Refer to text and adjust as outlined.

reverse belt tension, idle engine, then move drive clutch control to reverse and back to neutral. Make sure there is a positive release back to neutral. Repeat procedure with engine under full throttle. If tiller tines do not completely disengage with clutch control lever in neutral, adjust reverse belt tension.

To adjust reverse drive belt (10 – Fig. HB4), loosen nut in center of reverse idler pulley (6), then slide pulley up in slot to decrease tension or down to increase tension. Pulley should be moved in increments of 1/8-inch (3.2 mm). Retighten pulley nut then recheck belt tension.

FORWARD DRIVE BELTS. To check forward drive belt tension, idle

engine then engage drive clutch control into forward and back to neutral making sure there is a positive release back to neutral. Repeat procedure with engine under full throttle. If tiller creeps forward with control lever in neutral, decrease forward belt tension.

To adjust forward drive belt (9 – Fig. HB4), loosen nut in center of idler pulleys (4 & 5), then slide pulleys up in slot to increase tension or down to decrease tension. Pulley should be moved in increments of 1/8-inch (3.2 mm). Retighten pulley nut then recheck belt tension.

FORWARD TILLER SPEED
Forward tiller speed ranges are low

and high range. The forward drive belt (9 – Fig. HB4) must be relocated on pulleys to shift forward speed from low to high range or vice versa. To change belt from low to high pull up on engagement rod (1 – Fig. HB4) relieving tension on forward drive belt (9). Remove drive belt and install on appropriate pulleys. If adjustment is necessary refer to **FORWARD DRIVE BELT ADJUSTMENT** section.

OVERHAUL

ENGINE

Refer to Briggs and Stratton engine section for engine overhaul procedure. Engine model series is 130000.

CHAIN CASE

Overhaul of chain case assembly is evident after inspection of unit and referral to Fig. HB5.

Fig. HB4 – View of belt and pulley system.
1. Clutch control rod
2. Triple groove pulley
3. Idler arm
4. High speed idler pulley
5. Low speed idler pulley
6. Reverse idler pulley
7. High speed engine pulley
8. Reverse engine pulley
9. Forward drive belt
10. Reverse drive belt
11. Low speed engine pulley

Fig. HB5 – Exploded view of chain case components.
1. Output shaft
2. Hub caps
3. Woodruff key
4. Washers
5. Seals
6. Oil fill plug
6A. Oil level plug
6B. Slotted pipe plug
7. Bearings
8. Inner races
9. Spacer
10. Snap ring
11. Output sprocket
12. Lower chain
13. Idler sprocket assy.
14. Bearings
15. Idler sleeve
16. Upper chain
17. Chain case, right
18. Gasket
19. Bearings
20. Chain case, left
21. Bearing spacer
22. Snap rings
23. Seal
24. Input shaft

Fig. HB6 — Exploded view of Power Trac V.

1. Fender
2. Fender
3. PTO idler arm assy.
4. PTO idler pulley
5. PTO control rod
6. Spring adj. rod
6A. Drive lever spring
7. PTO control lever
8. PTO control lever springs
9. High speed idler pulley
10. Idler arm
11. Low speed idler pulley
12. Key
13. Triple groove pulley
14. Set screws
15. Reverse idler pulley
16. Idler arm assy.
17. Chain case assy.
18. Main frame assy.
19. Control rod
20. Engine mounting plate
21. Keys
22. Reverse engine pulley
23. Forward engine pulleys
24. Belt guide
25. Choke control rod
26. Throttle control cable
27. Starter cord

DRIVE BELTS

Use the following procedure to renew excessively worn or damaged drive belts. Refer to Fig. HB4. Remove hood, release tension on forward belt (9) by pulling up on engagement lever (1) and remove forward belt. Remove reverse idler pulley (6) then remove reverse belt (10). Install new belts by reversing removal procedure. Forward drive belt size is ½-inch x 53.5 inches long. Reverse drive belt size is ½-inch x 43.5 inches long. Check reverse and forward drive belt adjustment as previously outlined.

Fig. HB7 — Exploded view of tiller kit parts.

1. Inside tine mounting hub
2. Tine, right
3. Outside tine mounting hub
4. Tine, left
5. Drag bar
6. Drag bar ext. assy.
7. Chain
8. Pin tubes
9. Wheel mtg. strap
10. Wheel mtg. bracket
11. Tiller wheel pin

INTERNATIONAL

INTERNATIONAL HARVESTER COMPANY
401 North Michigan Avenue
Chicago, Illinois 60611

Model	Engine Make	Engine Series	Engine Horsepower	No. of Forward Speeds	Power Reverse?	Tilling Width (In.)	Drive Type
526	B&S	130000	5	1	Yes	26	Gear
526A	B&S	130000	5	1	Yes	11-26	Gear

LUBRICATION

ENGINE

All Models

Refer to appropriate Briggs and Stratton engine section for engine lubrication specifications. Recommended oil grade is SAE 30 or equivalent. Recommended fuel is either regular or low-lead gasoline having an octane rating of 90 or higher. The use of non-leaded gasolines reduces cylinder head deposits, but could shorten engine valve life if carburetor is adjusted too lean.

WHEELS AND CONTROLS

All Models

Lubricate transport wheels, pivot points and idler pulley hub at least every 15 hours of operation with SAE 30 oil. Caution should be taken in not getting oil on drive belts.

GEAR DRIVE

Oil level in gear case should be checked at least every 10 hours of operation. Gear case oil should be changed at beginning of each year. Recommended gear case oil is (EP) SAE 90 gear oil.

To check oil level in gear case place tiller on a level surface. Clean front of gear case housing. Remove level plug on front of case. Oil level should be at bottom of plug hole. If oil level is low on earlier 526 model, remove fill plug at top of gear case and add oil through fill hole until oil begins to run out level hole. Reinstall and tighten plugs. On later 526A model add oil through level hole until oil is flush with bottom of plug hole, then reinstall plug.

MAINTENANCE

Inspect all fasteners for looseness and retighten as needed. Check control levers, linkage and cables for freedom of movement and excessive play. Inspect drive belts for excessive stretching, wear, cracks, or any other damage. Install new belts if needed. Inspect all belt pulleys and renew if damaged or excessively worn.

ADJUSTMENT

CLUTCH CONTROL AND DRIVE BELT

Model 526

FORWARD DRIVE BELT. If tines turn when clutch lever is in neutral position, belt tension will need to be decreased. If drive belt slips on pulleys with clutch lever engaged, belt tension will need to be increased. Adjust belt by loosening idler pulley (8–Fig. I1) bolt and nut and sliding pulley in idler bracket slot. Slide pulley towards belt to increase tension and away from belt to decrease tension.

REVERSE DRIVE BELT. Place clutch control lever in forward running position. Lift reverse belt out of reverse idler pulley (3–Fig. I1) groove and place it on lip of idler pulley. Loosen idler

Fig. I1 — View of drive belt(s) and pulley arrangement for Model 526.

1. Engine pulley
2. Reverse belt restrictor
3. Reverse idler pulley
4. Reverse belt
5. Reverse arm
6. Forward belt
7. Belt guide bracket
8. Forward idler pulley
9. Forward belt restrictor

Fig. I2 — View of forward clutch control components for Model 526A. Similar parts are used for reverse clutch control.

1. Cable pulley
2. Idler spring
3. Loop

Fig. I3 — View showing forward belt adjustment procedure for Model 526A. Reverse belt is similarly adjusted.

D. Direction to decrease tension
N. Nut
I. Direction to increase tension

pulley bolt and move pulley up until belt is tight, then retighten idler pulley bolt. Reinstall belt back in pulley groove.

Model 526A

FORWARD DRIVE BELT AND REVERSE DRIVE BELT. Fig. I2 shows location of clutch control components for forward drive belt. Reverse belt clutch components are similar to forward and are adjusted in same manner as forward. To adjust belt tension refer to Fig. I3. If belt slips on pulleys when clutch lever is engaged, then loosen nut (N) and swing cable pulley (1 – Fig. I2) out to increase tension. If tines do not disengage with lever released, then loosen nut and swing pulley in slightly to decrease tension.

OVERHAUL

ENGINE

All Models

Engine model no. is stamped on blower housing. Refer to appropriate Briggs and Stratton engine section for overhaul procedures.

GEAR CASE

Model 526 and 526A

INSPECTION. On Model 526 refer to Fig. I4 for gear case parts breakdown and identification. On Model 526A refer to Fig. I5 for gear case parts breakdown and identification. Inspect and renew all components that are worn or damaged. Install new gaskets and seals. Lubricate gears and bearings with a light film of oil during reassembly. Keep all dirt and foreign matter out of gear case during reassembly. Refer to **LUBRICATION** section for lubricating requirements after reassembly and installation.

DRIVE BELTS

Model 526

Remove drive belt(s) cover. Place

Fig. I4 — Exploded view of gear case and tines for Model 526.

1. Gear housing	8. Grooved pin	15. Gear housing	22. Tine shaft
2. Oil fill plug	9. Shaft	16. Bushing	23. Inside spools
3. Oil level plug	10. Pin	17. Oil seal	24. Outside spools
4. Ball bearing	11. Needle bearing	18. Extension block	25. Tine, R. H.
5. Worm gear	12. Thrust washers	19. Needle bearings	26. Tine, L. H.
6. Driven gear	13. Ball bearing	20. Oil seals	27. Clevis pin
7. Worm spacer	14. Gasket	21. Felt washers	28. Cotter pin

Fig. I5 — Exploded view of gear case for Model 526A.

1. Snap ring
2. Housing plug
3. "O" ring
4. Shim (0.020 inch)
5. Shim (0.010 inch)
6. Front bearing cup
7. Bearing cone and roller
8. Front spacer
9. Woodruff key
10. Worm gear
11. Rear spacer
12. Retaining ring
13. Bearing cone and roller
14. Rear bearing cup
15. Worm shaft
16. Woodruff key
17. Tine shaft
18. Woodruff key
19. Oil seal
20. Needle bearing
21. Oil level plug
22. Gear housing
23. Cover gasket
24. Worm wheel gear
25. Needle bearing
26. Side cover
27. Oil seal

clutch control lever in neutral position. Loosen nut retaining forward drive belt restrictor (9 – Fig. I1) sufficiently enough to withdraw belt from idler pulley groove, then remove belt. To remove reverse belt, loosen nut retaining reverse belt restrictor (2), then remove belt. Install new belts in reverse order of disassembly. Forward drive belt size is ½-inch x 40 inches long. Reverse drive belt size is ½-inch x 45 inches long. Refer to **ADJUSTMENT** section for adjusting procedure.

Model 526A

Remove drive belt(s) cover. Unhook clutch engagement cable loop (3 – Fig. I2) from idler pulley spring (2), then remove forward drive belt. Use similar procedure on reverse drive belt and idler. Install new belts in reverse order of disassembly. Forward drive belt size is ½-inch x 34 inches long. Reverse drive belt size is ⅜-inch x 35 inches long. Refer to **ADJUSTMENT** section for adjusting procedure.

MERRY

MERRY TILLER, INC.
4500 5th Avenue South,
Birmingham, Alabama 35202

Model	Engine Make	Engine Series	Engine Horsepower	No. of Forward Speeds	Power Reverse?	Tilling Width (In.)	Drive Type
Scotsman G-76	B&S	80000	3	1	No	26	Chain
Custom G-77	Tec.	H40	4	1	No	26	Chain
Custom G-78	B&S	110000	4	1	No	26	Chain
Suburban G-80	B&S	130000	5	1	No	26	Chain
Suburban G-82	B&S	130000	5	1	Yes	26	Chain
Professional G-83	B&S	130000	5	1	No	37	Chain
Professional G-84	Wisc.	EY-18-3W	4.6	1	No	37	Chain
Professional G-87	Kohler	K91	4	1	No	37	Chain
Professional G-88	B&S	130000	5	1	Yes	37	Chain
Exporter G-90	Kohler	K91	4	1	No	48	Chain
Exporter G-91	B&S	130000	5	1	No	48	Chain
Exporter G-92	Wisc.	EY-18-3W	4.6	1	No	48	Chain
Minnie MM-1	B&S	60000	2	1	No	18	Chain
Minnie 3200	B&S	60000	2	1	No	18	Chain
Minnie 7100	B&S	60000	2	1	No	18	Chain
Scotsman 7200	B&S	80000	3	1	No	26	Chain
Custom 7300	B&S	110000	4	1	No	26	Chain
Suburban 7400	B&S	130000	5	1	No	26	Chain
Suburban 7402	B&S	130000	5	1	No	26	Chain
Suburban Rev. 7401	B&S	130000	5	1	Yes	26	Chain
Suburban Rev. 7403	B&S	130000	5	1	Yes	26	Chain
Professional 7500	B&S	130000	5	1	No	37	Chain
Professional 7501	Wisc.	EY-18-3W	4.6	1	No	37	Chain
Professional 7502	Kohler	K91	4	1	No	37	Chain
Exporter 7600	B&S	130000	5	1	No	48	Chain
Exporter 7601	Wisc.	EY-18-3W	4.6	1	No	48	Chain
Exporter 7602	Kohler	K91	4	1	No	48	Chain

LUBRICATION
ENGINE

All Models

Refer to appropriate Briggs and Stratton, Tecumseh, Wisconsin or Kohler engine section for engine lubrication specifications. Recommended oil grade is SAE 30 or equivalent. Recommended fuel is either regular or low-lead gasoline having an octane rating of 90 or higher. The use of non-leaded gasolines reduces cylinder head deposits, but could shorten engine valve life if carburetor is adjusted too lean.

CHAIN DRIVE

All Models

Chain case oil should be checked at least every 25 hours of operation. Recommended lubricant is SAE 90 gear oil.

To check oil level in chain case place tiller on a level surface. Clean dirt from off of chain case housing and remove oil level plug on bottom of left hand housing. Oil level should be at bottom of plug hole. If oil level is low remove fill plug on upper right hand side of chain case. Add oil slowly until it starts to run out of level plug hole, then reinstall plugs.

MAINTENANCE

Inspect all fasteners for looseness and retighten as needed. Check control levers, linkage and cables for freedom of movement and excessive play. Inspect drive belt(s) for excessive stretching, wear, cracks, or any other damage. Install new belt(s) if needed. Inspect all belt pulleys and renew if damaged or excessively worn. Lubricate transport wheels occasionally with SAE 30 oil.

ADJUSTMENT
CLUTCH CONTROL AND DRIVE BELT

All Models

Loosen hex nut on each side of idler link (3–Fig. ME1). Raise idler pulley to take slack out of belt. Hold idler pulley

Fig. ME1 — View of drive belt idler assembly.
1. Hex nuts   3. Idler link
2. Spring   4. Idler pulley

and pull down on idler link to take slack out of clutch cable, then retighten hex nuts. If clutch spring does not stretch when clutch lever is engaged, then clutch adjustment is too loose. Small adjustments may be made by adjusting chain links attached to clutch cable and cable spring.

OVERHAUL

ENGINE

All Models

Engine model no. is stamped on blower housing for Briggs and Stratton engines. Engine make and series no. is marked on data plate attached to engine for Tecumseh, Wisconsin and Kohler engines. Refer to appropriate engine section for overhaul procedures.

CHAIN CASE

Three different chain case models are used. The Model 1275 chain case is used on Models: Scotsman G-76; Custom G-77 and G-78; Suburban G-80 and G-82; Professional G-83, G-84, G-87 and G-88; Scotsman 7200; Custom 7300; Suburban 7400 and 7402; Suburban Rev. 7401 and 7403; Professional 7500, 7501 and 7502. The Model 2281 chain case is used on Models: Exporter G-90, G-91, G-92, 7600, 7601 and 7602. The Model 3260 chain case is used on Models: Minnie MM-1, 3200 and 7100.

All Models

OIL SEAL INSTALLATION. Remove tines from tine shaft. Use a seal puller or other appropriate tool to pull outer and inner seals out of case hub. Clean tine shaft with emery cloth. Install inner seal with lip facing toward inside and outer seal with lip facing toward outside. Drive new seals in until outer seal is flush with case hub.

INSPECTION. Chain case Model 1275 parts breakdown and identification is shown in Fig. ME2. For chain case Model 2281 refer to Fig. ME3. Refer to Fig. ME4 for parts breakdown and identification of Model 3260 chain case.

Inspect and renew all components that are worn or damaged. Install new gasket and seals. Lubricate chains, sprockets and bearings with a light film of oil during reassembly. Keep all dirt and foreign matter out of chain case during reassembly. Refer to **LUBRICATION** section for lubricating requirements after reassembly and installation.

Fig. ME2 — Exploded view of chain case Model 1275.

1. Right hand case assy.
2. Drive shaft seals
3. Oil fill plug
4. Tine shaft seals
5. Tine shaft needle bearings
6. Spacer
7. Chain
8. Tine shaft assy.
9. Idler sprocket
10. Idler sprocket bearing race
11. Idler sprocket bearings
12. Drive shaft bearings
13. Drive shaft sprocket
14. Drive shaft
15. Roll pin
16. Chain
17. Gasket
18. Left hand case assy.

Fig. ME3 — Exploded view of chain case Model 2281.

1. Tine shaft seals
2. Tine shaft needle bearings
3. Spacer
4. Right hand case assy.
5. Tine shaft
6. Chain
7. Nuts
8. Lockwashers
9. Flat washer
10. Oil fill plug
11. Soft plug
12. Drive shaft bearings
13. Drive shaft seal
14. Idler sprocket bearings
15. Inner race
16. Drive shaft assy.
17. Idler sprocket
18. Chain
19. Chain
20. Idler sprocket
21. Idler sprocket bearings
22. Inner race
23. Left hand case assy.
24. Bolt, 2-⅞ inch
25. Bolt, 2½ inch

Fig. ME4 — Exploded view of chain case Model 3260.

1. Tine shaft oil seals
2. Tine shaft needle bearings
3. Right hand case assy.
4. Spacer
5. Chain
6. Tine shaft
7. Idler sprocket bearings
8. Idler sprocket bearing race
9. Idler sprocket
10. Drive shaft bearings
11. Drive shaft
12. Chain
13. Gasket
14. Left hand case assy.
15. Drive shaft oil seal
16. Soft plug
17. Oil fill plug

DRIVE BELTS

Single Belt Models

Remove drive belt cover. Remove belt from pulleys and install new belt. Models G-76, G-77, G-78, G-80, G-83, G-84, G-87, 7200, 7300, 7400, 7402, 7500, 7501 and 7502 drive belt size is ½-inch x 50 inches long. Models G-90, G-91, G-92, 7600, 7601 and 7602 drive belt size is ½-inch x 41 inches long. Models MM-1, 3200 and 7100 drive belt size is ½-inch x 34 inches long. Refer to Fig. ME5 for belt routing and parts identification. Refer to **AD-JUSTMENT** section for adjusting procedure. Reinstall drive belt cover.

Fig. ME5 — View of single drive belt routing and parts identification.
1. Chain case drive pulley
2. Engine pulley
3. Idler pulley assy.
4. Drive belt

Two Belt Models

Remove drive belt cover. Remove forward drive belt from pulleys, then remove reverse drive belt from pulleys. Install new belts. Forward drive belt size is ½-inch x 50 inches long. Reverse drive belt size is ⅜-inch x 45 inches long. Refer to Fig. ME6 for belt routing and parts identification. Refer to **ADJUST-MENT** section for adjusting procedure. Reinstall drive belt cover.

Fig. ME6 — View of forward and reverse drive belt routing and parts identification.
1. Chain case drive pulley
2. Forward drive engine pulley
3. Reverse drive engine pulley
4. Forward drive belt idler assy.
5. Reverse drive belt idler assy.
6. Reverse drive belt
7. Forward drive belt

MIGHTY MAC

AMERIND-MACKISSIC, INC.
P.O. Box 111
Parker Ford, PA 19457

Model	Engine Make	Engine Series	Engine Horsepower	No. of Forward Speeds	Power Reverse?	Tilling Width (In.)	Drive Type
324	B&S	80000	3	1	No	24	Chain
524	B&S	130000	5	1	No	24	Chain
524R	B&S	13000	5	1	Yes	24	Chain
822RT	B&S	190000	8	1	Yes	24	Chain

LUBRICATION

ENGINE

All Models

Refer to Briggs and Stratton engine section for engine lubrication requirements. Recommended fuel is regular or low-lead gasoline having an octane rating of 90 or higher. Recommended oil is SAE 30.

CHAIN DRIVE

Models 324, 524 and 524R

Chain case oil should be checked at least every 25 hours of operation. Recommended lubricant is SAE 90 gear oil.

To check oil in chain case, place tiller on a level surface. Clean dirt from chain case housing and remove oil level plug (2 – Fig. MM1) on top or right side of housing. Oil level should be at bottom of plug hole. If oil is needed, add slowly until it starts to run out of plug hole, then reinstall plug.

Model 822RT

Chain case oil should be checked at least every 25 hours of operation. Recommended lubricant is SAE 90 gear oil or SAE 50 engine oil.

To check oil level in chain case, place tiller on a level surface. Clean dirt from chain case housing and remove oil level plug on right side. Oil should be at bottom of plug hole. If oil is needed, add slowly until it starts to run out of plug hole, then reinstall plug.

MAINTENANCE

Inspect all fasteners for looseness and retighten as needed. Check control levers, linkage and cables for freedom of movement and excessive play. Inspect drive belt(s) for excessive stretching, wear, cracks or any other damage. Install new belt(s) if needed. Inspect all belt pulleys and renew if damaged or excessively worn. Lubricate transport wheels occasionally with SAE 30 oil.

ADJUSTMENT

CLUTCH CONTROL AND DRIVE BELT

Models 324, 524 and 524R

FORWARD BELT. Loosen nuts holding idler shaft to frame, then slide idler arm up slightly to increase tension on belt. Retighten nuts. If necessary, adjust slack in control cable leading to clutch lever on handle bar by taking up a link in chain connecting cable to spring.

Model 524R

REVERSE BELT. To increase belt tension, loosen locknut and slide idler pulley further out on idler arm. If necessary, adjust slack in control cable leading to clutch lever on handle bar by taking up a link in chain connecting cable to spring.

Model 822RT

To check for proper engine belt tension, remove belt cover and press down on both belts so they touch the horizontal round bar on belt engagement lever. Forward idler pulley should move 1/4-1/2 inch (6.4-12-7 mm). If more movement is observed, loosen engine base plate and move engine to the rear 1/16-1/8 inch (1.6-3.2 mm). After moving engine, readjust linkage at bellcrank on forward belt idler and at collar under handle.

Fig. MM1—Exploded view of chain drive assembly for Models 324, 524 and 524R.

1. Seals	5. Sprocket	9. Chain	13. Bearings
2. Oil plug	6. Drive shaft	10. Gasket	14. Spacer
3. Right case	7. Bearings	11. Left case	15. Tine shaft
4. Bearings	8. Idler sprocket	12. Seal	16. Plug

MTD

MTD PRODUCTS
5965 Grafton Road,
Cleveland, Ohio 44136

Model	Engine Make	Engine Series	Engine Horsepower	No. of Forward Speeds	Power Reverse?	Tilling Width (In.)	Drive Type
030	B&S	80000	3	1	No	18	Chain
320	B&S	130000	5	1	No	20	Chain
355	B&S	130000	5	1	No	26	Gear
385	B&S	130000	5	1	Yes	26	Chain
386	B&S	130000	5	4	Yes	26	Chain
405	B&S	130000	5	5	Yes	21	Chain
408	B&S	190000	8	5	Yes	21	Chain
409	B&S	190000	8	5	Yes	21	Chain

LUBRICATION
ENGINE
All Models

Refer to appropriate Briggs and Stratton engine section for engine lubrication specification.

Recommended oil grade is SAE 30 or equivalent. Recommended fuel is either regular or low-lead gasoline having an octane rating of 90 or higher. The use of non-leaded gasolines reduces cylinder head deposits, but could shorten engine valve life if carburetor is adjusted too lean.

CHAIN DRIVE
All Models

Chain case is factory sealed and must be removed and disassembled in order to add or change grease in case. Refer to **OVERHAUL** section for servicing grease.

GEAR CASE
Model 355

Gear case oil should be checked at least every 10 hours of operation.

Fig. MT2— View of clutch control components for Model 030.

1. Clutch lever
2. Clutch cable
3. Hex nuts

Recommended lubricant is Pennant oil EP#35000 or suitable equivalent.

To check gear case oil place tiller on a level surface. Clean dirt from around front of gear case and remove oil level plug (1–Fig. MT1). Oil level should be at bottom of plug hole. If oil level is low remove fill plug (2), then add oil through fill hole until it begins to run out level hole. Reinstall and tighten plugs.

MAINTENANCE

Inspect all fasteners for looseness and retighten as needed. Check control levers, linkage and cables for freedom of movement and excessive play. Inspect drive belt(s) for excessive stretching, wear, cracks or any other damage. Install new belt(s) if needed. Inspect all belt pulleys and renew if damaged or excessively worn. Transport wheels on Models 030, 320, 355, 385 and 386

Fig. MT1— View of gear case oil level and plugs for Model 355.

1. Oil level plug
2. Fill plug
3. Breather plug
4. Oil level

Fig. MT3— View of clutch adjusting components for Model 320.

1. Hex nuts
2. Clutch cable
3. Bracket

Fig. MT4— View of clutch control components for Models 355, 385, 386, 405, 408 and 409.

1. Clutch lever
2. Threaded control rod
3. Adjustment ferrule
4. Bracket

should be lubricated occasionally with SAE 30 oil.

ADJUSTMENT
CLUTCH CONTROL AND DRIVE BELT

Models 030 and 320

For Model 030 refer to Fig. MT2 for clutch components identification. For Model 320 refer to Fig. MT3 for clutch components identification.

Loosen and turn hex nuts to adjust clutch, then check for correct adjustment. For Model 030 place clutch lever in neutral position. For Model 320 make sure clutch engagement lever is in released position. Unhook spark plug lead and pull on starter rope handle. If tines do not turn, then adjustment is correct. If tines do turn, then clutch cable will need to be adjusted.

Models 355, 385 and 386

Remove hair pin clip from ferrule (3 – Fig. MT4), then remove ferrule from bracket (4). Turn ferrule on control rod (2) to adjust clutch. Reinstall ferrule in bracket and install hair pin clip. To check for correct clutch adjustment place clutch lever (1) in neutral position. Unhook spark plug lead and pull on starter rope handle. If tines do not turn, then adjustment is correct. If tines do turn, then clutch rod will need to be adjusted.

GEAR CASE

Model 355

Gear case bearings should be adjusted approximately every five hours of operation. Adjust by removing cotter pin (17 – Fig. MT10), then turning adjustment cap (16) in until snug. Do not overtighten. Reinstall cotter pin, then check adjustment by starting tiller and engaging tines. If engine stalls out, then bearing adjustment is too tight and adjustment cap should be loosened slightly.

ENGINE POSITION

Model 386

Loosen engine securing hex bolts and slide engine in slots to adjust position. If there is no reverse or a slippage in reverse, then engine assembly will need to be slid back until engine disc and friction disc on variable speed pulley make contact. If neutral cannot be obtained, then engine assembly will need to be slid forward. Refer to **CLUTCH CONTROL AND DRIVE BELT AD-**

Fig. MT5 — Exploded view of chain case for Model 030.

1. Chain case, L.H.
2. Oil seal
3. Dust cover
4. Bolt 2½ inches long
5. Input pulley
6. Roll pin
7. Gasket
8. Flange bearings
9. Washers
10. Spacer
11. Tine shaft assy.
12. Chain, 0.375 inch pitch x 50 links
13. Inner race
14. Hub and sprocket assy.
15. Chain, ½-inch pitch x 38 links
16. Input shaft assy.
17. Chain case, R.H.
18. Expansion ring
19. Hex nut
20. Lockwasher
21. Flat washer

Fig. MT6 — Exploded view of chain case for Model 320.

1. Chain case, L.H.
2. Bearings
3. Bearing housing
4. Dust caps
5. V-Ring seals
6. Gasket
7. Thrust washers
8. Step spacer
9. Tine shaft and sprocket
10. Chain, ⅝-inch pitch x 38 links
11. Inner race
12. Sprocket
13. Chain, ⅜-inch pitch x 70 links
14. Spacer
15. Input shaft and sprocket
16. Snap ring

Fig. MT7 — Exploded view of chain case for Model 385 and 386.

1. Chain case, L.H.	10. Spacer	17. Hex flanged bearings
2. Gasket	11. Tine shaft assy.	18. Spacer
3. Bearings	12. Chain, ⅝-inch pitch x 28 links	19. Sprocket shaft
4. Bearing housing	13. Sprocket shaft	20. Sprocket sleeve assy.
5. Flat washer	14. Sprocket	21. Roll pin
6. Spacer	15. Flange bearings	22. Chain, ½-inch pitch x 34 links
7. Input pulley	16. Chain, ½-inch pitch x 48 links	23. Sprocket
8. Oil seal		24. Spacer
9. Flat washer		25. Input shaft
		26. Square key
		27. Flat washer
		28. Chain case, R.H.
		29. Gasket
		30. Bearing housing assy.

JUSTMENT section for clutch rod adjusting procedure.

OVERHAUL
ENGINE

All Models

Engine model no. is stamped on blower housing. Refer to appropriate Briggs and Stratton engine section for overhaul procedures.

CHAIN CASE

All Models

OIL SEAL INSTALLATION. The chain case is factory sealed and no provision is made for checking or adding lubricant. Chain case must be separated as described in following **INSPECTION** paragraph to accurately add specific amount of lubricant. Seals may be renewed as follows:

Remove tines from tine shaft. Use a seal puller or other appropriate tools to remove seal(s) from case hub. Clean tine shaft with emery cloth. Drive new seal(s) in until outside face is flush with case hub. On models with two seals on each side install inner seal with lip facing toward inside and outer seal with lip facing toward outside. On Models 405, 408 and 409 remove wheels to install axle shaft seals.

INSPECTION. For Model 030 refer to Fig. MT5 for parts breakdown and identification. For Model 320 refer to Fig. MT6 for parts breakdown and identification. For Models 385 and 386 refer to Fig. MT7 for parts breakdown and identification. For Model 405 refer to Fig. MT8 for parts breakdown and identification. For Models 408 and 409 refer to Fig. MT9 for parts breakdown and identification.

Inspect and renew all components that are worn or damaged. Install new gasket(s) and seals. Lubricate chains, sprockets and bearings with a light film of grease during reassembly. Keep all dirt and foreign matter out of chain case during reassembly.

Recommended lubricant for all models is Plastilube #0 grease or suitable equivalent. Capacity for Model 030 is 16 ounces. Capacity for Model 320 is 12 ounces. Capacity for Models 385 and 386 is 14 ounces. Capacity for Models 405, 408 and 409 is 28 ounces. To fill chain case with grease, lay right half of case on its side, add grease and assemble left half to right. Complete reassembly and reinstall in tiller frame.

Fig. MT8 — Exploded view of chain case for Model 405.

1. Chain case, L.H.	9. Spacer	16. Inner race
2. Seals	10. Axle shaft assy.	17. Flange bearings
3. Seals	11. Chain, ½-inch pitch x	18. Sprocket
4. Bearing housing	42 links	19. Chain, ⅝-inch pitch x
5. Side plate, L.H. and	12. Inner race	52 links
R.H.	13. Flange bearings	20. Flange bearings
6. Gasket	14. Chain, ½-inch pitch x	21. Flat washers
7. Flange bearings	58 links	22. Spacer
8. Flat washers	15. Sprocket	23. Tine shaft assy.

24. Chain, ½-inch pitch x 58 links
25. Ball bearings
26. Spacer
27. Sprocket
28. Spacer
29. Input shaft
30. Square keys
31. Chain case, R.H.

Fig. MT9 — Exploded view of chain case for Models 408 and 409. Shift parts (5 through 12) are used on both right hand wheel drive engagement and left hand tine engagement.

1. Chain case, L.H.		20. Sprocket bearing
2. Bearing housing		sleeve assy.
3. Gasket	13. Oil seals	21. Hub sleeve
4. Oil seals	14. Flange bearings	22. Flange bearings
5. Shift yoke	15. Chain, ⅝-inch pitch x	23. Sprocket assy.
6. Gasket	52 links	24. Chain, ½-inch pitch x
7. Cap plug	16. Sprocket bearing	58 links
8. Detent ball	sleeve assy.	25. Flange bearings
9. Spring	17. Stepped spacer	26. Flat washers
10. Shift housing	18. Clutch shaft assy.	27. Axle shaft assy.
11. Clutch dog	19. Chain, ½-inch pitch x	28. Chain, ½-inch pitch x
12. Clutch dog driver	58 links	42 links

29. Spacer
30. Flange bearings
31. Flat washers
32. Tine shaft assy.
33. Spacer
34. Ball bearings
35. Spacer
36. Sprocket
37. Spacer
38. Input shaft
39. Square keys
40. Chain case, R.H.

GEAR CASE

Model 355

OIL SEAL INSTALLATION. Remove tines from tine shaft. Use a seal puller to remove seals from case hub. Clean tine shaft with emery cloth. Drive new seals in until outside face is flush with case hub.

REMOVE AND DISASSEMBLE. Refer to Fig. MT10 for parts breakdown and identification. Inspect and renew all components that are worn or damaged. Install new gaskets and seals. Lubricate gears and bearings with a light film of oil during reassembly. Keep all dirt and foreign matter out of gear case during reassembly. Refer to **LUBRICATION** section for lubricating requirements after reassembly and installation. Refer to **GEAR CASE ADJUSTMENT** section for bearing preload adjusting procedure.

DRIVE BELTS

Model 030

Refer to Fig. MT11 for belt routing and parts identification. Place clutch lever in forward position, then unhook extension spring (3) from drive belt cover. Remove drive belt cover. Remove belt from pulleys and install new belt. Drive belt size is 3/8-inch x 29 inches long. Reinstall drive belt cover, then rehook extension spring in cover. Refer to **CLUTCH CONTROL AND DRIVE BELT ADJUSTMENT** section for adjusting procedure.

Model 320

Refer to Fig. MT12 for belt routing and parts identification. Remove drive belt cover. Remove drive belt from chain case pulley (2), then remove belt from idler pulley (3) and engine pulley (1). Install new drive belt, making sure belt is positioned inside two pins at engine pulley. Drive belt size is 1/2-inch x 39 inches long. Reinstall drive belt cover. Refer to **CLUTCH CONTROL AND DRIVE BELT ADJUSTMENT** section for adjusting procedure.

Model 355

Refer to Fig. MT13 for belt(s) routing and parts identification. Remove drive belt cover, then remove wire belt retainer at front of gear case pulley. Remove forward drive belt from engine pulley (1) and gear case pulley (2). Remove retaining nut from reverse idler pulley (3), then pull pulley out away from idler bracket. Slip reverse belt off idler pulley and gear case pulley. Install new drive belt(s). Reassemble in reverse order of disassembly. Forward drive belt size is 1/2-inch x 37 inches long. Reverse drive belt size is 1/2-inch x 44 inches long. Refer to **CLUTCH CONTROL AND DRIVE BELT ADJUSTMENT** section for adjusting procedure.

Model 385

Refer to Fig. MT14 for belt(s) routing and parts identification. Remove drive belt cover. Loosen belt wire finger (2) retaining bolt and nut. Place clutch lever in reverse position, then remove forward drive belt from pulleys. Place clutch lever in neutral position, then remove reverse drive belt from chain case pulley. Place clutch lever in reverse position. Remove reverse idler pulley (5) retaining nut, then slip pulley and belt off idler bracket together. Install new belts, then reassemble in reverse order

Fig. MT10—Exploded view of gear case for Model 355.

1. Gear case
2. Sleeve bearing
3. Oil seal
4. Snap ring
5. Breather plug and star washer
6. Oil fill plug
7. Oil level plug
8. Bearing cups
9. Bearing cones
10. Spacers
11. Worm shaft
12. Worm gear
13. Drive key
14. Snap ring
15. "O" ring
16. Adjustment plug
17. Cotter pin
18. Flange bearing
19. Washers
20. Drive keys
21. Tine shaft
22. Snap ring
23. Worm gear
24. "O" ring
25. Flange cover with bearing
26. Oil seals

Fig. MT11—View of drive belt routing and parts identification for Model 030.

1. Engine pulley
2. Idler pulley
3. Extension spring
4. Chain case pulley
5. Clutch cable
6. Drive belt

Fig. MT12—View of drive belt routing and parts identification for Model 320.

1. Engine pulley
2. Chain case pulley
3. Idler assy.
4. Extension spring
5. Clutch cable assy.
6. Drive belt

of disassembly. Forward drive belt size is ½-inch x 37 inches long. Reverse drive belt size is ½-inch x 41 inches long. Refer to **CLUTCH CONTROL AND DRIVE BELT ADJUSTMENT** section for adjusting procedure.

Model 386

Refer to Fig. MT15 for belt(s) routing and parts identification. Remove drive belt cover. Push idler pulley (8) forward, then slip reverse belt off chain case pulley, idler pulley and variable speed pulley. Place shift lever in forward speed position, then lift forward drive belt from engine pulley and variable speed pulley. Install new belts, make sure forward drive belt is positioned inside two pins at engine pulley. Forward drive belt size is ½-inch x 19 inches long. Rear

drive belt size is ½-inch x 28 inches long. Reassemble in reverse order of disassembly. Refer to **ENGINE POSITION ADJUSTMENT** section and **CLUTCH CONTROL AND DRIVE BELT ADJUSTMENT** section for adjusting procedure.

Models 405, 408 and 409

Refer to Fig. MT16 for belt(s) routing and parts identification. Remove drive belt cover. Place clutch lever in reverse position, then remove forward belt (13)

from engine pulley towards engine. Slip belt off variable speed pulley (4) and remove belt. Place clutch lever in second speed position, then remove rear drive belt (14) from chain case pulley (11) and variable speed pulley. Model 405 forward drive belt size is ⅝-inch x 26 inches long. Rear drive belt size is ⅝-inch x 52 inches long. Models 408 and 409 forward drive belt size is ⅝-inch x 27 inches long. Rear drive belt size is ⅝-inch x 52 inches long. Install new belts, then reassemble in reverse order of disassembly.

Fig. MT14—View of drive belt(s) routing and parts identification for Model 385.

1. Engine pulley
2. Belt wire finger
3. Clutch plate
4. Control rod
5. Reverse idler assy.
6. Spring
7. Forward idler assy.
8. Clutch control rod assy.
9. Reverse belt
10. Forward belt
11. Chain case pulley

Fig. MT15—View of drive belt(s) routing and parts identification for Model 386.

1. Engine pulley
2. Variable speed pulley
3. Reinforcement plate
4. Friction wheel assy.
5. Drive belt
6. Drive belt
7. Chain case pulley
8. Idler pulley
9. Pivot arm assy.
10. Control rod
11. Idler arm
12. Extension spring
13. Front belt guard support

Fig. MT16—View of drive belt(s) routing and components for Models 405, 408 and 409.

1. Drive belt(s) cover support assy.
2. Square key
3. Engine pulley
4. Variable speed assy.
5. Friction wheel assy.
6. Spacer
7. Friction disc
8. Belt keeper
9. Idler pulley
10. Spacer
11. Chain case input pulley
12. Drive belt(s) cover
13. Drive belt
14. Drive belt

Fig. MT13—View of drive belt(s) routing and parts identification for Model 355.

1. Engine pulley
2. Gear case pulley
3. Reverse idler assy.
4. Forward idler assy.
5. Extension spring
6. Reverse drive belt
7. Forward drive belt

MTD

Model	Engine Make	Engine Series	Engine Horsepower	No. of Forward Speeds	Power Reverse?	Tilling Width (In.)	Drive Type
410A	B&S	130000	5	5	Yes	21	Chain
412A	B&S	190000	8	5	Yes	21	Chain
418A	B&S	190000	8	5	Yes	21	Chain

LUBRICATION

ENGINE

All Models

Refer to appropriate Briggs and Stratton engine section for engine lubrication specification.

Recommended oil grade is SAE 30 or equivalent. Recommended fuel is either regular or low-lead gasoline having an octane rating of 90 or higher. The use of non-leaded gasolines reduces cylinder head deposits, but could shorten engine valve life if carburetor is adjusted too lean.

CHAIN DRIVE

All Models

Chain case is factory sealed and must be removed and disassembled in order to add or change grease in case. Refer to OVERHAUL section for servicing grease.

MAINTENANCE

Inspect all fasteners for looseness and retighten as needed. Check control levers, linkage and cables for freedom of movement and excessive play. Inspect drive belt(s) for excessive stretching, wear, cracks or any other damage. Install new belt(s) if needed. Inspect all belt pulleys and renew if damaged or excessively worn.

ADJUSTMENT

GEAR SHIFT LEVER

All Models

Place tiller drive wheels in freewheeling position. Put tine depth bar all the way down to raise tines off ground. Start tiller engine, then move gear shift lever to each of five forward speed positions. Return lever to neutral position and turn engine off. Remove hair pin clip from ferrule, then remove ferrule

from gear shift lever. Place shift lever in first (1) forward speed position and pull lever to rear of position slot. Thread ferrule on control rod to align with shift lever hole, then reinstall ferrule in lever and install hair pin clip.

OVERHAUL

ENGINE

All Models

Engine model no. is stamped on blower housing. Refer to appropriate Briggs and Stratton engine section for overhaul procedures.

CHAIN CASE

All Models

OIL SEAL INSTALLATION. Remove tines from tine shaft. Use a seal puller to remove seal(s) from case hub. Clean tine shaft with emery cloth. Drive new seal in until outside face is flush with case hub. Remove drive wheels to install axle shaft seals.

INSPECTION. Refer to Fig. MT21 for parts breakdown and identification. Inspect and renew all components that are worn or damaged. Install new gaskets and seals. Lubricate chains,

Fig. MT21 — Exploded view of chain case for Models 410, 412 and 418. Shift parts (5 through 12) are used on both right hand wheel drive engagement and left hand tine engagement.

1. Chain case, L.H.
2. Bearing housing
3. Gasket
4. Oil seals
5. Shift yoke
6. Gasket
7. Cap plug
8. Detent ball
9. Spring
10. Shift housing
11. Clutch dog
12. Clutch dog driver
13. Oil seals
14. Flange bearing
15. Chain, ⅝-inch pitch x 52 links
16. Sprocket bearing sleeve assy.
17. Stepped spacer
18. Clutch shaft assy.
19. Chain, ½-inch pitch x 58 links
20. Sprocket bearing sleeve assy.
21. Hub sleeve
22. Flange bearings
23. Sprocket assy.
24. Chain, ½ inch pitch x 58 links
25. Flange bearings
26. Flat washers
27. Axle shaft assy.
28. Chain, ½-inch pitch x 42 links
29. Spacer
30. Flange bearings
31. Flat washers
32. Tine shaft assy.
33. Spacer
34. Ball bearings
35. Spacer
36. Sprocket
37. Spacer
38. Input shaft
39. Square keys
40. Chain case, R.H.

sprockets and bearings with a light film of grease during reassembly. Keep all dirt and foreign matter out of chain case during reassembly. Recommended lubricant is Plastilube #0 grease or suitable equivalent. Capacity is 28 ounces. To fill chain case with grease, lay right half of case on its side, add grease and assemble left half to right. Complete reassembly and reinstall in tiller frame.

DRIVE BELTS

All Models

Refer to Fig. MT22 for belt(s) routing and parts identification. Remove drive belt cover and engine brace. Place gear shift lever in neutral position. Remove three cap screws securing friction disc (4) on variable speed assembly (3). Slip belt off variable speed pulley, then remove two cap screws and washers securing belt guard (11) on engine. Remove belt guard, then remove belt off

Fig. MT22 — View of drive belt(s) routing and parts identification for Models 410, 412 and 418.

1. Engine pulley	4. Friction disc	7. Chain case input pulley
2. Friction wheel	5. Idler pulley	8. Drive belt
3. Variable speed assy.	6. Idler bracket	9. Drive belt
		10. Drive belt cover
		11. Drive belt guard

engine pulley. Place gear shift lever in a forward speed position. Lift up on idler pulley (5) and remove belt from under pulley. Slip belt off chain case input pulley (7) and variable speed pulley (3).

Install new drive belts. Forward drive belt size is ⅝-inch x 27 inches long. Rear drive belt size is ⅝-inch x 51 inches long. Reassemble in reverse order of disassembly.

MURRAY

THE MURRAY OHIO MANUFACTURING COMPANY
Box 268
Brentwood, Tennessee 37027

Model	Engine Make	Engine Series	Engine Horsepower	No. of Forward Speeds	Power Reverse?	Tilling Width (In.)	Drive Type
1000	B&S	60000	2	1	No	11-24	Chain
1190	B&S	130000	5	1	No	14-28	Chain
1202	B&S	130000	5	1	Yes	14-28	Chain
1203	B&S	130000	5	1	Yes	14-28	Chain
1290	B&S	130000	5	1	No	14-28	Chain
1302	B&S	130000	5	1	Yes	14-28	Chain
1303	B&S	130000	5	1	Yes	14-28	Chain

LUBRICATION

ENGINE

All Models

Refer to appropriate Briggs and Stratton engine section for engine lubrication specifications. Recommended oil grade is SAE 30 or equivalent. Recommended fuel is either regular or low-lead gasoline having an octane rating of 90 or higher. The use of non-leaded gasolines reduces cylinder head deposits, but could shorten engine valve life if carburetor is adjusted too lean.

CHAIN DRIVE

All Models

Chain case oil should be checked at least every 25 hours of operation. Recommended oil is SAE 30 API SE engine oil.

To check oil level, clean case and remove oil level plug on right hand side of case. Raise transport wheels to their highest position. Oil level should be at bottom of plug hole. If oil level is low add oil until level is flush with bottom of plug hole, then reinstall oil level plug.

MAINTENANCE

Inspect all fasteners for looseness and

Fig. MU2 — View of clutch control linkage for Models 1202, 1203, 1302 and 1303.
F. Forward drive lever   R. Reverse drive lever

retighten as needed. Check control levers, linkage and cables for freedom of movement and excessive play. Inspect drive belt(s) for excessive stretching, wear, cracks or any other damage. Install new belt(s) if needed. Inspect all belt pulleys and renew if damaged or excessively worn. Lubricate transport wheels occasionally with SAE 30 oil.

ADJUSTMENT

CLUTCH CONTROL

All Models

FORWARD DRIVE. Refer to Fig. MU1 for Models 1000, 1190 and 1290 and Fig. MU2 for Models 1202, 1203, 1302 and 1303 for clutch control parts and identification. With drive lever disengaged tines should not turn. If tines continue to turn, then reposition clutch cable in cable guide. If drive belt slips when lever is engaged, then reposition clutch spring in drive lever.

Fig. MU1 — View of clutch control linkage for Models 1000, 1190 and 1290.
1. Drive lever
2. Spring
3. Clutch cable

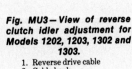

Fig. MU3 — View of reverse clutch idler adjustment for Models 1202, 1203, 1302 and 1303.
1. Reverse drive cable
2. Cable hook
3. Reverse drive idler

Models 1202, 1203, 1302 and 1303

REVERSE DRIVE. Refer to Fig. MU3 for clutch control parts and identification. If belt slippage occurs when reverse clutch lever is engaged, then reposition cable hook in forward most hole in reverse idler lever.

OVERHAUL

ENGINE

All Models

Engine model no. is stamped on blower housing. Refer to appropriate Briggs and Stratton engine section for overhaul procedures.

CHAIN CASE

All Models

INSPECTION. For Model 1000 refer to Fig. MU4 for parts breakdown and identification. For other models refer to Fig. MU5 for parts breakdown and identification. Inspect and renew all components that are worn or damaged. Install new gaskets and seals. Lubricate gears, chains and bearings with a light film of oil during reassembly. Keep all dirt and foreign matter out of chain case during reassembly. Refer to **LUBRICATION** section for lubricating requirements after reassembly and installation.

DRIVE BELTS

Model 1000

Refer to Fig. MU6 for drive belt parts and identification. Remove drive belt guard, then loosen engine pulley set screw and remove pulley. Remove idler pulley retaining nut, then remove pulley and drive belt. Drive belt size is ½-inch x 26 inches long. Install new belt and reassemble in reverse order of disassembly.

Model 1190 and 1290

Refer to Fig. MU7 for drive belt parts and identification. Remove drive belt guard, then remove hex nut securing belt guide (2) and remove guide from around engine pulley. Remove idler pulley (1) hex nut and remove idler pulley from idler bracket (4). Slide belt off of pulleys and install a new belt. Drive belt size is ½-inch x 48 inches long. Complete reassembly in reverse order of disassembly.

Fig. MU4 — Exploded view of chain case for Model 1000.

1. Bearing caps	6. Flange locknuts	10. Right hand housing assy.	14. Chain
2. Oil seal (0.625 shaft)	7. Left hand housing assy.	11. Bolts	15. Sprocket assy.
3. Oil seals (one-inch shaft)	8. Gasket	12. Oil level plug	16. Washer
4. Felt washers	9. Tine shaft assy.	13. Bearings	17. Chain
5. Dust caps			18. Retaining rings
			19. Input shaft

Fig. MU5 — Exploded view of chain case for all models, except Model 1000.

1. Dust caps	6. Left hand housing and bearing assy.	9. Gasket	14. Chain
2. Felt washers	7. Retaining rings	10. Thrust washer	15. Tine shaft
3. Flange bearing assy.	8. Rear belt guard bracket	11. Input shaft	16. Right hand housing and bearing assy.
4. Oil seals		12. Chain	17. Oil level plug
5. Gaskets		13. Idler shaft assy.	

Fig. MU6 — View of drive belt components for Model 1000.

1. Belt guard
2. Engine pulley
3. Set screw
4. Idler pulley
5. Transmission pulley
6. Idler bracket
7. Drive belt

Model 1202, 1203, 1302 and 1303

Refer to Fig. MU8 for drive belt parts and identification. Remove drive belt guard. On Models 1203 and 1303 remove tin shield (8) on front of tiller. Remove belt guide (4) from around engine pulley. Remove reverse belt from reverse idler and input pulley (6). Drive belt size is ½-inch x 39 inches long. Remove idler pulley (3) retaining nut and remove pulley from idler bracket. Remove forward drive belt from engine pulley (5) and transmission pulley (7). Drive belt size is ½-inch x 48 inches long. Install new belts and reassemble in reverse order of disassembly.

Fig. MU7 — View of drive belt components for Models 1190 and 1290.

1. Idler pulley
2. Belt guide
3. Transmission pulley
4. Idler bracket
5. Engine pulley
6. Drive belt

Fig. MU8 — View of drive belt components for Models 1202, 1203, 1302 and 1303.

1. Reverse drive belt
2. Forward drive belt
3. Forward idler pulley
4. Belt guide
5. Crankshaft (forward) pulley
6. Reverse drive pulley
7. Forward drive pulley
8. Shield
9. Camshaft (reverse) pulley
10. Reverse idler pulley

J.C. PENNEY

J.C. PENNEY CO., INC.
11800 West Burleigh Street,
Milwaukee, Wisconsin 53201

The following J.C. Penney tillers were manufactured for J.C. Penney Co., Inc., by MTD Products, Cleveland, Ohio and by Atlas Tool & Manufacturing Co., St. Louis, Missouri. Service procedures for these J.C. Penney models will not differ greatly from those given for similar MTD and Atlas models. However, parts are not necessarily interchangeable and should be obtained from J.C. Penney Co., Inc.

J.C. Penney Model	J.C. Penney Catalog No.	Atlas Section	MTD Section
3040	812-0628	12-5100	. . . .
3041	812-0313	. . . .	405
3046	812-0644	. . . .	408

ROTO-HOE

The ROTO-HOE Co.
100 Auburn Rd.
Newbury, OH 44065

Model	Engine Make	Engine Series	Engine Horsepower	No. of Forward Speeds	Power Reverse?	Tilling Width (In.)	Drive Type
SP	Tec.	H35	3.5	2	No	12-24	Chain
SP	Tec.	H50	5	2	No	12-24	Chain
220	Tec.	H35	3.5	1	No	12-24	Chain
220	Tec.	HS50	5	1	No	12-24	Chain
904	B&S	110000	4	1	Yes	15.25	Chain
910	B&S	110000	4	5	Yes	16.5-24	Chain
910	B&S	130000	5	5	Yes	16.5-24	Chain
990	B&S	130000	5	5	Yes	16.5-24	Chain
990	Tec.	H60	6	5	Yes	16.5-24	Chain
990	Tec.	HM80	8	5	Yes	16.5-24	Chain
990	Kohler	K-181	8	5	Yes	16.5-24	Chain

LUBRICATION

ENGINE

Refer to appropriate Briggs and Stratton, Tecumseh or Kohler engine section for engine lubrication specification.

Recommended oil grade is SAE 30 or equivalent. Recommended fuel is either regular or low-lead gasoline having an octane rating of 90 or higher.

CHAIN AND WHEEL DRIVE

All Models

Lubricate grease fittings every 25 hours of operation with a good grade multi-purpose grease. Chains and transmissions are packed with grease at the time of manufacture and should not require additional lubrication.

Oil transport wheel bearings on front tine models every 25 hours of operation.

MAINTENANCE

Inspect all fasteners for looseness and retighten as needed. Check control levers, linkage and cables for freedom of movement and excessive play. Inspect drive belt(s) for excessive stretching, wear, cracks, or any other damage. Install new belt(s) if needed. Inspect all belt pulleys and renew if damaged or excessively worn.

Fig. RH1—Exploded view of chain drive for Model SP.

1. Belt
2. Belt
3. Pulley (5 in.)
4. Washers
5. Pulley (8-in.)
6. Bronze bearing
7. Tube & plate assy.
8. Frame
9. Shaft
10. Washer
11. Sprocket
12. Pin
13. Chain
14. Gasket
15. Chain case
16. Cover
17. Sprocket & shaft assy.
18. Bearing housing
19. Bearings
20. Dust seals
21. Bearing housings
22. Seals
23. Bearings
24. Spacers
25. Sprocket
26. Chain
27. Gasket
28. Chain case

Fig. RH2—Exploded view of chain drive for Model 220.

1. Bearing & housing assy.
2. Chain case assy.
3. Gasket
4. Chain
5. Washer
6. Sprocket & shaft
7. Sprocket & shaft
8. Frame
9. Bronze bearing
10. Housing & bearing assy.
11. Belt
12. Block & set screw
13. Pulley

Fig. RH3 — Exploded view of chain drive for Model 904.

1. Intermediate chain
2. Sprocket
3. Bearing
4. Bearing housing assy.
5. Bearing
6. Frame
7. Shaft
8. Shaft & sprocket

9. Bronze bearing
10. Bearing housing assy.
11. Bronze bearing
12. Pulley (5 in.)
13. Pulley (8 in.)
14. Chain
15. Chain case assy.

16. Sprocket & shaft, tiller drive
17. Chain, wheel drive
18. Chain, tiller drive
19. Washers
20. Sprocket & shaft, wheel drive

21. Sprocket
22. Bearing housing
23. Bearing
24. Bearing housing
25. Bearing
26. Dust cap

Fig. RH4 — Exploded view of wheel drive components for Models 910 and 990.

1. Transmission
2. Pulley
3. Pulley
4. Belt
5. Frame
6. Gasket
7. Chain case
8. Wheel drive shaft
9. Sprocket
10. Chain
11. Bearing carrier
12. Pulley (to engine)
13. Pulley (to tiller)

Fig. RH5 — Exploded view of chain drive for tiller used on Models 910 and 990.

1. Pulley (6 in.)
2. Belt
3. Bronze bearing
4. Bearing housing
5. Frame

6. Gasket
7. Dust shield
8. Bearing housing
9. Washers

10. Sprocket & shaft
11. Chain
12. Gasket
13. Chain case

14. Bearing
15. Wiper bearing
16. Bearing housing
17. Bearing
18. Shaft & sprocket

ADJUSTMENT

CHAIN

Model 904

Remove chain guard cover (15 – Fig. RH3) from left hand side and adjust bearing equally on both sides of unit. Slots for adjustment are provided on bearing housing (22); note that a similar bearing is located on opposite side of frame. Align square serrated washers with serrations on bearing housing before tightening bolts.

SHIFT CONTROL AND DRIVE BELT

Model 904

Shift control adjustments are provided at both top and bottom of shift control handle near idler arm assembly.

To adjust drive belt tension, remove cotter pins at either end or both ends of shift control rod and reengage in next position.

OVERHAUL

ENGINE

All Models

Engine model number is stamped on blower housing for Briggs and Stratton engines and on an attached data plate for Kohler and Tecumseh engines. Refer to appropriate Briggs and Stratton, Kohler or Tecumseh engine section for overhaul procedures.

TRANSMISSION

Models 910 and 990

Transmission is a Peerless 700 series with four forward speeds and one reverse speed.

Thoroughly clean outside of transmission and remove screw (5 – Fig. RH6), spring (4) and detent ball (3) from upper case half (1). Remove six cap screws and separate case halves (1 and 41). Remove shifter shaft and fork assembly (26). Lift chain, shaft and gear assemblies (8 through 37) out of lower case half (41). Remove snap rings (38 and 46) from input shaft (44) and remove input shaft and pinion gear (39) assembly.

Check chain (25) for stretching and check gears for broken teeth or other damage. Inspect shafts, bushings and thrust washers for excessive wear or scoring. Inspect keys (19) for excessive wear in shaft slots. Replace all components that are excessively worn or damaged.

Fig. RH7—Input shaft needle bearings must be installed flush to 0.005-inch (0.13 mm) below case surface.

Fig. RH8—Install shifter collar and shifter (drive) keys on output shaft as shown. Thick side of collar must face shoulder on shaft.

Fig. RH9—View showing correct installation of thrust washers and gears on output shaft. The 45° inside chamfer on thrust washers must face the shoulder on the shaft.

Fig. RH6—Exploded view of Peerless 700 series gearbox used on Models 910 and 990. Note that transmission shown has 5 speeds; transmission used in Model 910 and 990 tillers is similar but has 4 speeds.

1. Case, upper half	13. Gear, 22T	25. Chain
2. Filler plug	14. Gear, 25T	26. Shift rod & fork assy.
3. Ball	15. Gear, 30T	26A. Thrust race
4. Spring	16. Gear, 37T	27. Spacer
5. Screw	17. Thrust washer	28. Gear, 30T
6. Gasket	18. Shaft	29. Gear, 28T
8. Bushing	19. Key	30. Washer
9. Washer	20. Collar	31. Gear, 25T
10. Spacer	21. Sprocket, 18T	32. Gear, 15T
11. Gear, 20T	22. Thrust race	33. Spacer
12. Thrust washer	23. Sprocket	34. Gear, 12T
	24. Snap ring	
35. Gear, 42T	41. Case, lower half	
36. Countershaft	42. Needle bearings	
37. Sprocket	43. "O" ring	
38. Snap ring	44. Input shaft	
39. Pinion gear	45. Thrust race	
40. Thrust race	46. Snap ring	

Reassemble by reversing disassembly procedure. Install a new gasket (6). When installing shift collar (20) and keys (19) on shaft (18), the thin side of collar must face towards outer end of shaft. Refer to Fig. RH8. When assembling gears on shaft, note that the 45 degree chamfer on thrust washers (12–Fig. RH6) must face shoulder on shaft (18) and that flat side of gears must also face shoulder of shaft as shown in Fig. RH9. Input shaft needle bearings (42–Fig. RH6) must be installed flush or 0.005-inch (0.13 mm) below inside and outside surfaces of case (41) as shown in Fig. RH7.

SEARS

SEARS, ROEBUCK & COMPANY
Sears Tower
Chicago, Illinois 60684

Model	Engine Make	Engine Series	Engine Horsepower	No. of Forward Speeds	Power Reverse?	Tilling Width (In.)	Drive Type
29852	B&S	60000	2	1	No	15	Chain
29943	B&S	80000	3	1	No	17	Chain
29945	B&S	130000	5	1	Yes	24	Chain
29936	Craftsman	.....	6	1	Yes	24	Chain
29937	Craftsman	.....	6	1	No	24	Chain
29966	Craftsman	.....	6	2	Yes	21	Gear & Chain
29968	Craftsman	.....	8	2	Yes	21	Gear & Chain
29958	B&S	190000	8	2	No	28	Gear
299130	Craftsman	744012	3.5	1	Yes	14	Chain
299150	B&S	130000	5	1	Yes	17	Chain
299382	Craftsman	736062	6	1	Yes	24	Chain

LUBRICATION

ENGINE

All Models

Refer to appropriate Briggs and Stratton engine section for Briggs and Stratton engine lubrication specifications. Refer to appropriate Tecumseh engine section for Craftsman engine lubrication specifications.

Recommended oil grade is SAE 30 or equivalent. Recommended fuel is either regular or low-lead gasoline having an octane rating of 90 or higher. The use of non-leaded gasolines reduces cylinder head deposits, but could shorten engine valve life if carburetor is adjusted too lean.

CHAIN DRIVE

All Models

Chain case lubricant cannot be added on any models except Models 29966 and 29968. Chain case on other models is factory sealed and must be removed and disassembled in order to add or change grease in case.

GEAR CASE

Model 29958

Gear case oil should be checked at least every 10 hours of operation. Recommended lubricant is SAE 30 heavy duty detergent oil or suitable equivalent.

To check gear case oil place tiller on a level surface. Clean dirt from around gear case housing and remove oil level plug (1–Fig. SE1). Oil level should be at bottom of plug hole. If oil level is low add oil through level hole until it begins to run out hole. Reinstall and tighten plug.

Models 29966, 29968, 299130, 299150 and 299382

Gear case is factory sealed and must be removed and disassembled in order to add or change grease in case. Refer to **OVERHAUL** section for servicing grease.

MAINTENANCE

Inspect all fasteners for looseness and retighten as needed. Check control levers, linkage and cables for freedom of movement and excessive play. Inspect drive belt(s) for excessive stretching, wear, cracks or any other damage. In- stall new belt(s) if needed. Inspect all belt pulleys and renew if damaged or excessively worn. Transport wheels on Models 29852, 29943, 29945, 29937,

Fig SE2 – View of clutch control components for Model 29852.

1. Adjusting clip
2. Clutch lever in released position
3. Clutch lever in engaged position

Fig. SE3 – View of clutch adjusting components for Models 29937 and 29943.

1. Idler spring   2. Chain

Fig. SE1 – View of oil level plug for Model 29958. Oil level plug is shown at (1).

TINE CONTROL "OFF" POSITION

TINE CONTROL "RUNNING" POSITION

29958 and 299382 should be lubricated occasionally with SAE 30 oil.

ADJUSTMENT

CLUTCH CONTROL

Model 29852

Refer to Fig. SE2 for view of clutch control components. Adjustment is achieved by repositioning clutch cable in adjusting clip (1). With clutch lever in released position idler pulley arm should just touch drive belt cover. To check for correct adjustment, make sure clutch lever is in released position and pull on starter rope handle. If tines do not turn, then adjustment is correct. If tines do turn, then clutch cable will need to be adjusted.

Fig. SE5—View of clutch operation and adjusting components for Model 29958.

1. Clutch rod
2. Turnbuckle
3. Lockwasher
4. Wing nut
5. Clutch lever in released position
6. Clutch lever in engaged position

Models 29937 and 29943

Refer to Fig. SE3 for view of clutch adjustment components. Adjustment is achieved by repositioning chain (2) in idler spring loop (1). To check for correct adjustment, make sure clutch lever is in released position and pull on starter rope handle. If tines do not turn, then

Fig. SE4—View of clutch operation and adjusting components for Models 29936 and 29945.

1. Clutch control cable
2. Retaining clip screw

adjustment is correct. If tines do turn, then chain will need to be adjusted.

Models 29936 and 29945

Refer to Fig. SE4 for view of clutch adjustment components. Adjustment is achieved by sliding clutch cable (1) in retaining clip (2). To check for correct adjustment, make sure clutch lever is in released position and pull on starter rope handle. If tines do not turn, then adjustment is correct. If tines do turn, then clutch cable will need to be adjusted.

Model 29958

Refer to Fig. SE5 for view of clutch adjustment components. Adjustment is achieved by loosening wing nut (4) and turning turnbuckle (2) on clutch rod (1). To check for correct adjustment, make sure clutch lever is in released position and pull on starter rope handle. If drive belt does not turn, then adjustment is correct. If drive belt does turn, then turnbuckle will need to be adjusted.

Models 29966 and 29968

TINE DRIVE BELT. Refer to Fig. SE6 for view of belt adjustment com-

Fig. SE6—View of tine drive belt adjusting components for Models 29966 and 29968.

1. Adjustment nuts
2. Idler arm swivel
3. Tine control spring
4. Adjustment rod
5. Washer

Fig. SE7—View of correct wheel drive cable adjustment and components.

1. Control cable
2. Clip & screw
3. Extension spring
4. Idler pulley assy.
5. Ground drive input pulley

ponents. Place tine engagement lever in disengaged position, then remove drive belt cover. Place engagement lever in engaged position. Turn adjustment nuts (1) until there is a one-inch distance be-

tween idler arm swivel (2) and washer (5). Reinstall drive belt cover.

GROUND DRIVE BELT. Refer to Fig. SE7 for view of clutch adjustment

components. Adjustment is achieved by sliding control cable (1) in retaining clip (2). There should be a 5/8 inch (15.9 mm) stretch in extension spring (3) when clutch lever is completely engaged.

Models 299130 and 299150

Refer to Fig. SE7A. Extension spring (1) should stretch (A) 5/8 inch (15.9 mm) when clutch control handle is held down. Adjustment is made by loosening clip (2) and sliding cable in or out as needed.

Model 299382

Refer to Fig. SE15. Adjust belt guide (7) position so there is 3/16-inch (4.8 mm) clearance between belt guide and belt when clutch control lever is held down. Align engine and transmission pulleys as shown in Figs. SE17 and SE18.

OVERHAUL
ENGINE
All Models

Engine model number is stamped on blower housing for Briggs and Stratton engines. Engine make and series number is marked on data plate attached to engine for Craftsman engines. Refer to appropriate Briggs and Stratton engine section for overhaul procedures. Refer to appropriate Tecumsech engine section for Craftsman engine overhaul procedures.

CHAIN CASE
All Models

On all models except Models 29966, 29968, 299130 and 299150, chain case is factory sealed and must be replaced as a complete unit if service is required. Chain case parts breakdown and identification is shown in Fig. SE8 for Models 29966 and 29968 or in Fig. SE10A for Models 299130 and 299150.

OIL SEAL INSTALLATION. Remove tines from tine shaft. Use a seal puller to remove seals out of case hub. Clean tine shaft with emery cloth. Drive new seals in until outside face is flush with case hub.

INSPECTION. Inspect and renew all components that are worn or damaged. Install new gasket and seals. Lubricate chains, sprockets and bearings with a light film of grease during reassembly. Keep all dirt and foreign matter out of chain case during reassembly. Recom-

Fig. SE7A – View of clutch control extension spring (1) showing 5/8-inch (15.88 mm) stretch (A) on Models 299130 and 299150.

Fig. SE8 – Exploded view of tine drive chain case components for Models 29966 and 29968.

1. Cups
2. Seals
3. Seals
4. Chain case cover, R.H.
5. Needle bearing
6. Gasket
7. Chain
8. Washers
9. Spacer
10. Intermediate shaft
11. Needle bearings
12. Sprocket
13. Tine shaft assy.
14. Thrust bearing races
15. Input shaft assy.
16. Needle bearing
17. Chain case cover, L.H.

76

1. Oil seals
2. Needle bearings
3. Gear case shield, L.H.
4. Gear case, L.H.
5. Gasket
6. Thrust caps
7. Tine shaft assy.
8. Chain
9. Gear case, R.H.
10. Gear case shield, R.H.
11. Needle bearings
12. Needle bearing
13. Pipe plug
14. Gasket
15. Thrust bearing races
16. Third reduction shaft gears
17. Second reduction shaft & gears
18. Reverse idler shaft
19. Locknut
20. High speed pinion
21. Woodruff key
22. Snap rings
23. Input shaft
24. Low speed pinion
25. Steel balls
26. Detent springs
27. Shift lever yokes
28. Shift block guide (Three Grooves)
29. Shift block guide (Two Grooves)
30. Gasket
31. Gearshift gate reinforcement
32. Cotter pin
33. Washer
34. Seal
35. Washer
36. Spring
37. Shift lever guide ball
38. Gear shift cover
39. Shift lever cap
40. Gear shift lever
41. Shift knob

Fig. SE9 — Exploded view of gear case and shift lever components for Model 29958.

1. Cups
2. Seals
3. Seals
4. Gear case, R.H.
5. Gasket
6. Spacer
7. Output shaft assy.
8. Spacer
9. Washers
10. Spacers
11. Gear cluster
12. Shaft
13. Washers
14. Washer
15. Gear cluster
16. Shaft
17. Thrust bearing
18. Crescent ring
19. Needle bearings
20. Thrust bearing races
21. Gear cluster
22. Spacer
23. Reverse gear
24. Gear
25. Shaft
26. Needle bearings
27. Thrust bearing races
28. Gear assy.
29. Input shaft
30. "E" ring
31. Gear
32. Needle bearing
33. Reverse idler shaft
34. Upper shift shaft
35. Seal washers
36. Shift arm assy.
37. Shift fork
38. Steel ball
39. Shift fork spring
40. Gear case, L.H.
41. Lower shift shaft

Fig. SE10 — Exploded view of ground drive gear case for Models 29966 and 29968.

Fig. SE10A – Exploded view of chain case used on Models 299130 and 299150.

1. Left chain case	10. Bearing	29. Reverse gear
2. Right chain case	11. Bushing	30. Shaft
3. Gasket	12. Wheel shaft & gear	31. Cup
4. Clip	13. Chain	32. Shift arm
5. Shift fork	14. Sprocket	33. Spiral ring
6. Detent ball &	15. Washer	34. Seal
spring	16. Reverse idler shaft	35. Seal
7. Shift shaft	16A. Spacer	36. Spacer
8. Spacer	17. Reverse idler gear	37. Tine shaft &
8A. Seal	18. Needle bearing	sprocket
9. "O" Ring	19. Clip	38. Spacer
	20. Bearing	
	21. Thrust bearing	
	race	
	22. Input pinion	
	23. Input shaft	
	24. Bearing	
	25. Chain	
	26. Bearing	
	27. Sprocket	
	28. Gear	

mended lubricant for all models except Models 299130 and 299150 is six ounces of Plastilube #1 grease or suitable equivalent. Recommended lubricant for Models 299130 and 299150 is eight ounces of Plastilube #1 grease or suitable equivalent. To fill chain case with grease, lay right half of case on its side, add grease and assemble left half to right half. Complete reassembly and reinstall in tiller frame.

GEAR CASE

Model 29958

OIL SEAL INSTALLATION. Remove tines from tine shaft. Use a seal puller to remove seals from case hub. Clean tine shaft with emery cloth. Drive new seals in until outside face is flush with case hub.

INSPECTION. Refer to Fig. SE9 for parts breakdown and identification. Inspect and renew all components that are worn or damaged. Install new gasket and seals. Lubricate gears and bearings with a light film of oil during reassembly. Keep all dirt and foreign matter out

Fig. SE11 – View of single drive belt and components for Models 29852, 29943, 29937 and 29958.

1. Engine pulley
2. Idler pulley
3. Transmission pulley
4. Drive belt

Fig. SE12 – View of drive belt arrangement and components for Models 29936 and 29945.

1. Engine pulley
2. Idler pulley
3. Transmission pulley
4. Reverse isler pulley
5. Reverse drive belt
6. Forward drive belt
7. Reverse idler arm

Fig. SE13 — View of tine drive belt arrangement and components for Models 29966 and 29968.

1. Rear pulley
2. Idler pulley
3. Front pulley
4. Drive belt

Fig. SE14 — View of ground drive belt arrangement and components

1. Engine pulley
2. Idler pulley
3. Ground drive input pulley
4. Drive belt

Fig. SE15 — View of drive belt arrangement and components for Model 299382.

1. Forward belt
2. Reverse belt
3. Transmission pulley
4. Idler pulley
5. Engine pulley
6. Reverse idler pulley
7. Belt guide

of gear case during reassembly. Refer to **LUBRICATION** section for lubrication requirements after reassembly and installation.

Models 29966, 29968, 299130 and 299150

OIL SEAL INSTALLATION. Remove drive wheels from output shaft. Using a seal puller pull seals out of case hub. If seal puller is not available use an awl and screwdriver to pry seals out. Clean tine shaft with emery cloth. Drive new seals in until outside face is flush with case hub.

INSPECTION. Refer to Fig. SE10 for parts breakdown and identification for Models 29966 and 29968. Refer to Fig. SE10A for parts breakdown and identification for Models 299130 and 299150. Inspect and renew all components that are worn or damaged. Install new gasket and seals. Lubricate gears and bearings with a light film of grease during reassembly. Keep all dirt and foreign matter out of gear case during reassembly. Recommended lubricant is Plastilube #1 grease or equivalent. Lubricant capacity is six ounces for Models 29966 & 29968 and eight ounces for Models 299130 & 299150. To fill gear case with grease, lay right half of case on its side, add grease and assemble left half to right half. Complete reassembly and reinstall in tiller frame.

DRIVE BELTS

Models 29852, 29943, 29937 and 29958

Refer to Fig. SE11 for belt routing and parts identification. Remove drive belt cover, then slip drive belt off engine pulley and chain case input pulley. Install new drive belt. Drive belt size for Models 29852 and 29943 is ⅜-inch x 39 inches long. Drive belt size for Model 29937 is ½-inch x 42 inches long. Drive belt size for Model 29958 is ½-inch x 37 inches long. Reinstall drive belt cover. Refer to appropriate **CLUTCH CONTROL ADJUSTMENT** section for readjustment of clutch linkage.

Models 29936 and 29945

Refer to Fig. SE12 for belt(s) arrangement and parts identification. Remove drive belt cover, then remove bolt and nut securing reverse idler pulley (4) to idler arm (7). Remove reverse drive belt from pulleys. To remove forward drive belt, loosen drive belt guide nut and swing belt guide away from belt. Slip drive belt from transmission pulley, then from engine pulley. Install new drive

Fig. SE16 — View showing proper alignment of belt pulleys on Model 299382. Distance (A) between engine pulley and crankcase should be 5/16-inch (7.9 mm).

1. Reverse belt
2. Reverse idler pulley
3. Idler arm pin
4. Forward belt
5. Engine pulley
6. Crankcase face

Fig. SE17 — View showing specified clearance (CA) of 1 9/16-inch (39.7 mm) between transmission input hub (1) and transmission pulley hub (2) on Model 299382.

Fig. SE18 — View showing specified clearance (A) of 5/16-inch (7.9 mm) between engine pulley (1) and reverse idler arm assembly (2) on Model 299382.

belts. Forward drive belt size is ½-inch x 41 inches long. Reassemble in reverse order of disassembly. Refer to **CLUTCH CONTROL ADJUSTMENT** section for adjusting procedures.

Models 29966 and 29968

TINE DRIVE. Refer to Fig. SE13 for belt routing and parts identification. Place tine engagement lever in disengaged position. Place control handle to highest position, then remove drive belt cover. Loosen drive belt guides, then slip drive belt off pulleys. Install new drive belt. Refer to **CLUTCH CONTROL ADJUSTMENT** section for belt adjusting procedures. Reassemble in reverse order of disassembly.

GROUND DRIVE. Refer to Fig. SE14 for belt routing and parts identification. Remove drive belt cover, then loosen belt guides. Slip belt off engine pulley and ground drive input pulley. Install new drive belt. Refer to **CLUTCH CONTROL ADJUSTMENT** section for adjusting procedures. Reassemble in reverse order of disassembly.

Models 299130 and 299150

Refer to Fig. SE14 for belt routing and parts identification. Remove hairpin clip and rivet from left-hand side wheel and slide wheel assembly out approximately 1½ inch (38.1 mm). Remove drive belt cover, then loosen belt guides. Slip belt away from idler pulley (2) and remove belt from engine pulley (1) and input shaft pulley (3). Install new drive belt and retighten belt guides. Reassemble in reverse order of disassembly. Refer to **CLUTCH CONTROL ADJUSTMENT** section for adjusting procedures.

Model 299382

Refer to Fig. SE15 for belt routing and parts identification. Remove belt guard. Unbolt and remove reverse idler pulley (6) and remove reverse belt (2). Loosen and move belt guide (7) away from forward belt (1). Roll belt off transmission pulley (3), then remove from engine pulley (5). Reassemble in reverse order of disassembly. Note that reverse belt is installed inside out. Refer to **CLUTCH CONTROL ADJUSTMENT** section for adjusting procedures.

SNAPPER

MCDONOUGH POWER EQUIPMENT
McDonough, Georgia 30253

(Front Tine Models)

Model	Engine Make	Engine Series	Engine Horsepower	No. of Forward Speeds	Power Reverse?	Tilling Width (In.)*	Drive Type
300T	B&S	80000	3	1	No	26	Chain
300T	Tec.	H30	3	1	No	26	Chain
500T	B&S	130000	5	1	No	26	Chain
500T	Tec.	H50	5	1	No	26	Chain
301T	B&S	80000	3	1	No	26	Chain
301TR	B&S	80000	3	1	No	26	Chain
401T	B&S	110000	4	1	No	26	Chain
401TR	B&S	110000	4	1	No	26	Chain
501T	Tec.	H50	5	1	No	26	Chain
501TR	Tec.	H50	5	1	No	26	Chain
501TC	B&S	130000	5	1	No	26	Chain
501TRC	B&S	130000	5	1	No	26	Chain

* On some models extension tines may be added to extend tilling width to 36 inches.

LUBRICATION

ENGINE

All Models

Refer to appropriate Briggs and Stratton or Tecumseh engine section for engine lubrication specifications. Recommended oil grade is SAE 30 or equivalent. Recommended fuel is either regular or low-lead gasoline having an octane rating of 90 or higher. The use of non-leaded gasolines reduces cylinder head deposits, but could shorten engine valve life if carburetor is adjusted too lean.

CHAIN DRIVE

All Models

Chain case oil should be checked at least every time engine oil is changed. SAE 90 is recommended oil.

To check chain case oil, place tiller on a level surface. Clean case housing and remove oil level plug and washer (24 – Fig. S4). Oil level should be at bottom of plug hole. If oil level is low remove plastic oil fill plug (4). Add oil through fill hole until oil begins to run out oil level hole, then replace plugs.

MAINTENANCE

Inspect all fasteners for looseness and retighten as needed. Check control levers, linkage and cables for freedom of movement and excessive play. Inspect drive belt(s) for excessive stretching, wear, cracks, or any other damage. Install new belt(s) if needed. Inspect all belt pulleys and renew if damaged or excessively worn. Transport wheels should be lubricated occasionally with SAE 30 oil.

ADJUSTMENT

CLUTCH CONTROL

All Models

Small clutch adjustment may be done by repositioning spring (2 – Fig. S1) in chain links (3). If clutch spring does not stretch when clutch lever is engaged, then chain will need to be shortened. If correct clutch engagement and disengagement cannot be obtained by adjusting chain links, then adjustment of idler link (2 – Fig. S2 and S3) will need to be done. For single belt models refer to Fig. S2 and two belt models refer to Fig. S3 for idler assembly breakdown and identification. To adjust: loosen two hex nuts (1 – Fig. S2 and S3) on each side of idler link (2). Raise idler pulley to take slack out of belt. Hold idler pulley and pull down on idler link to take slack out of clutch cable, then retighten hex nuts. Adjust spring (2 – Fig. S1) and chain (3) if clutch is too tight or too loose.

BELT ADJUSTMENT

Single Belt Models

Remove drive belt cover. Loosen engine mounting bolts. Slide engine forwards or backwards to adjust belt tension. Belt should slip on pulleys when clutch is not engaged. Retighten engine mounting bolts, then reinstall drive belt cover.

Fig. S1 – View of clutch lever (1), spring (2) and chain links (3) for clutch control and adjustment.

Fig. S2 – Exploded view of drive belt idler assembly for single belt models.

1. Hex nut
2. Idler link
3. Washer
4. Mounting bracket
5. Idler pulley

Two Belt Models

Remove drive belt cover. Loosen engine and speed reducer mounting bolts. Slide engine or reducer forward or backwards to adjust belt(s) tension. Belt from engine to reducer should be adjusted tight. Belt from reducer to chain drive should slip on pulleys when clutch is not engaged. Retighten mounting bolts, then reinstall drive belt cover.

OVERHAUL

ENGINE

All Models

Engine model no. is stamped on blower housing for Briggs and Stratton engines. Engine make and series no. is marked on data plate attached to engine for Tecumseh engines. Refer to appropriate Briggs and Stratton or Tecumseh engine section for overhaul procedures.

CHAIN CASE

All Models

OIL SEAL INSTALLATION. Remove tines from tine shaft. Use a seal puller to remove outer and inner seals (7 – Fig. S4) from case hub. Clean tine shaft with emery cloth. Install inner seal with lip facing toward inside and outer seal with lip facing toward outside. Drive new seals in until outer seal is flush with case hub.

REMOVE AND DISASSEMBLE. Unbolt handle bar tie bars from chain case. Remove two lower handle bar bolts and nuts. Lift handle bar assembly from chain case and place to the side. Tip tiller forward until engine is resting on ground. Remove chain case to side rail bolts and nuts. Remove side rail to hitch assembly bolts. Remove transport wheels, skid arm and hitch from tiller as a unit. Remove drive belt cover, then remove belt from input pulley. Withdraw chain case from frame. Remove tines from tine shaft. Loosen set screw in drive pulley hub and remove pulley and Woodruff key. Drain out chain case oil. Split chain case in half and withdraw chain sprocket assembly out as a unit. Refer to Fig. S4 for chain case parts breakdown and identification. Inspect and renew all components that are worn or damaged. Install new gasket and seals. Lubricate chains, sprockets and bearings with a light film of oil during reassembly. Keep all dirt

Fig. S3 – Exploded view of drive belt idler assembly for two belt models.

1. Hex nut
2. Idler link
3. Washer
4. Mounting bracket
5. Idler pulley
6. Idler pulley arm
7. Locknut
8. Bolt, washer and race assy.
9. Reduction pulley
10. Washer
11. Belt guide
12. Hex nut

Fig. S4 – Exploded view of chain case assembly.

1. Right side case half
2. Bronze bushings
3. Welch plug
4. Oil fill plug
5. Cap screw (2½ inches long)
6. Spacer clips
7. Oil seals
8. Case half spacer
9. Needle bearings
10. Nylon spacer
11. Gasket
12. Shim washer
13. Primary drive chain
14. Drive shaft
15. Sprocket
16. Tine shaft
17. Final drive chain
18. Race
19. Roller bearing
20. Spacer
21. Left side case half
22. Oil seal
23. Locknut
24. Oil level check plug and washer

and foreign matter out of chain case during reassembly. Refer to **LUBRICATION** section for lubricating requirements after reassembly and installation.

DRIVE BELTS

Single Belt Models

Remove drive belt cover. Remove belt from pulleys and install new belt. Drive belt is ½-inch x 51 inches long. Loosen engine mounting bolts and slide engine, belt should slip on pulleys when clutch is not engaged. Retighten engine mounting bolts. Refer to **CLUTCH CONTROL ADJUSTMENT** section for adjusting procedure. Reinstall drive belt cover.

Two Belt Models

Loosen engine mounting bolts. Slide engine backwards to lower tension on belt. Remove engine to reducer belt, then remove reducer to chain drive belt. Install new belts. Reducer to chain drive belt is ½-inch x 37 inches long. Reducer to engine belt is ½-inch x 26.5 inches long. Belt from reducer to chain drive should slip on pulleys when clutch is not engaged. Reposition speed reducer mounting bracket to adjust belt tension. Belt from engine to reducer should be adjusted tight. Retighten mounting bolts. Refer to **CLUTCH CONTROL ADJUSTMENT** section for adjusting procedure. Reinstall drive belt cover.

SNAPPER
(Rear Tine Models)

Model	Engine Make	Engine Series	Engine Horsepower	No. of Forward Speeds	Power Reverse?	Tilling Width (In.)	Drive Type
RT5	B&S	130000	5	4	Yes	20	Chain
RT8	B&S	190000	8	4	Yes	20	Chain
RT8S	B&S	190000	8	4	Yes	20	Chain
R5000	B&S	130000	5	4	Yes	20	Chain
R5001	B&S	130000	5	4	Yes	20	Chain
R8000	B&S	190000	8	4	Yes	20	Chain
R8001	B&S	190000	8	4	Yes	20	Chain
R8001S	B&S	19000	8	4	Yes	20	Chain

CAUTION: Frequently, the performance of maintenance, adjustment or repair operations on a rotary tiller is more convenient if tiller is standing on end. This procedure can be considered a recommended practice providing the following safety recommendations are performed:

1. Drain fuel tank or make certain that fuel level is low enough so that fuel will not drain out.
2. Close fuel shut-off valve if so equipped.
3. Remove battery on models so equipped.
4. Disconnect spark plug wire and tie out of way.
5. Although not absolutely essential, it is recommended that crankcase oil be drained to avoid flooding the combustion chamber with oil when engine is tilted.
6. Secure tiller from tipping by lashing unit to a nearby post or overhead beam.

LUBRICATION

ENGINE

All Models

Refer to appropriate Briggs and Stratton engine section for engine lubrication specifications. Recommended oil grade is SAE 30 or equivalent. Recommended fuel is either regular or low-lead gasoline having an octane rating of 90 or higher.

CONTROL MECHANISM

Apply a suitable grease at least twice a year to sliding surfaces of shift mechanism and drive components.

TINE CHAIN DRIVE

The oil level in the chain drive should be checked at the same recommended intervals as the engine oil. Oil level should be even with bottom edge of oil plug hole (P – Fig. S10). To add oil remove plastic plug (G – Fig. S11) on side of chain case. Do not overfill. Approximate capacity of chain case is one quart (0.95 L). Recommended oil is Snapper 00 or a suitable equivalent.

PRIMARY CHAIN DRIVE

The primary chain drive is lubricated during assembly with Snapper 00 oil and does not normally require new lubricant.

GEAR DRIVE

The gear drive is lubricated during assembly with Snapper 00 oil and does not normally require new lubricant.

MAINTENANCE

Inspect all fasteners for looseness and retighten as needed. Check control levers, linkage and cables for freedom of movement and excessive play. Inspect drive belt(s) for excessive stetching, wear, cracks, or any other damage. Install new belt(s) if needed. Inspect all belt pulleys and renew if damaged or excessively worn.

ADJUSTMENT

CLUTCH CONTROL

To check adjustment, position tiller on front end. Measure lengths of both springs at end of each control cable with clutch disengaged. Pull clutch control to engaged position (towards handlebar) and remeasure lengths of springs. The springs should be ¼-½ inch (6.4-12.7 mm) longer when extended from the clutch disengaged to the clutch engaged positions. Adjust clutch spring length by rotating adjusting nuts located at upper and lower ends of cables. If wheels or

Fig. S10 — View showing location of oil level plug on the tine chain case.

Fig. S11 — View showing location of oil fill plug on tine chain case.

tines turn when clutch control is in disengaged position, clutch spring length is too great and should be readjusted. If clutch springs will not adjust properly, check drive belt adjustment and drive disc.

TINE DRIVE BELT

To adjust drive belt, position tiller on front end. Move belt cover away so belt is accessible. Pull clutch control towards handlebar so clutch is engaged. Note position of idler arm attached to crossmember (19–Fig. S12). The idler arm should be nearly parallel with the crossmember when the belt is tight. If not parallel, loosen cap screw securing idler pulley (L–Fig. S13) adjacent to chain case pulley. Move idle pulley (L) so idler arm is parallel with crossmember (19–Fig. S12) when the belt is tight, then tighen pulley cap screw.

WHEEL DRIVE DISC

Power for the tiller's wheels is transmitted through two discs, a drive disc and a driven disc. The drive disc is attached to the engine's crankshaft while the driven disc is attached to the primary chain case input shaft. As the primary chain case is moved from side to side through the shift mechanism, the driven friction disc contacts a different spot on the drive disc to change ground speed. Moving the driven disc to the opposite side of the drive disc reverses direction.

To check friction disc adjustment, position tiller on front end. Shift speed lever to first speed and then to reverse speed. The driven disc should be equidistant from the center of the drive disc in first and reverse positions (see Fig. S14). The driven disc must also be outside the indentation in the center of the drive disc. To position disc away from indentation, loosen screws securing shift quadrant (22–Fig. S12) to the frame, move the quadrant forward then retighten screws. Recheck disc movement and position.

Fig. S12—Exploded view of tractor unit components.

1. Stand-up bar		20. Idler
2. Weight	8. Clutch yoke	21. Boot
3. Wheel hub	9. Lever	22. Shift quadrant assy.
4. Dust cap	10. Spring	23. Thrust washer
5. Transmission & left frame	11. Braces	24. Nylon thrust washer
6. Primary chain case	12. Bellcrank	25. Bearing
7. Shift link	13. Shift link	26. Right frame
	14. Stud	
	15. Washer (5 hp)	
	16. Cable clip	
	17. Spacer (5 hp)	
	18. Rod	
	19. Idler bracket assy.	

Fig. S13—View showing location of idler pulley (L) which may be relocated to adjust tine drive belt as outlined in text.

Fig. S14—The driven disc should not contact indentation (D) in first or reverse speed. Refer to text for adjustment. The driven disc should be approximately equidistant from drive disc center in first and reverse speeds.

1. Nut
2. Belleville washers
3. Pulley
4. Left chain case half
5. Ball bearing
6. Washer
7. Key
8. Input shaft & sprocket
9. "O" ring
10. Right chain case half
11. Oil fill plug
12. Shaft
13. Bearing (2)
14. Intermediate sprocket
15. Spacer stud
16. Tine shaft & sprocket
17. Spacer
18. Gasket
19. Needle bearing
20. Seals (2)

Fig. S15—Exploded view of tine chain case. Two seals (20) are located in each case half.

16. Axle
17. Thrust washer
18. Drive tube
19. Plastic washer
20. Bolt
21. Boot

Fig. S16—Exploded view of transmission assembly.

1. Gasket
2. Cover
3. Boot retainer
4. Oil fill plug
5. Left frame
6. Thrust washer
7. Shaft
8. Gear
9. Gear
10. Hex tube
11. Bearing
13. Bearing
15. Spacer

OVERHAUL

ENGINE

The engine model number is stamped on the engine's blower housing. Refer to the appropriate Briggs and Stratton engine section for overhaul information.

TINE CHAIN CASE

OIL SEAL INSTALLATION. Position tiller on front end. Remove tines from tine shaft. Use a seal puller to remove outer and inner seals (20–Fig. S15) from case hub. Clean tine shaft with emery cloth. Install inner seal with lip facing toward inside and outer seal with lip facing outside. Drive new seals in until outer seal is flush with case hub.

R&R AND OVERHAUL. Position tiller on front end. Remove tines from tine shaft. Remove spring and grip from depth bar. Detach drive belt from chain case pulley. Unscrew retaining bolt and remove depth bar. Unscrew chain case pulley retaining nut (1–Fig. S15) and remove pulley (3). Remove screws securing chain case mounting brackets to tine cover. Remove nuts securing front bracket to chain case and note position of spacers. Remove pulley shield and cover attaching pin. Remove chain case along with mounting brackets then detach brackets from chain case.

Drain lubricant from chain case. Separate chain case halves and remove chain sprocket assembly as a unit. Refer to Fig. S15 for an exploded view of chain case assembly. Inspect all components for damage and excessive wear.

Reassemble and reinstall chain case by reversing disassembly and removal procedure while noting the following: Install needle bearings (19) by driving against numbered end of bearing; numbered end of bearing must be to inside of case half. Install ball bearings (5) so numbered end of bearing is to inside of case half. Install nylon spacer (17) so cupped side is towards sprocket (16). Install new gasket and seals. Lubricate chains, sprockets and bearings with oil during assembly. Alternate from side to side when tightening the case screws. Tighten case screws to 8-10 ft.-lbs. (10.8-13.5 N·m). Tighten center through-bolt to 18-26 ft.lbs. (24.4-35.2 N·m). Install Belleville washers (2) with concave side towards pulley. Refill with oil as outlined in **LUBRICATION** section.

TRANSMISSION

R&R AND OVERHAUL. Although not necessary, the tiller unit should be separated from the tractor unit to ease disassembly.

The transmission is located on the left frame and may be removed for overhaul as follows: Remove the front stand-up bar and both wheels and hubs. Loosen clamps securing left boot. Remove bolts and screws securing left frame (5–Fig. S16) to tractor unit components then separate left frame from tractor.

To disassemble transmission, remove through-bolt (20) and screws retaining cover (2) to frame. Refer to Fig. S16 and disassemble transmission while noting location of components.

Reassemble and reinstall transmission by reversing disassembly and removal sequences. Note that split washers may be installed at right end of hex shaft adjacent to bearing (25–Fig. S12) so shaft end play does not exceed 1/16 in. (1.6 mm). Fill transmission with 4 oz. of Snapper 00 oil or equivalent after installation.

PRIMARY CHAIN CASE

R&R AND OVERHAUL. To remove the primary chain case, remove the transmission as previously outlined. Detach shift link (7–Fig. S12), twist unit sideways and remove primary chain

Fig. S17— Exploded view of primary chain case. Bushings (20) and spacers (1) are used on early models in place of bearings (14) and spacers (15).

1. Snap ring
2. Roller
3. Case half
4. Ball bearing
5. Input shaft & sprocket
6. Shims
7. Belleville washer
8. Bolt
9. Key
10. Hub
11. Locknut
12. Driven disc
13. Locknut
14. Needle bearing
15. Spacer
16. Sprocket & shaft
17. Gasket
18. Case half
19. Oil fill plug
20. Bushing
21. Spacer

case. Drain grease from case. Refer to Fig. S17 and disassemble chain case.

Press bearings or bushings (4, 14 or 20) towards inside of case half if they must be removed. Press bearings or bushings towards outside of case half when installing. Early models may be equipped with bushings (20) which should be discarded and replaced with needle bearings (14). Note that different thrust washers (15 and 21) must also be installed if bushings are replaced with bearings. Install spacers (15) so cupped side is towards sprocket (16). Two shims (6) are located on each side of input sprocket (5).

Reinstall primary chain case by reversing disassembly procedure. Fill chain case with 2 oz. of Snapper 00 oil or equivalent.

TROY-BILT

GARDEN WAY MFG. CO.
102nd St. & 9th Ave.
Troy, NY 12180

Model	Engine Make	Engine Series	Engine Horsepower	No. of Forward Speeds	Power Reverse?	Tilling Width (In.)	Drive Type
Junior	Tec.	.....	3½	2	Yes	14	Gear
Pony	B&S	130000	5	2	Yes	16	Gear
Horse	Clinton	498-0301-280	4½	4	Yes	20	Gear
Horse	Tec.	.....	6	4	Yes	20	Gear
Horse	Kohler	K-161	7	4	Yes	20	Gear
Horse	B&S	190000	8	4	Yes	20	Gear
Horse	Kohler	K-181	8	4	Yes	20	Gear

LUBRICATION

ENGINE

All Models

Refer to Briggs and Stratton, Tecumseh, Kohler or Clinton engine section for engine lubrication specifications. Recommended oil grade is SAE 30 oil with SF classification. Recommended fuel is either regular or low-lead gasoline having an octane rating of 90 or higher.

WHEELS AND CONTROLS

All Models

At least every 10 hours of operation, lubricate wheel shafts and pivot points with SAE 30 oil and apply a thin coat of grease to engine mounting bars and belt adjustment block. Do not get oil or grease on drive belts.

GEAR DRIVE

All Models

Oil level in gear housing should be checked at least every 30 hours of operation. With tiller in a level position, gear housing oil level should be even with oil level plug hole on left side of transmission. If oil level is low, add oil through fill plug hole at top of transmission case until oil flows out of oil level plug hole. Recommended gear oil is SAE 90 or SAE 140.

MAINTENANCE

All Models

Inspect drive belt(s) and renew if frayed or stretched to the point where adjustment is no longer effective.

On Horse models, reverse disc should be inspected at least every 30 hours of operation. Replace disc if there are any chunks of rubber missing from outside diameter or if there are any flat spots if the disc is made of fiber material. Periodically check tires for a specified pressure of 10-20 psi.

ADJUSTMENT

Horse Models

BELT TENSION. To adjust belt tension, push forward/reverse shift lever all the way down and lock in forward position, then loosen mounting bolt for the yellow colored adjustment block. Press down hard on shift lever until roller moves down below forward detent notch and onto lower surface of adjustment block. In this position, roller should be ¼-inch (6.4 mm) from adjustment block mounting bracket. Slide adjusting block up or down to obtain proper adjustment. Retighten mounting bolt.

REVERSE DISC. With shift lever in neutral position, tab on motor mount should be resting on top of reverse plunger adjusting bolt and reverse disc should be at least 3/16-inch (4.8 mm) above flat surface of transmission drive pulley. Move plunger up or down as needed to obtain specified clearance between reverse disc and transmission drive pulley.

Pony and Junior Models

FORWARD BELT TENSION. Tension is applied to forward belt by a forward idler pulley which in turn is adjusted by a screw at the idler pivot. Screw head must always be ⅛-¼ inch (3.2-6.4 mm) above pivot when shift lever is in "forward" position. Adjust as needed. The unit can be set up for additional adjustment if belt is overly stretched. This can be accomplished by placing shift lever in neutral and turning adjustment screw all the way in, then by removing belt from top pulley. Remove retainer pin and washer from idler on left side. Remove pin from outside hole in adjustable link and reinstall in inside hole. Reinstall washer and retainer pin and make adjustment with adjusting screw as previously outlined.

REVERSE BELT TENSION. Tension is applied to reverse belt by the reverse idler pulley. To adjust, remove reverse belt from engine pulley, then remove retainer pin and washer from idler on right side. Remove pin from outside hole in adjustable link and reinstall through inside hole. Reinstall retainer pin and washer, then reinstall reverse belt.

OVERHAUL

ENGINE

All Models

Engine model number is stamped on blower housing or on a plate which is attached to blower housing on Briggs and Stratton, Tecumseh or Kohler engines. On Clinton engines, model number is stamped on air baffle at rear of cylinder. Refer to appropriate Briggs and Stratton, Tecumsech, Kohler or Clinton engine sections for overhaul procedures.

GEAR CASE

All Models

WHEEL SHAFT OIL SEAL INSTALLATION. Support gear case

Fig. TB1 — Exploded view of transmission assembly used on Horse models.

1. Plug & "O" ring assy.	10. Gasket	20. Shims	29. Lever
2. Roll pin	11. Cover	22. Bushing	30. "O" rings
3. "O" ring	12. Neutral spring	23. Wheel shaft	31. Key, clutch-to-wheel shaft
4. Shims	13. Neutral plunger	24. High speed gear	32. Plug
5. Bearings	14. Nut	25. Dog clutch, high speed	33. Shifter shaft eccentric
6. Washers	15. Bolt	26. Dog clutch, low speed	34. Shifter shaft fork pivot
7. Shaft	16. Clip	27. Low speed gear	35. Shift fork
8. Snap ring	17. Seal	28. Roll pin	
9. Gear (bronze)	18. Shim		
9A. Pinion gear	19. Snap ring		

36. Shift fork shoes	44. Seals
37. Seal	45. Bearing outer races
38. Cap	
39. Gasket	46. Bearing cones & rollers
40. Bearing outer race	47. Gear (bronze)
41. Bearing cone & roller	48. Tine shaft
42. Drive shaft, welded type	49. Gasket
	50. Housing cover
43. Cap	51. Shims
	52. Gasket

Fig. TB2 — Assembled drive shaft first used on tiller serial number 14159 and occasionally used on later models.

1. Bearing outer races	4. Snap ring	7. Shaft
2. Bearing cones & rollers	5. Spacer	8. Woodruff keys
3. Shim	6. Worm gear, front	9. Spacer
		10. Worm gear, rear
		11. Spacer

(43 – Fig. TB1) and remove wheel. Drive a screwdriver or chisel into seal (17) at an angle and pry seal out of casting bore. Polish wheel shaft (23) with emery cloth to remove rust or burrs. Check to be sure there is at least one wheel shaft shim 0.062-inch (1.57 mm) thick or two 0.030-inch (0.76 mm) thick shims inside seal bore. Apply non-hardening gasket sealer to outside surface of seal and coat lip of seal with a light coat of grease. Drive new seal into casting bore until it is almost flush with outside edge of bore. Repeat procedure for opposite side if necessary.

TINE SHAFT OIL SEAL IN-STALLATION. Remove tine hood and tine assemblies. To remove left side oil seal, remove the five housing cover screws and pry cover off housing. With cover removed, tap seal out from inside. If right seal is to be removed, remove housing cover. Use a soft hammer and tap shaft and gear assembly out of housing.

With shaft and gear assembly removed, inspect components for wear or damage and renew if needed. Clean rust and burrs off shaft when installing seal on either side.

Before installing seals, reinstall shaft and gear assembly in housing. Install gasket on housing cover and reinstall cover on housing. Check shaft assembly for a slight amount of end play. End play is adjusted by installing either the available 0.010-inch (0.254 mm) gasket or the 0.030-inch (0.762 mm) gasket or any combination thereof. When proper end play is determined, coat housing cover cap screws with nonhardening sealer and reinstall. To install new seals, coat outside diameter of seal with nonhardening gasket sealer and coat in-

side lip of seal with a light coat of grease. Tap seals into casting bores until seal is almost flush with outside edge of bore.

FRONT TRANSMISSION OIL SEAL. Remove engine assembly along with transmission drive pulley and

pulley shim. Remove the three cap screws and bearing cap. With cap removed, push out oil seal from inside. Using an emery cloth, clean any rust or burrs off shaft. Using a new gasket, reinstall bearing cap without seal. Coat cap screw threads with nonhardening gasket sealer before installation. Coat outside diameter of seal with nonhardening gasket sealer and coat sealing lip of seal with a light coat of grease. Tap seal into cap and align front edge of seal with front edge of bearing cap.

INSPECTION. Refer to Figs. TB1 through TB7 for parts breakdown and identification. Inspect and renew all components that are worn or damaged. Install new gaskets, snap rings, "O" rings and seals. Lubricate gears with a light film of oil during reassembly. Keep all dirt and foreign matter out of chain case during reassembly. Refer to **LUBRICATION** section for lubricant requirements after reassembly.

Fig. TB3—Assembled drive shaft used on models with serial numbers 14158 and below and on models with serial numbers 14518 through 14717.

1. Bearing outer races	5. Spacer
2. Bearing cones & rollers	6. Worm gear, front
3. Shim	7. Thrust bushing
4. Snap ring	8. Shaft

9. Woodruff keys	12. Spacer
10. Washer, locking tab	13. Worm gear, rear
11. Adjustment nut	14. Spacer

REVERSE DISC

Horse Models

Loosen disc mounting bolt as far as possible, then pry disc away from engine pulley. Slide disc backward and angle enough to remove bolt past reverse plunger, then remove disc. Reinstall by reversing removal procedure.

DRIVE BELTS

Horse Models

FORWARD DRIVE BELT. To replace drive belt, first place shift lever in neutral position, then work belt away from lower and upper pulleys. Place shift lever in forward position and work belt out between reverse disc and lower pulley assembly. Reinstall by reversing removal procedure. Replacement belt 9245 is available only from Troy-Bilt.

Pony and Junior Models

FORWARD AND REVERSE BELT. Remove belt cover and refer to Fig. TB8 for component identification. Place forward/reverse lever in neutral position and remove reverse belt (1) from engine pulley (3) and idler pulley. Remove forward belt (7) from forward engine pulley (4 and 5). Remove reverse belt from transmission pulley and remove from tiller. Remove forward belt from transmisson pulley and remove from tiller. Reinstall belts by reversing removal procedure. Replacement belts are available only from Troy-Bilt. Stock numbers for Pony models are: forward

Fig. TB6—Exploded view of transmission assembly used on Pony models.

1. Pulley	11. Bearing roller	20. Spring
2. Washer	12. Gear	21. Seal
3. Seal	13. Drive shaft	22. Lever
4. Snap ring	14. Bearing race	23. Oil seals
5. Thrust washer	15. Shim	24. Snap rings
6. Bushing	16. Cover	24A. Shims
7. Thrust washer	17. Gasket	25. Bushings
8. Snap ring	18. Housing	26. Key
9. Input pinion	19. Shift shaft	27. Wheel shaft
10. Bearing race		

28. Gear	
29. Shim	
29A. Bearings	
30. Clutch hub	
30A. Key	
31. Tine shaft	
32. Worm gear	
33. Gasket	
34. Cover	
35. Seal	

Fig. TB8 — View of belt assembly used on Pony and Junior models.

1. Reverse belt
2. Forward engine shaft
3. Reverse engine shaft
4. Low speed sheaves
5. High speed sheaves
6. Input shaft
7. Forward belt

Fig. TB7 — Exploded view of transmission assembly used on Junior models.

1. Cover	10. Cap, rear bearing	18. Spacer	25. Key
2. Gasket	11. Drive shaft	19. Key	26. Tine shaft
3. Cover	12. Retainers	20. Wheel shaft	26A. Worm gear
4. Gasket	13. Seals	20A. Worm gear	27. Spacers
5. Seal	14. Snap rings	21. Shims	28. Bushings
6. Cap, front bearing	15. Shims	22. Bearing	29. Shims
7. Gasket	16. Bushings	23. Washer	30. Snap rings
8. Housing assy.	17. Spacer	24. Bearing race	31. Seals
9. Gasket			

belt—20565, reverse belt—9493, set of both forward and reverse belts—4922. Stock numbers for Junior models are: forward belt—50161, reverse belt—50134, set of both forward and reverse belts—50180.

OVERHAUL

Horse Models

Transmission assembly consists of a main gearbox at the front and a tine drive gearbox at the rear which are connected by a driveshaft tube. Newer

models have a clutch in between the two gearboxes which may be disconnected.

REMOVE AND REINSTALL. Remove throttle cable, belt(s), and reverse disc. If equipped with an electric starter, disconnect key switch wiring, charging system wire and battery cables, then remove battery. Disconnect positive cable at starter and remove the two battery bracket screws on top of the transmission cover, then remove battery bracket and starter solenoid as an assembly. Remove control yoke bolts from engine mount and engine mount

bar lock bolts. Support engine with blocks of wood and tap engine mount bars down and out of housing. Engine may now be lifted away from transmission.

Remove "T" bar handlebar mounting bolt and remove handlebars as an assembly. Remove control yoke pivot point bolts from each side of transmission and remove yoke as an assembly. Disconnect depth regulator bar from transmission and remove the two bolts from rear of tine transmission end cap (43—Fig. TB1). Remove the two rear transmission bolts which hold the tine hood front bracket in place. Disconnect wheel shift linkage from transmission shift lever. Lift tine hood assembly away from transmission. Remove tine retaining stud in each side and using a soft hammer, tap tine assemblies off shaft. To remove wheels, tap roll pins out of wheel shafts, then remove wheels.

Reassemble tiller by reversing disassembly procedure.

OVERHAUL. Remove outer snap ring and pull transmission pulley off drive shaft, then remove inner snap ring from drive shaft. Drain gear oil from transmission. Remove the two remaining bolts and remove the top cover (11—Fig. TB1). Remove front bearing cap (38) and rear bearing cap (43). When removing rear bearing cap, note the number and thickness of the bearing adjusting shims (51). Place shift lever (29) in neutral position. Using a soft hammer, tap drive shaft (42) and rear bearing race (40) out towards the rear.

Remove roll pins (2). Using pliers, remove pinion shaft plugs (1). Remove shims (4) and keep in order for left and right sides. Using a hammer and brass drift, carefully tap pinion shaft (7) out through left side plug hole, then remove bronze gear (9) and pinion gear (9A) as an assembly. Left pinion bearing (5) will be removed as the pinion shaft is removed. The right side bearing may be tapped out with a hammer handle.

Remove left side wheel shaft oil seal (17), shims (18 and 20) and snap ring (19). Align keyway on high speed gear (24) with key on wheel shaft (23). Note that high speed gear and high speed gear dog clutch (25) may be marked on outside edge to show keyway position.

With keyways aligned, use a soft hammer and tap wheel shaft (23) out through right side of transmssion case (53). As shaft moves out, shims (18 and 20), seal (17), snap ring (19) and bushing (22) will also be removed from right side. As wheel shaft is removed, lift low speed gear (27), low speed dog clutch (26), high speed dog clutch (25) and high speed gear (24) out of transmission case.

If necessary, bushing (22) on left side of housing may be tapped out with a pipe or brass drift of the proper diameter. Remove shift fork shoes (36) from shift fork (35). Remove plug (32) at rear of case under shift lever (29). Thread a rear bearing cap retaining screw into threaded hole in shift fork shaft (34) and pull shaft out of case, then lift shift fork (35) out of case. Drive roll pin (28) out of shift lever and remove lever from eccentric shaft (33), then using a soft hammer, tap eccentric shaft into case and remove.

Remove the five screws from tine shaft housing cover (50) and remove cover and gasket (49). Using a soft hammer, tape tine shaft (48), bronze gear

(47) and bearings (46) out of housing as an assembly.

Inspect gears and dog clutches for broken teeth or other obvious damage. Inspect shafts for scoring or damage around keyways. Inspect bearings for roughness. Replace components as necessary.

Reassemble by reversing disassembly procedure. During reassembly, replace all seals, gaskets and "O" rings. Reinstall wheel shaft bushings (22–Fig. TB1) flush with outside edge of bores and with oil pick-up grooves facing towards inside of housing. Specified wheel shaft (23) side play is 0.005-0.015 inch (0.13-0.38 mm). During initial assembly, manufacturer recommends using any combination of shims (20) equaling 0.030-inch (0.76 mm) on the right side. Install shims for end play adjustment on the left side. Install wheel shaft snap rings (19) with flat side facing away from housing. When installing shims (18) between snap ring and outer wheel shaft seal (17), manufacturer recommends using one 0.62 inch (1.57 mm) shim or two 0.030-inch (0.76 mm) shims on each side. Refer to WHEEL SHAFT OIL SEAL INSTALLATION paragraph for oil seal installation procedure.

Bronze gear (9) must be centered in housing when pinion shaft (7) and pinion gear (9A) are installed. Centering and side play of pinion shaft is adjusted with shims (4). Shims are available in thicknesses of 0.010 inch (1.57 mm).

Specified drive shaft end play is 0.002-0.010 inch (0.05-2.54 mm). Drive shaft end play is adjusted with shims (51) which are available in thicknesses of 0.005 (0.13 mm), 0.010 inch (0.25 mm) and 0.030 inch (0.76 mm). Refer to FRONT TRANSMISSION OIL SEAL paragraph for seal installation procedure.

Tine shaft (48) should be installed so that there is a very slight amount of side

play. Adjustment is controlled by thickness of gasket (49). Gaskets are available in thicknesses of 0.010 inch (0.25 mm) and 0.030-inch (0.76 mm). Adjust by trial and error using the thinnest gasket first. Maximum thickness of gasket(s) should be a combination of the thin and thick gaskets totaling 0.040-inch (1.02 mm). If proper tine shaft side play is not attainable by using gaskets, shims are available for installation between bearing cone (46) and bronze gear (47). These shims are available in thicknesses of 0.005-inch (0.13 mm), 0.010-inch (0.25 mm) and 0.015 inch (0.38 mm). Refer to TINE SHAFT OIL SEAL INSTALLATION paragraph for seal installation procedure.

Transmission oil capacity is approximately 6.375 pounds (2.89 Kg).

ASSEMBLED ADJUSTABLE DRIVE SHAFT. Some models are equipped with an assembled drive shaft as shown in Fig. TB3. To remove the assembled drive shaft, remove front and rear bearing caps. Bend up tabs on lockwasher (10). Using a soft hammer, tap shaft rearward until rear bearing outer race falls out. Tap rear bearing cone (2), spacer (14) and worm gear (13) off end of shaft. With shaft moved rearward, use a brass drift and hammer to tap front bearing outer race out of transmission housing. Shaft may now be removed through front of house. Unthread spacer (12) from nut (11) and slide spacer off shaft (8). Remove front bearing cone (2), shim (3) and snap ring (4), then slide spacer (5) and worm gear (6) off shaft.

Reassemble by reversing disassembly procedure. Specified drive shaft end play is 0.002-0.010 inch (0.05-0.25 mm). Adjust end play by turning adjusting nut (11). After adjustment bend over two or three tabs on lockwasher (10).

WARDS

MONTGOMERY WARD
Montgomery Ward Plaza
Chicago, Illinois 60671

The following Wards tillers were manufactured for Montgomery Ward by the Gilson Brothers Company, Plymouth, Wisconsin and by MTD Products, Cleveland, Ohio. Service procedures for these models will not differ greatly from those given for similar Gilson and MTD models. However, parts are not necessarily interchangeable and should be obtained from Montgomery Ward.

Wards Model	Gilson Section	MTD Section
39000	51095	.....
39011	51143	.....
39023	.....	320
39025	.....	385
39031	51142	.....
1580	51097	.....
39032	51134	.....
39008	51135	.....
39095	.....	410A
39098	.....	412A
39103	.....	412A

WARDS

Model	Engine Make	Engine Series	Engine Horsepower	No. of Forward Speeds	Power Reverse?	Tilling Width (In.)	Drive Type
39083	B&S	110000	4	1	Yes	14	Chain
39084	B&S	130000	5	1	Yes	18	Chain
39096	B&S	130000	5	1	No	18	Chain
39097	B&S	130000	5	1	No	18	Chain

LUBRICATION

ENGINE

All Models

Refer to Briggs and Stratton engine section for lubrication specifications. Recommended oil grade is SAE 30 or equivalent. Recommended fuel is either regular or low-lead gasoline having an octane rating of 90 or higher.

DRIVE CONTROLS AND WHEELS

All Models

Clean and lubricate friction points with SAE 30 oil after each eight to fifteen

Fig. MW1 – View of control components for Models 39083 and 39084.
1. Throttle lever
2. Tine clutch lever
3. Drive clutch lever

Fig. MW2 – View of control components for Model 39097.
1. Drive clutch lever
2. Throttle lever
3. Tine clutch lever

Fig. MW3 — View of drive clutch cable adjusting nuts on Models 39083 and 39084.

1. Adjusting nuts
2. Lockwashers
3. Forward cable
4. Reverse cable

Fig. MW4 — View of drive clutch cable adjusting nuts on Models 39096 and 39097.

1. Nuts   2. Slot

Fig. MW3A — View of drive cables on Models 39083 and 39084.

1. Reverse cable
2. Forward cable
3. Forward idler

Fig. MW5 — Typical view of tine clutch cable and adjusting nuts.

1. Upper nut
2. Lockwasher
3. Lower nut

hours of operation. Do not get oil on belts.

Models 39096 and 39097

Lubricate wheel pawl and ratchet drive at least twice a season with a silicone type lubricant.

CHAIN CASES

Chain cases are factory sealed and must be removed and disassembled in order to add or change lubricant. Refer to OVERHAUL section.

MAINTENANCE

Inspect all fasteners for looseness and retighten as needed. Check control levers, linkage and cables for freedom of movement or excessive play. Inspect drive belt(s) for excessive stretching, wear, cracks or any other damage. Install new belt(s) if needed. Inspect all pulleys and renew if damaged or excessively worn.

ADJUSTMENT

DRIVE CLUTCH

Models 39083 and 39084

PRIMARY ADJUSTMENT. Move lever (3 – Fig. MW1) to forward position, then adjust hex nuts (1 – Fig. MW3) so cables are tight.

To check adjustment, place tiller against a solid object, move control lever to neutral position and start engine. Tiller should not move in either direction. If tiller moves forward, adjust forward cable (3 – Fig. MW3) by loosening hex nut on top and tightening hex nut on bottom. If tiller moves in reverse, adjust reverse cable (4) by loosening hex nut on bottom and tightening hex nut on top. If tiller has no movement in neutral position, check clutch operation in the forward and reverse positions. If there is no movement in the forward position, adjust forward cable by loosening bottom hex nut and tightening upper hex nut. If there is no movement in the reverse position, adjust reverse cable by loosening upper hex nut and tightening lower hex nut.

SECONDARY ADJUSTMENT. If there is no adjustment left at upper ends of cables, the lower ends may be adjusted as follows: If tiller will not move

Fig. MW6 — View of belt and pulley system on Models 39083 and 39084.

1. Tine belt
2. Idler pulley
3. Forward drive belt
4. Idler pulley
5. Reverse drive belt
6. Two-step engine pulley
7. Wire belt keeper
8. Forward engine pulley
9. Idler pulley
10. Wheel chain case pulley
11. Tine chain case pulley

Fig. MW7 — View of belt and pulley system on Models 39096 and 39097.

1. Tine chain case pulley
2. Tine belt
3. Idler pulley
4. Wheel drive belt
5. Engine pulley, rear
6. Engine pulley, front
7. Idler pulley
8. Wheel chain case pulley

forward, refer to Fig. MW3A and loosen hex nut in back of forward cable bracket and tighten hex nut at front. If tiller will not move in reverse, loosen hex nut in front of reverse cable bracket and tighten nut at rear.

When making secondary adjustments on either forward or reverse cable, recheck neutral adjustment at upper end of cable.

Models 39096 and 39097

Refer to Fig. MW4 and with clutch lever in "up" position, adjust bottom hex nut at cable bracket so there is only a slight amount of slack in control cable. Tighten upper hex nut. With lever held down, control cable should be straight.

TINE CLUTCH

All Models

Refer to Fig. MW5. With tine clutch control lever in released position, adjust bottom hex nut (3) at cable bracket so that there is a slight amount of slack in control cable, then tighten upper hex nut (1). With control lever held down, control cable should be straight.

OVERHAUL

ENGINE

All Models

Engine model number is stamped on blower housing. Refer to appropriate Briggs and Stratton engine section for overhaul procedure.

CHAIN CASE

All Models

OIL SEAL INSTALLATION. Chain cases are factory sealed and no provision is made for checking or adding lubricant. Chain case must be separated as described in the following INSPEC-

TION paragraph to accurately add specific amounts of lubricant. Seals may be renewed as follows:

Remove tines or wheels from shaft. Use a seal puller or other appropriate tool to remove seal(s) from case hub. Clean tine/wheel shaft with emery cloth. Drive new seal(s) in until outside face is flush with case hub. Install inner seal

Fig. MW8 — Exploded view of wheel chain drive assembly used on Models 39083, 39084, 39096 and 39097.

1. Chain case
2. Gasket
3. Input shaft & sprocket
4. Sprocket
5. Bearings
6. Sleeves
7. Sprocket
8. Wheel shaft & sprocket assy.
9. Washer
10. Flange bearing
11. Seals
12. Dust caps
13. Bearing
14. Bearing housing
15. Chain

DRIVE BELTS
Models 39083 and 39084

Refer to Fig. MW6 for belt routing and parts identification. Remove drive belt cover. Lift up idler pulley (2) and slip tine (belt(s) off chain case pulley (11) and two-step engine pulley (6). Lift up small idler pulley (4) and slip reverse drive belt (5) off outside sheave of wheel chain case pulley (10). Loosen and rotate wire keeper (7) away from forward engine pulley (8). Lift forward drive belt (3) off forward engine pulley and lift away from inside groove of wheel chain case pulley. Reverse procedure to install new belts. Tine drive belt size is ½-inch x 54 inches long. Forward drive belt size is ½-inch x 43 inches long. Reverse drive belt size is ½-inch x 39 inches long. Manufacturer recommends that only belts constructed with Kevlar Tensile be used.

Models 39096 and 39097

Refer to Fig. MW7 for belt routing and parts identification. Remove drive belt cover. Lift tine drive belt (2) out from under idler pulley (3). Loosen hex bolt on rear engine pulley (5) and slide pulley out far enough to remove belt, then slide belt off tine case pulley (1). To remove wheel drive belt (4), remove hex bolt, lockwasher and flat washer from rear engine pulley (5). Slide rear pulley off shaft. Loosen the two set screws on front engine pulley (6). Remove locknut on idler pulley (7). Slide idler and front engine pulleys out on their respective shafts and remove. Remove belt from wheel chain case pulley (8). Reverse procedure to install new belts. Tine drive belt size is ½-inch x 54 inches along. Wheel drive belt size is ½-inch x 43 inches long. Manufacturer recommends that only belts constructed with Kevlar Tensile be used.

Fig. MW9—Exploded view of the chain drive assembly used on Models 39083, 39084, 39096 and 39097.

1. Chain case
2. Gasket
3. Input shaft & sprocket
4. Spacer
5. Snap ring
6. Bearing
7. Chain
8. Sprocket
9. Bearing
10. Sleeve
11. Tine shaft & sprocket assy.
12. Washer
13. Flange bearing
14. Seal
15. Dust cap
16. Bearing housing
17. Bearing

with lip facing towards inside and outer seal with lip facing towards outside.

INSPECTION. For wheel chain case, refer to Fig. MW8 for parts breakdown and identification. For tine chain case, refer to Fig. MW9 for parts breakdown and identification.

Inspect and renew all components that are worn or damaged. Install new gasket(s) and seals. Lubricate chains, sprockets and bearings with a light film

of grease during reassembly. Keep all dirt and foreign matter out of chain case during reassembly.

Recommended lubricant for all models is Plastilube #0 grease or suitable equivalent. Wheel chain case capacity for all models is 10 ounces. Tine chain case capacity for all models is 12 ounces. To fill chain case with lubricant, lay left half of case on its side, add lubricant and assemble right half to left. Complete reassembly and reinstall in tiller frame.

WHITE

WHITE MOTOR CORPORATION
1830 White Boulevard
Libertyville, IL 60048

Model	Engine Make	Engine Series	Engine Horsepower	No. of Forward Speeds	Power Reverse?	Tilling Width (In.)	Drive Type
Roto Boss 200	B&S	60000	2	1	No	6½-18	Chain
Roto Boss 300	B&S	80000	3	1	No	10-18	Chain
Roto Boss 350	B&S	90000	3.5	1	Yes	12-26	Gear
Roto Boss 500	B&S	130000	5	1	Yes	14-26	Chain
Roto Boss 800	B&S	190000	8	4	Yes	12-26	Chain
Roto Boss 802	B&S	190000	8	5	Yes	20	Chain

LUBRICATION

ENGINE

All Models

Refer to appropriate Briggs and Stratton engine section for engine lubrication specifications.

Recommended oil grade is SAE 30 or equivalent. Recommended fuel is either regular or low-lead gasoline having an octane rating of 90 or higher. The use of non-leaded gasolines reduces cylinder head deposits, but could shorten engine valve life if carburetor is adjusted too lean.

CHAIN DRIVE

All Models

Chain case is factory sealed and must be removed and disassembled in order to add or change lubricant in case. Refer to **OVERHAUL** section.

GEAR CASE

Model 350

Gear case oil should be checked at least every 10 hours of operation. Recommended lubricant is Pennant oil EP#35000 or suitable equivalent.

To check gear case oil place tiller on a level surface. Clean dirt from around front of gear case and remove oil level plug (1 – Fig. W1). Oil level should be at bottom of plug hole. If oil level is low add oil through plug hole until it begins to run out, then replace and tighten plug.

MAINTENANCE

Inspect all fasteners for looseness and retighten as needed. Check control levers, linkage and cables for freedom of movement and excessive play. Inspect drive belt(s) for excessive stretching, wear, cracks, or any other damage. Install new belt(s) if needed. Inspect all belt pulleys and renew if damaged or excessively worn. Transport wheels on Models 200, 300, 350, 500 and 800 should be lubricated occasionally with SAE 30 oil.

ADJUSTMENT

CLUTCH CONTROL AND DRIVE BELT

Models 200 and 300

Loosen and turn hex nuts (3 – Fig. W2) to adjust clutch. To check for correct clutch adjustment place clutch lever (1) in neutral position. Unhook spark plug lead and pull on starter rope handle. If tines do not turn, then adjustment is correct. If tines do turn, then clutch cable should be adjusted.

Fig. W1 – View of oil plugs and oil level for Model 350 gear case.
1. Oil level plug
2. Oil level
3. Breather plug

Fig. W2 – View of clutch control components for Models 200 and 300.
1. Clutch lever
2. Clutch cable
3. Cable adjusting nuts

Fig. W3 – View of clutch control components for Models 350, 500, 800 and 802.
1. Clutch lever
2. Threaded control rod
3. Adjustment ferrule
4. Bracket

Models 350, 500, 800 and 802

Remove hair pin clip from ferrule (3 – Fig. W3), then remove ferrule from bracket (4). Turn ferrule up or down control rod (2) to adjust clutch. Reinstall ferrule in bracket and install hair pin clip. To check for correct clutch adjustment place clutch lever (1) in neutral position. Unhook spark plug lead and pull on starter rope handle. If tines do not turn, then adjustment is correct. If tines do turn, then clutch rod will need to be adjusted.

GEAR CASE

Model 350

Gear case bearing adjustment should be accomplished approximately every five hours of operation. Adjust by removing cotter pin (17 – Fig. W8), then turning adjustment cap (16) in until snug. Do not over-tighten. Reinstall cotter pin, then check adjustment by starting tiller and engaging tines. If engine stalls, then bearing adjustment is too tight and adjustment cap should be loosened slightly.

OVERHAUL

ENGINE

All Models

Engine model no. is stamped on blower housing. Refer to appropriate Briggs and Stratton engine section for overhaul procedures.

CHAIN CASE

All Models

OIL SEAL INSTALLATION. Remove tines from tine shaft. Using a seal puller pull seal(s) out of case hub. If seal puller is not available use an awl and screwdriver to pry seals out. Clean tine shaft with emery cloth. Drive new seal(s) in until outside face is flush with case hub. On models with two seals on each side install inner seal with lip facing toward inside and outer seal with lip facing toward outside. On Model 802 remove wheels to install axle shaft seals.

INSPECTION. On Models 200 and 300 refer to Fig. W4 for parts breakdown and identification. For Model 500 refer to Fig. W5, for Model 800 refer to Fig. W6 and for Model 802 refer to Fig. W7.

Inspect and renew all components that are worn or damaged. Install new gasket and seals. Lubricate chains, sprockets and bearings with a light film

Fig. W4 – Exploded view of chain case for Models 200 and 300.

1. Chain case, L.H.
2. Oil seals
3. Dust covers
4. Bolt, 2½ inches long
5. Input pulley
6. Roll pin
7. Gasket
8. Flange bearings
9. Washers
10. Spacer
11. Tine shaft assy.
12. Chain, 0.375 inch pitch x 50 links
13. Inner race
14. Hub and sprocket assy.
15. Chain, 0.50 inch pitch x 38 links
16. Input shaft assy.
17. Chain case, R.H.
18. Expansion ring
19. Hex nut
20. Lockwasher
21. Flat washer

Fig. W5 – Exploded view of chain case for Model 500.

1. Chain case, L.H.
2. Gasket
3. Bearings
4. Bearing housing
5. Flat washer
6. Spacer
7. Input pulley
8. Oil seal
9. Flat washer
10. Spacer
11. Tine shaft assy.
12. Chain, ⅝-inch pitch x 28 links
13. Sprocket shaft
14. Sprocket
15. Flange bearing
16. Chain, ½-inch pitch x 48 links
17. Hex flanged bearing
18. Spacer
19. Sprocket shaft
20. Sprocket sleeve assy.
21. Roll pin
22. Chain, ½-inch pitch x 34 links
23. Sprocket
24. Spacer
25. Input shaft
26. Square key
27. Flat washer
28. Chain case, R.H.
29. Gasket
30. Bearing housing assy.

Fig. W6 – Exploded view of chain case for Model 800.

1. Chain case, L.H.
2. Ball bearing, L.H and R.H.
3. Bearing housing, L.H. and R.H.
4. Oil seal, L.H. and R.H.
5. Bearing housing with bearing, L.H. and R.H.
6. Gasket
7. Input shaft
8. Spacer
9. Roll pin
10. Sprocket
11. Chain, #35-2 x 36-¾ inches long
12. Flange bearings
13. Sprocket shaft
14. Sprocket
15. Chain case, R.H.
16. Chain, #40-2 x 34 inches long
17. Roll pins
18. Tine shaft
19. Sprocket

of grease during reassembly. Keep all dirt and foreign matter out of chain case during reassembly.

Recommended lubricant for Models 200 and 300 is 16 ounces of Plastilube #0 grease or suitable equivalent. Recommended lubricant for Model 500 is 14 ounces of Plastilube #0 grease or suitable equivalent. Recommended lubricant for Model 800 is Lubriplate No. 310 or suitable equivalent. Adequately lubricate chains and gears during reassembly. Recommended lubricant for Model 802 is 28 ounces of Plastilube #1 grease or suitable equivalent. To fill chain case with grease, lay right half of case on its side, add grease and assemble left half to right. Complete reassembly and reinstall in tiller frame.

GEAR CASE

Model 350

OIL SEAL INSTALLATION. Remove tines from tine shaft. Use a seal puller to remove seal(s) from case hub. Clean tine shaft with emery cloth. Drive new seal(s) in until outside face is flush with case hub.

REMOVE AND DISASSEMBLE. Refer to Fig. W8 for parts breakdown and identification. Inspect and renew all components that are worn or damaged. Install new gaskets and seals. Lubricate gears and bearings with a light film of oil during reassembly. Keep all dirt and foreign matter out of gear case during reassembly. Refer to **LUBRICATION** section for lubricating requirements after reassembly and installation. Refer to **GEAR CASE ADJUSTMENT** section for bearing preload adjusting procedure.

DRIVE BELTS

Models 200 and 300

Refer to Fig. W9 for belt routing and parts identification. Place clutch lever in forward position, then unhook extension spring (3) from drive belt cover. Remove drive belt cover. Remove belt from pulleys and install new belt. Drive belt size is ⅜-inch x 29 inches long. Reinstall drive belt cover, then rehook extension spring in cover. Refer to **CLUTCH CONTROL AND DRIVE BELT ADJUSTMENT** section for adjusting procedure.

Model 350

Refer to Fig. W10 for belt(s) routing and parts identification. Place clutch lever in neutral position. Remove four cap screws securing engine bed to mounting plate assembly, then remove

Fig. W7—Exploded view of chain case for Model 802. Shift parts (5 through 12) are used on both sides.

1. Chain case, L.H.	13. Oil seals	21. Hub sleeve
2. Bearing housing	14. Flange bearings	22. Flange bearings
3. Gasket	15. Chain, ⅝-inch pitch	23. Sprocket assy.
4. Oil seals	x 52 links	24. Chain, ½-inch pitch x
5. Shift yoke	16. Sprocket bearing	58 links
6. Gasket	sleeve assy.	25. Flange bearings
7. Cap plug	17. Stepped spacer	26. Flat washers
8. Detent ball	18. Clutch shaft assy.	27. Axle shaft assy.
9. Spring	19. Chain, ½-inch pitch	28. Chain, ½-inch pitch x
10. Shift housing	x 58 links	42 links
11. Clutch dog	20. Sprocket bearing	29. Spacer
12. Clutch dog driver	sleeve assy.	30. Flange bearings

31. Flat washers
32. Tine shaft assy.
33. Spacer
34. Ball bearings
35. Spacer
36. Sprocket
37. Spacer
38. Input shaft
39. Square keys
40. Chain case, R.H.

Fig. W8—Exploded view of gear case for Model 350.

1. Gear case
2. Sleeve bearing
3. Oil seal
4. Snap ring
5. Breaker plug and star washer
6. Oil fill plug
7. Oil level plug
8. Bearing cups
9. Bearing cones
10. Spacers
11. Worm shaft
12. Worm gear
13. Drive key
14. Snap ring
15. "O" ring
16. Adjustment plug
17. Cotter pin
18. Flange bearing
19. Washers
20. Drive keys
21. Tine shaft
22. Snap ring
23. Worm gear
24. "O" ring
25. Flange cover with bearing
26. Oil seals

Fig. W9— View of drive belt routing and components for Model 200 and 300.

1. Engine pulley
2. Idler pulley
3. Extension spring
4. Chain case pulley
5. Clutch cable
6. Drive belt

engine bed with engine assembly. Remove front belt guard. Remove forward drive belt from pulleys. Drive belt size is ½-inch x 30 inches long. Place clutch lever in forward position, then remove reverse belt from pulleys. Drive belt size is ½-inch x 25 inches long. Install new belts, then reassemble in reverse order of disassembly. Refer to **CLUTCH CONTROL AND DRIVE BELT ADJUSTMENT** section for adjusting procedure.

Model 500

Refer to Fig. W11 for belt(s) routing and parts identification. Remove drive belt cover. Loosen belt wire finger (2) retaining bolt and nut. Place clutch lever in reverse position, then remove forward drive belt from pulleys. Drive belt size is ½-inch x 37 inches long. Place clutch lever in neutral position, then remove reverse drive belt from chain case pulley. Place clutch lever in reverse position. Remove reverse idler pulley (5) retaining nut, then slip pulley and belt off of idler bracket together. Drive belt size is ½-inch x 41 inches long. Install new belts, then reassemble in reverse order of disassembly. Refer to **CLUTCH CONTROL AND DRIVE BELT ADJUSTMENT** section for adjusting procedure.

Model 800

Refer to Fig. W12 for belt(s) routing and parts identification. Remove drive belt cover. Place tine depth bar across top of transport wheel hanger, then place tip of bar under variable speed bracket assembly (8). Stand on back of bar, using wheel hanger as a fulcrum apply upward pressure on bracket. Slack should be present in belts if enough pressure is applied. Remove rear drive belt (6) first, then remove forward drive

Fig. W10— View of drive belt(s) routing and components for Model 350.

1. Engine pulley
2. Reverse pulley
3. Extension spring
4. Forward idler assy.
5. Reverse idler assy.
6. Gear case pulley
7. Spring
8. Belt clip
9. Belt pusher
10. Forward belt
11. Reverse belt

Fig. W11— View of drive belt(s) routing and components for Model 500.

1. Engine pulley
2. Belt wire finger
3. Clutch plate
4. Control rod
5. Reverse idler assy.
6. Spring
7. Forward idler assy.
8. Clutch control rod assy.
9. Reverse belt
10. Forward belt
11. Chain case pulley

Fig. W12— View of drive belt(s) routing and components for Model 800.

1. Engine pulley
2. Friction wheel assy.
3. Drive belt
4. Variable speed pulley assy.
5. Friction disc
6. Drive belt
7. Chain case pulley
8. Variable speed bracket assy.

belt (3). Rear drive belt size is ⅝-inch x 35 inches long. Forward drive belt size is ⅝-inch x 28 inches long. Install new belts, then reassemble in reverse order of disassembly. Refer to **CLUTCH CONTROL AND DRIVE BELT ADJUSTMENT** section for adjusting procedure.

Model 802

Refer to Fig. W13 for belt routing and parts identification. Remove drive belt cover. Place clutch lever in reverse position, then remove forward belt (13) from engine pulley towards engine. Slip belt off variable speed pulley (4) and remove belt. Drive belt size is ⅝-inch x 27 inches long. Place clutch lever in second (2) speed position, then remove rear drive belt (14) from chain case pulley (11) and variable speed pulley. Drive belt size is ⅝-inch x 52 inches long. Install new belts, then reassemble in reverse order of disassembly. Refer to **CLUTCH CONTROL AND DRIVE BELT ADJUSTMENT** section for adjusting procedure.

Fig. W13 — View of drive belt routing and components for Model 802.
1. Drive belt(s) cover support assy.
2. Square key
3. Engine pulley
4. Variable speed assy.
5. Friction wheel assy.
6. Spacer
7. Friction disc
8. Belt keeper
9. Idler pulley
10. Spacer
11. Chain case input pulley
12. Drive belt(s) cover
13. Drive belt
14. Drive belt

DRIVE BELTS

Make & Model	Mfg. Part No.	Dayco No.	Gates No.	Size*	Make & Model	Mfg. Part No.	Dayco No.	Gates No.	Size*
ARIENS					**JOHN DEERE**				
RT214	72109	L432	6832	1/2X32	216	M81805			17/32X49
RT320	72109	L432	6832	1/2X32	324				
RT324	72109	L432	6832	1/2X32	Fwd.	M45680	L433	6833	1/2X33
RT424					Rev.	M46030	L433	6833	1/2X33
Fwd.	72056	L432	6832	1/2X32	524				
Rev.	72085	L332	6832	3/8X32	Fwd.	M45680	L433	6833	1/2X33
RT424X					Rev.	M45681	L432	6832	1/2X32
Fwd.	72056	L432	6832	1/2X32	624				
Rev.	72085	L332	6732	3/8X32	Fwd.	M45680	L433	6833	1/2X33
RT524					Rev.	M45681	L432	6832	1/2X32
Fwd.	72056	L432	6832	1/2X32					
Rev.	72085	L332	6732	3/8X32	**FORD**				
RT524C	72109	L432	6832	1/2X32	1005				
RT524S					Fwd.	2435	L437	6837	1/2X37
Fwd.	72056	L432	6832	1/2X32	Rev.	6184	L339	6739	3/8X39
Rev.	72043	L332	6732	3/8X32	1013	9304	L429	6829	1/2X29
RT5020					1023				
Fwd.	72056	L432	6832	1/2X32	Fwd.	1110	L435	6835	1/2X35
Rev.	72099	L331	6731	3/8X31	Rev.	6163	L337	6737	3/8X37
RT7020					1105 & 1200	36019	L320	6720	3/8X20
Fwd.	72056	L432	6832	1/2X32	1114 & 1134				
Rev.	72099	L331	6731	3/8X31	Trac	200555	L346	6746	3/8X46
RT8020					Tine	200554	L338	6738	3/8X38
Fwd.	72056	L432	6832	1/2X32					
Rev.	72085	L332	6732	3/8X32	**GILSON**				
RT8028					51080	28673			
Fwd.	72056	L432	6832	1/2X32	51081				
Rev.	72085	L332	6732	3/8X32	Fwd.	1110			
					Rev.	6163			
					51082				
					Fwd.	1110			
					Rev.	6163			
					51083				
					Upper	26344			
ATLAS					Lower	26345			
2100	107-38	L436	6836	1/2X36	51084	28673			
3010	107-37	L431	6831	1/2X31	51085				
3011	107-37	L431	6831	1/2X31	Fwd.	1110			
3100	107-38	L436	6836	1/2X36	Rev.	6163			
3150	107-38	L436	6836	1/2X36	51088				
5012	107-37	L431	6831	1/2X31	Fwd.	1110			
5013	107-37	L431	6831	1/2X31	Rev.	6163			
5015					51095	33622			
Fwd.	107-37	L431	6831	1/2X31	51097				
Rev.	107-37	L431	6831	1/2X31	Fwd.	1110			
5016					Rev.	6163			
Fwd.	107-37	L431	6831	1/2X31	51104	35900			
Rev.	107-37	L431	6831	1/2X31	51105	36019			
5021					51114				
Fwd.	107-37	L431	6831	1/2X31	Trac	200555			
Rev.	107-37	L431	6831	1/2X31	Tine	200554			
5022					51116	9304			
Fwd.	107-37	L431	6831	1/2X31	51134				
Rev.	107-37	L431	6831	1/2X31	Trac	200555			
5100					Tine	200554			
Fwd.	107-38	L436	6836	1/2X36	51135				
Rev.	107-39	L432	6832	1/2X32	Fwd.	208526			
5300	107-38	L436	6836	1/2X36	Rev.	208525			
					Tine	208527			
					51142	208301			
					51143				
CLINTON					Fwd.	208301			
500-T-14	10228**	L327	6727	3/8X27	Rev.	208626			

Make & Model	Mfg. Part No.	Dayco No.	Gates No.	Size*
HABAN				
861-002				
Fwd.	10467	L4535	68535	1/2X53.5
Rev.	10371	L4435	68435	1/2X43.5
INTERNATIONAL				
526				
Fwd.	59-004	L440	6840	1/2X40
Rev.	59-003	L445	6845	1/2X45
526A				
Fwd.	73-692	L434	6834	1/2X34
Rev.	73-691	L335	6735	3/8X35
MERRY				
G-76	2059	L450	6850	1/2X50
G-77	2059	L450	6850	1/2X50
G-78	2059	L450	6850	1/2X50
G-80	2059	L450	6850	1/2X50
G-82				
Fwd.	2059	L450	6850	1/2X50
Rev.	2313	L345	6745	3/8X45
G-83	2059	L450	6850	1/2X50
G-84	2059	L450	6850	1/2X50
G-87	2059	L450	6850	1/2X50
G-88				
Fwd.	2059	L450	6850	1/2X50
Rev.	2313	L345	6745	3/8X45
G-90	2278	L441	6841	1/2X41
G-91	2278	L441	6841	1/2X41
G-92	2278	L441	6841	1/2X41
MM-1	3292	L434	6834	1/2X34
3200	3292	L434	6834	1/2X34
7100	3292	L434	6834	1/2X34
7200	2059	L450	6850	1/2X50
7300	2059	L450	6850	1/2X50
7400	2059	L450	6850	1/2X50
7401				
Fwd.	2059	L450	6850	1/2X50
Rev.	2313	L345	6745	3/8X45
7402	2059	L450	6850	1/2X50
7403				
Fwd.	2059	L450	6850	1/2X50
Rev.	2313	L345	6745	3/8X45
7500	2059	L450	6850	1/2X50
7501	2059	L450	6850	1/2X50
7502	2059	L450	6850	1/2X50
7600	2278	L441	6841	1/2X41
7601	2278	L441	6841	1/2X41
7602	2278	L441	6841	1/2X41
MTD				
030	754-216	L329	6729	3/8X29
320	754-190	L439	6839	1/2X39
355				
Fwd.	754-154	L437	6837	1/2X37
Rev.	754-189	L444	6844	1/2X44
385				
Fwd.	754-154	L437	6837	1/2X37
Rev.	754-201	L441	6841	1/2X41
386				
Fwd.	754-254	L419	6819	1/2X19
Rear	754-231	L428	6828	1/2X28
405				
Fwd.	754-224	L526	6926	5/8X26
Rear	754-221	L552	6952	5/8X52

Make & Model	Mfg. Part No.	Dayco No.	Gates No.	Size*
MTD Cont.				
408				
Fwd.	754-220	L527	6927	5/8X27
Rear	754-221	L552	6952	5/8X52
409				
Fwd.	754-220	L527	6927	5/8X27
Rear	754-221	L552	6952	5/8X52
410				
Fwd.	754-220	L527	6927	5/8X27
Rear	754-268	L551	6951	5/8X51
412				
Fwd.	754-220	L527	6927	5/8X27
Rear	754-268	L551	6951	5/8X51
418				
Fwd.	754-220	L527	6927	5/8X27
Rear	754-268	L551	6951	5/8X51
MURRAY				
1000	75370	L426	6826	1/2X26
1190	75121	L448	6848	1/2X48
1202				
Fwd.	75121	L448	6848	1/2X48
Rev.	75147	L339	6739	3/8X39
1203				
Fwd.	75121	L448	6848	1/2X48
Rev.	75147	L339	6739	3/8X39
1290	75121	L448	6848	1/2X48
1302				
Fwd.	75121	L448	6848	1/2X48
Rev.	75147	L339	6739	3/8X39
1303				
Fwd.	75121	L448	6848	1/2X48
Rev.	75147	L339	6739	3/8X39
SEARS				
29852	9179R	L339	6739	3/8X39
29936				
Fwd.	4833H	L441	6841	1/2X41
Rev.	2614J			
29937	9180R	L442	6842	1/2X42
29943	9179R	L339	6739	3/8X39
29945				
Fwd.	4833H	L441	6841	1/2X41
Rev.	2614J			
29958	4897H1	L437	6837	1/2X37
29966				
Tine	4454J			
Trac	4376J			
29968				
Tine	4454J			
Trac	4376J			
SNAPPER				
300T	1-1969	L451	6851	1/2X51
500T	1-1969	L451	6851	1/2X51
301T	1-1969	L451	6851	1/2X51
301TR				
Fwd.	1-2248	L4265	68265	1/2X26.5
Rear	1-2249	L437	6837	1/2X37
401T	1-1969	L451	6851	1/2X51
401TR				
Fwd.	1-2248	L4265	68265	1/2X26.5
Rear	1-2249	L437	6837	1/2X37
501T	1-1969	L451	6851	1/2X51

Make & Model	Mfg. Part No.	Dayco No.	Gates No.	Size*	Make & Model	Mfg. Part No.	Dayco No.	Gates No.	Size*
SNAPPER Cont.					**WHITE**				
501TR					200	45527	L329	6729	3/8X29
Fwd.	1-2248	L4265	68265	1/2X26.5	300	45527	L329	6729	3/8X29
Rear	1-2249	L437	6837	1/2X37	350				
501TC	1-1969	L451	6851	1/2X51	Fwd.	05118	L430	6830	1/2X30
501TRC					Rev.	05096	L425	6825	1/2X25
Fwd.	1-2248	L4265	68265	1/2X26.5	500				
Rear	1-2249	L437	6837	1/2X37	Fwd.	41327	L437	6837	1/2X37
					Rev.	41165	L441	6841	1/2X41
TROY-BILT					800				
Horse					Fwd.	05908	L528	6928	5/8X28
Fwd.	9245				Rear	05843	L535	6935	5/8X35
Pony					802				
Fwd.	20565				Fwd.	54089	L527	6927	5/8X27
Rev.	9493				Rear	54100	L552	6952	5/8X52
Junior									
Fwd.	50161								
Rev.	50134								
Set	50180								

* All belt dimensions are in inches.

** Notched belt is preferred.

METRIC CONVERSION

Cubic meters	= .02832	x	Cubic Feet
Cubic meters	x 1.308	=	Cubic Yards
Cubic meters	= .765	x	Cubic Yards
Liters	x 61.023	=	Cubic Inches
Liters	= .01639	x	Cubic Inches
Liters	x .26418	=	U.S. Gallons
Liters	= 3.7854	x	U.S. Gallons
Grams	x 15.4324	=	Grains
Grams	= .0648	x	Grains
Grams	x .03527	=	Ounces, avoirdupois
Grams	= 28.3495	x	Ounces, avoirdupois
Kilograms	x 2.2046	=	Pounds
Kilograms	= .4536	x	Pounds
Kilograms per square centimeter	x 14.2231	=	Pounds per square Inch
Kilograms per square centimeter	= .0703	x	Pounds per square Inch
Kilograms per cubic meter	x .06243	=	Pounds per cubic Foot
Kilograms per cubic meter	= 16.01890	x	Pounds per cubic Foot
Metric tons (1,000 kilograms)	x 1.1023	=	Tons (2,000 Pounds)
Metric tons (1,000 kilograms)	= .9072	x	Tons (2,000 Pounds)
Kilowatts	= 1.3405	x	Horsepower
Kilowatts	x .746	=	Horsepower
Millimeters	x .03937	=	Inches
Millimeters	= 25.400	x	Inches
Meters	x 3.2809	=	Feet
Meters	= .3048	x	Feet
Kilometers	x .621377	=	Miles
Kilometers	= 1.6093	x	Miles
Square centimeters	x .15500	=	Square Inches
Square centimeters	= 6.4515	x	Square Inches
Square meters	x 10.76410	=	Square Feet
Square meters	= .09290	x	Square Feet
Cubic centimeters	x .061025	=	Cubic Inches
Cubic centimeters	= 16.3866	x	Cubic Inches
Cubic meters	x 35.3156	=	Cubic Feet

BRIGGS & STRATTON

BRIGGS & STRATTON CORPORATION
Milwaukee, Wisconsin 53201

HP	Crankshaft	Basic Model (Series)	Bore	Stroke	Displacement
2 (1.49 kW)	Horizontal	60000	2.4 in. (60.3 mm)	1.5 in. (38.1 mm)	6.65 cu. in. (108.97 cc)
3 (2.24 kW)	Horizontal	80000	2.4 in. (60.3 mm)	1.75 in. (44.45 mm)	7.75 cu. in. (126 cc)
3.5 (2.61 kW)	Vertical	90000	2.6 in. (65.1 mm)	1.75 in. (44.45 mm)	9.02 cu. in. (147.8 cc)
4 (2.98 kW)	Horizontal	110000	2.8 in. (70.6 mm)	1.9 in. (47.6 mm)	11.39 cu. in. (186.6 cc)
5 (3.73 kW)	Vertical	130000	2.6 in. (65.1 mm)	2.4 in. (61.9 mm)	12.57 cu. in. (207.6 cc)
5 (3.73 kW)	Horizontal	130000	2.6 in. (65.1 mm)	2.4 in. (61.9 mm)	12.57 cu. in. (207.6 cc)
7 (5.22 kW)	Horizontal	170000	3.0 in. (76.2 mm)	2.4 in. (60.3 mm)	16.70 cu. in. (273.7 cc)
8 (5.97 kW)	Horizontal	190000	3.0 in. (76.2 mm)	2.75 in. (69.85 mm)	19.44 cu. in. (318.6 cc)

All engines covered in this section have aluminum cylinder blocks with either plain aluminum cylinder bore or with a cast iron sleeve integrally cast into the block.

MAINTENANCE

SPARK PLUG. On models with five horsepower or less, use AC 45, Autolite 295, Champion J-8 or equivalent plug. If resistor type plugs are necessary to decrease radio interference, use Champion RJ-8 or equivalent. Seven horsepower and eight horsepower models use AC GC46, Autolite A71, Champion J-8 or equivalent plug. If resistor type plugs are necessary to decrease radio interference, use Champion XJ-8 or equivalent. On all models, set gap to 0.030 inch (0.76 mm). Briggs & Stratton Corporation recommends that plugs not be cleaned by abrasive blasting method as this may introduce some abrasive

material into the engine which could cause extensive damage.

FLOAT TYPE (FLO-JET) CARBURETORS. Three different float type carburetors are used. They are called a "two-piece" (See Fig. B60), a small "one-piece" (See Fig. B64) or a large "one-piece" (See Fig. B66) carburetor depending upon the type of construction.

Float type carburetors are equipped with adjusting needles for both idle and power fuel mixtures. Counterclockwise rotation of the adjusting needles richens the mixture. For initial starting adjustment, open the main needle valve (power fuel mixture) 1½ turns on the two-piece carburetor and 2½ turns on the small one-piece carburetor. Open the idle needle ½ to ¾ turn on the two-piece carburetor and 1½ turns on the small one-piece carburetor. On the large one-piece carburetor, open both needle valves 1⅛ turns. Start the engine and when it is warm, make final adjustments

as follows: Set the speed control for desired operating speed, turn main needle clockwise until engine misses, and then turn it counterclockwise just past the smooth operating point until the engine begins to run unevenly. Return the speed control to idle positon and adjust the idle speed stop screw un-

Fig. B61—Checking upper body of "two-piece" carburetor for warpage.

Fig. B62—Carburetor float setting should be within specifications shown. To adjust float setting, bend tang with needle nose pliers as shown in Fig. B63.

Fig. B60—Cross-sectional view of typical B&S "two-piece" carburetor. Before separating upper and lower body sections, loosen packing nut and unscrew nut and needle valve as a unit. Then, using special screwdriver, remove nozzle.

Fig. B63— Bending tang with needle nose pliers to adjust float setting. Refer to Fig. B62 for method of checking float setting.

Fig. B65 — Disassembling the small "one-piece" float type carburetor. Pry out welch plug, remove choke butterfly (disc), remove choke shaft and needle valve; venturi can then be removed as shown in left view.

Fig. B64— Cross-sectional view of typical B&S small "one-piece" float type carburetor. Refer to Fig. B65 for disassembly views.

Fig. B66 — Cross-sectional view of B&S large "one-piece" float type carburetor.

Fig. B67 — Cutaway view of typical suction type (Vacu-Jet) carburetor. Inset shows fuel metering holes which are accessible for cleaning after removing needle valve. Be careful not to enlarge the holes when cleaning them.

til the engine idles at 1750 rpm. Then adjust the idle needle valve until the engine runs smoothly. Reset the idle speed stop screw, if necessary. The engine should then accelerate without hesitation or sputtering. If it does not accelerate properly, turn the main needle valve counterclockwise slightly to provide a richer fuel mixture.

The float setting on all float type carburetors should be within dimensions shown in Fig. B62. If not, bend the tang on float as shown in Fig. B63 to adjust float setting. If any wear is visible on the inlet valve or the inlet valve seat, install a new valve and seat assembly. On large one-piece carburetors, the renewable inlet valve seat is pressed into the carburetor body until flush with the body.

NOTE: The upper and lower bodies of the two-piece float type careburetor are locked together by the main nozzle. Refer to cross-sectional view of carburetor in Fig. B60. Before attempting to separate the upper body from the lower body, loosen packing nut and unscrew nut and needle valve. Then, using special screwdriver (B&S tool No. 19061 or 19062), remove nozzle.

If a 0.002-inch (0.05 mm) feeler gage can be inserted between upper and lower bodies of the two-piece carburetor as shown in Fig. B61, the upper body is warped and should be replaced.

Check throttle shaft for wear on all float type carburetors. If 0.10-inch (0.25 mm) or more free play (shaft to bushing clearance) is noted, install new throttle shaft and/or throttle shaft bushings. To remove worn bushings, turn a 1/4-inch x 20 tap into bushing and pull bushing from body casting with the tap. Press new bushings into casting by using a vise and, if necessary, ream bushings with a 7/32-inch drill bit.

SUCTION TYPE (VACU-JET) CARBURETORS. A typical suction type (Vacu-Jet) carburetor is shown in Fig. B67. This type carburetor has only one fuel mixture adjusting needle. Turning the needle clockwise leans the fuel-air mixture. Adjust suction type carburetors with fuel tank approximately one-half full and with engine warm and running at approximately 3000 rpm at no load. Turn needle valve clockwise until engine begins to run unevenly from a too-lean fuel-air mixture, then turn needle valve counterclockwise, counting

Fig. B68 — Removing brass fuel feed pipe from suction type carburetor. Press new brass pipe into carburetor until it projects 2.28-2.31 inches (57.9-58.7 mm) from carburetor face. Nylon fuel feed pipe is threaded into carburetor.

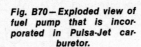

Fig. B70 — Exploded view of fuel pump that is incorporated in Pulsa-Jet carburetor.

the number of turns, until engine begins to run unevenly from a too-rich fuel-air mixture. Turn needle valve back clockwise one-half the number of turns that it took to go from a too-lean to a too-rich fuel-air condition. This should result in a correct adjustment for full load operation. Adjust idle speed to 1750 rpm.

To remove the suction type carburetor, first remove carburetor and fuel tank as an assembly, then remove carburetor from fuel tank. When reinstalling carburetor on fuel tank, use a new gasket and tighten retaining screws evenly.

The suction type carburetor has a fuel feed pipe extending into fuel tank. The pipe has a check valve to allow fuel to feed up into the carburetor, but prevents fuel from flowing back into the tank. If check valve is inoperative and cleaning in alcohol or acetone will not free the check valve, renew the fuel feed pipe. If feed pipe is made of brass, remove as shown in Fig. B68. Using a vise, press new pipe into carburetor so that it extends 2.28-2.31 inches (57.9-58.7 mm) from carburetor body. If pipe is made of nylon (plastic), screw pipe out of carburetor body with wrench. When installing new nylon feel pipe, be careful not to overtighten.

NOTE: If soaking carburetor in cleaner for more than one-half hour, be sure to remove all nylon parts and "O" ring, if used, before placing the carburetor in cleaning solvent.

PUMP TYPE (PULSA-JET) CARBURETORS. The pump type (Pulsa-Jet) carburetor is basically a suction type carburetor incorporating a fuel pump to fill a constant level fuel sump in top of fuel tank. Refer to schematic view in Fig. B69. This makes a constant fuel-air mixture available to engine regardless of fuel level in tank. Adjustment of the pump type carburetor fuel mixture needle valve is the same as outlined for suction type carburetors in previous paragraph, except that fuel level in tank is not important.

To remove the pump type carburetor, first remove the carburetor and fuel tank as an assembly; then, remove carburetor from fuel tank. When reinstalling carburetor on fuel tank, use a new gasket or pump diaphragm as required and tighten retaining screws evenly.

Fig. B70 shows an exploded view of the pump unit used on some carburetors.

On other carburetors pump diaphragm is placed between the carburetor and fuel tank as shown in Fig. B71.

The pump type carburetor has two fuel feed pipes; the long pipe feeds fuel into the pump portion of the carburetor from which fuel then flows to the constant level fuel sump. The short pipe extends into the constant level sump and feeds fuel into the carburetor venturi via fuel mixture needle valve.

As check valves are incorporated in the pump diaphragm, fuel feed pipes on pump type carburetors do not have a check valve. However, if the fuel screen in lower end of pipe is broken or clogged and cannot be cleaned, the pipe or screen housing can be renewed. If pipe is made of nylon, unscrew old pipe and install new pipe with a wrench; be careful not to overtighten new pipe. If pipe is made of brass, clamp pipe lightly in a vise and drive old screen housing from pipe with screwdriver or small chisel as shown in Fig. B72. Drive a new screen housing onto pipe with a soft faced hammer.

NOTE: If soaking carburetor in cleaner for more than one-half hour, be sure to remove all nylon parts and "O" ring, if used, before placing carburetor in cleaning solvent.

NOTE: Be sure air cleaner retaining screw is in place if engine is being operated (during tests) without air cleaner installed. If screw is not in place, fuel may lift up through the screw hole and enter carburetor throat as the screw hole leads directly into the constant level fuel sump.

Fig. B69 — Fuel flow in Pulsa-Jet carburetor. Fuel pump incorporated in carburetor fills constant level sump below carburetor (F) and excess fuel flows back into tank. Fuel is drawn from sump through inlet (I) past fuel mixture adjusting needle by vacuum in carburetor.

Fig. B71 — Pump type (Pulsa-Jet) carburetor diaphragm is installed between carburetor and fuel tank.

Fig. B72 — To renew screen housing on pump type carburetors with brass feed pipes, drive old screen housing for pipe as shown. To hold pipe, clamp lightly in a vise.

Fig. B73—Metering holes in pump type carburetors are accessible for cleaning after removing fuel mixture needle valve. On models with intake pipe, carburetor is sealed to pipe with "O" ring.

Fig. B76—Choke-A-Matic control on float type carburetor. Remote control can be attached to speed slide.

Fig. B77—Typical Choke-A-Matic control on suction type carburetor. Remote control can be attached to speed lever.

Fig. B78—Choke-A-Matic control in choke and stop positions on float carburetor.

INTAKE TUBE. Intake tube is attached between carburetor and engine intake port in one of three methods. First method: Carburetor is sealed to intake tube with an "O"ring as shown in Fig. B73. Second method: Intake tube is threaded in engine intake port. A gasket is used between engine intake port cover and engine casting as shown in Fig. B74. Third method: Intake tube is bolted to engine intake port and a gasket is used between intake tube and engine casting as shown in Fig. B75.

CHOKE-A-MATIC CARBURETOR CONTROLS. Engines equipped with float, suction or pump type carburetors may be equipped with a control unit with which the carburetor choke and throttle and the magneto grounding switch are operated from a single lever (Choke-A-Matic carburetors). Refer to Figs. B76

Fig. B79—Choke-A-Matic control in choke and stop positions on suction carburetor. Bend choke link if necessary to adjust control.

Fig. B74—Intake tube is threaded into intake port of engine; a gasket is placed between intake port cover and intake port.

Fig. B80—On Choke-A-Matic control, choke actuating lever (A) should just contact choke link or shift (B) when control is at "FAST" position. If not, loosen screw (C) and move control wire housing (D) as required.

Fig. B75—Fuel intake tube is bolted to engine intake port and a gasket is placed between tube and engine.

Fig. B81—When Choke-A-Matic control is in "START" or "CHOKE" position, choke must be completely closed as shown in view A. When control is in "STOP" position arm should contact stop switch (View B.)

through B82 for views showing the different types of Choke-A-Matic carburetor controls.

To check operation of Choke-A-Matic carburetor controls, move control lever to "CHOKE" position; carburetor choke slide or plate must be completely closed. Then, move control lever to "STOP"

position; magneto grounding switch should be making contact. With the control lever in "RUN", "FAST", or "SLOW" position, carburetor choke should be completely open. On units with remote controls, synchronize movement of remote lever to carburetor control lever by loosening screw (C – Fig.

B80 or Fig. B82) and moving control wire housing (D) as required; then, tighten screw to clamp the housing securely. Refer to Fig. B83 to check remote control wire movement.

AUTOMATIC CHOKE (THERMOSTAT TYPE). A thermostat operated choke is used on some models equipped with the two-piece carburetor. To adjust choke linkage, hold choke shaft so thermostat lever is free. At room temperature, stop screw in thermostat collar should be located midway between thermostat stops. If not, loosen stop screw, adjust the collar and tighten stop screw. Loosen set screw (S – Fig. B84) on thermostat lever. Then, slide lever on shaft to ensure free movement of choke unit. Turn thermostat shaft clockwise until stop screw contacts thermostat stop. While holding shaft in this position, move shaft lever until choke is open exactly 1/8 inch (3.2 mm) and tighten lever set screw. Turn thermostat shaft counterclockwise until stop screw contacts thermostat stop as shown in Fig. B85. Manually open choke valve until it stops against top of choke link opening. At this time, choke valve should be open at least 3/32-inch (2.4 mm), but not more than 5/32-inch (4.0 mm). Hold choke valve in wide open position and check

Fig. B82 – On Choke-A-Matic control, lever (A) should just contact choke shaft arm (B) when control is in "FAST" position. If not, loosen screw (C) and move control wire housing (D) as required, then tighten screw.

Fig. B85 – Automatic choke on two-piece Flo-Jet carburetor in "Cold" position.

Fig. B83 – For proper operation of Choke-A-Matic controls, remote control wire must extend to dimension shown and have a minimum travel at 1 3/8 inches (34.9 mm).

Fig. B86 – Diagram showing vacuum operated automatic choke used on some vertical crankshaft engines in closed (engine not running) position.

Fig. B84 – Automatic choke used on some models equipped with a two-piece Flo-Jet carburetor showing unit used in "Hot" position.

Fig. B87 – Diagram showing vacuum operated automatic choke in open (engine running) position.

Fig. B88 — Fuel tank outlet used on smaller engines with float type carburetor.

Fig. B91 — Exploded view of governor unit used on two and three horsepower horizontal crankshaft models.

Fig. B89 — Fuel tank outlet used on larger B&S engines.

Fig. B92 — View of governor linkage used on two and three horsepower horizontal crankshaft engines using a mechanical governor. Governor spring should be hooked in governor lever as shown in inset.

position of counterweight lever. Lever should be in a horizontal position with free end towards right.

AUTOMATIC CHOKE (VACUUM TYPE). A spring and vacuum operated automatic choke is used on some vertical crankshaft engines. A diaphragm under carburetor is connected to the choke shaft by a link. The compression spring works against the diaphragm, holding choke in closed position when engine is not running. See Fig. B86. As engine starts, increased vacuum works against the spring and pulls the diaphragm and choke link down holding choke in open (running) position shown in Fig. B87.

During operation, if a sudden load is applied to engine or a lugging condition develops, a drop in intake vacuum occurs, permitting choke to close partially. This provides a richer fuel mixture to

meet the condition and keeps the engine running smoothly. When the load condition has been met, increased vacuum returns choke valve to normal running (fully open) position.

FUEL TANK OUTLET. Small models with float type carburetors are

equipped with a fuel tank outlet as shown in Fig. B88. On larger engines, a fuel sediment bowl is incorporated with fuel tank outlet as shown in Fig. B89. Clean any lint and dirt from tank outlet screens with a brush. Varnish or other gasoline deposits may be removed by use of a suitable solvent. Tighten packing nut or remove nut and shut-off valve, then renew packing if leakage occurs around shut-off valve stem.

GOVERNOR. All models are equipped with either a mechanical (flyweight type) or an air vane (pneumatic) governor. Refer to following appropriate paragraph for service and adjustment information on the governor unit being serviced.

MECHANICAL GOVERNOR. Three different designs of mechanical governors are used.

On two and three horspower engines a governor unit as shown in Fig. B90 is used. An exploded view of this governor unit is shown in Fig. B91. The governor housing is attached to inner side of crankcase cover and the governor gear is driven from the engine camshaft gear. Use Figs. B90 and B91 as a disassembly and assembly guide. Renew any parts that bind or show excessive wear. After governor is assembled, refer to Fig. B92 and adjust linkage as follows: Loosen screw clamping governor lever to governor crank. Turn governor lever counterclockwise so that carburetor throttle is in wide open position and while holding lever, turn governor crank as far counterclockwise as possible and tighten screw clamping lever to crank. Governor crank can be turned with screwdriver. Check linkage to be sure it is free and that the carburetor throttle will move from idle to wide open position.

Fig. B90 — Removing governor unit from inside crankcase cover on two and three horsepower horizontal crankshaft models.

Fig. B93 — Installing crankcase cover on four horsepower and larger engines with mechanical governor. Governor crank (C) must be in position shown. A thrust washer (W) is placed between governor (G) and crankcase cover.

On four horsepower and larger engines the governor gear and weight unit (G–Fig. B93) is supported on a pin in engine crankcase cover and the governor crank is installed in a bore in the engine crankcase. A thrust washer (W) is placed between governor gear and crankcase cover. When assembling crankcase cover to crankcase, be sure governor crank (C) is in position shown in Fig. B93. After governor unit and crankcase cover is installed, refer to Fig. B94 for installation of linkage. Before attempting to start engine, refer to Fig. B95 and adjust linkage as follows: Loosen bolt clamping governor lever to governor crank. Set control lever in high speed position, then, using screwdriver, turn governor crank as far clockwise as possible and tighten governor lever clamp bolt. Check to be sure carburetor throttle can be moved from idle to wide open position and that linkage is free.

On vertical crankshaft engines having a mechanical governor, the governor weight unit is integral with the lubricating oil slinger and is mounted on lower end of camshaft gear as shown in Fig. B96. With engine upside down, place governor and slinger unit on camshaft gear as shown, place spring washer on camshaft gear and assemble engine base to crankcase. Assemble linkage as shown in Fig. B97; then, refer to Fig. B98 and adjust linkage as follows: With bolt clamping governor lever to governor crank loose and control lever in high speed position, turn governor crank with screwdriver as far clockwise as possible and tighten governor lever clamping bolt.

AIR VANE (PNEUMATIC) GOVERNORS. Some models are equipped with an air vane governor; refer to Fig. B99 for schematic operational views of a typical unit.

Vane should stop $1/8$-$1/4$ inch (3.2-6.35 mm) from magneto coil (See Fig. B100, illustration 2) when linkage is assembled and attached to carburetor throttle shaft. If necessary to adjust, spring the vane while holding the shaft. With wide open throttle, the link from the air vane arm to the carburetor throttle should be in a vertical position on horizontal crankshaft models and in a horizontal position on vertical crankshaft models. (See Fig. B100, illustration 3 and 4). Check linkage for binding; if binding

Fig. B94—Cutaway drawing of governor and linkage used on four horsepower and larger models.

Fig. B97—Schematic drawing of mechanical governor and linkage used on some vertical crankshaft mechanical governed models.

Fig. B95—Linkage adjustment on four horsepower and larger horizontal crankshaft mechanical governor models. Refer to text for procedure.

Fig. B96—View showing vertical crankshaft mechanical governor unit. Drawing is of lower side of engine with oil sump (engine base) removed; note spring washer location.

Fig. B98—View showing adjustment of vertical crankshaft mechanical governor; refer to text for procedure.

Fig. B99— Views showing operating principle of air vane (pneumatic) governor. Air from flywheel fan acts against air vane to overcome tension of governor spring; speed is adjusted by changing spring tension.

Fig. B102— Adjustment of breaker point gap on models having breaker point separate from condenser.

Fig. B100— Air vane governors and linkage. ILL. 1, the governor vane should be checked for clearance in all positions. ILL. 2, the vane should stop (⅛-¼-inch (3.2-6.4 mm) from the magneto coil. ILL. 3, with wide open throttle, the link connecting vane arm to throttle lever should be in a vertical position on vertical cylinder engines and in a horizontal position (ILL. 4) on horizontal cylinder engines. Bend link slightly (ILL. 5) to remove any binding condition in linkage.

condition exists, bend links slightly to correct. Refer to Fig. B100, illustration 5.

NOTE: Some engines are equipped with a nylon governor vane which does not require adjustment.

MAGNETO. The breaker contact gap is 0.020 inch (0.51 mm) on all models. Condenser capacity on all models is 0.18-0.24 mfd.

Breaker points and condenser are accessible after removing engine flywheel and breaker cover.

On some models, one breaker contact point is an integral part of the ignition condenser and the breaker arm is pivoted on a knife edge retained in a slot in pivot post. On these models, breaker contact gap is adjusted by moving the condenser as shown in Fig. B101. On other models, breaker contact gap is adjusted by relocating position of breaker contact bracket; refer to Fig. B102.

On all models, breaker contact arm is actuated by a plunger held in a bore in engine crankcase and riding against a cam on engine crankshaft. Plunger can

be removed after removing breaker points. Renew the plunger if worn to a length of 0.870 inch (22.10 mm) or less. If breaker point plunger bore in crankcase is worn, oil will leak past plunger. Check bore with B&S plug gage No. 19055; if plug gage will enter bore ¼-inch (6.4 mm) or more, bore should be reamed and a bushing installed. Refer to Fig. B103 for method of checking bore and to Fig. B104 for steps in reaming bore and installing bushing if bore is worn. To ream bore and install bushing, it is necessary that the breaker points, armature and ignition coil and the crankshaft be removed.

Armature and ignition coil are located outside flywheel and armature to flywheel air gap should be as follows:

Series 60000 & 80000
　Two Leg Armature . . .0.006-0.010 in.
　　　　　　　　　　(0.15-0.25 mm)
　Three Leg Armature . .0.012-0.016 in.
　　　　　　　　　　(0.30-0.41 mm)
Series 90000
　& 110000. . . . . .0.006-0.010 in.
　　　　　　　　　　(0.15-0.25 mm)

Fig. B101— View showing breaker point adjustment on models having breaker point integral with condenser. Move condenser to adjust point gap.

Fig. B103— If Briggs & Stratton plug gage #19055 can be inserted in breaker plunger bore a distance of ¼-inch (6.35 mm) or more, bore is worn and must be rebushed.

Fig. B104 — Views showing reaming plunger bore to accept bushing (left view), installing bushing (center) and finish reaming bore (right) of bushing.

Fig. B106 — Cylinder head screw tightening sequence. Long screws are used in positions 2, 3 and 7.

Fig. B106A — Tightening sequence on models with nine cylinder head screws. Long screws are used in positions, 1, 7 and 9.

Series 130000 . . . . 0.010-0.014 in.
(0.25-0.36 mm)

Series 170000 & 190000
Two Leg Armature . . . 0.010-0.014 in.
(0.25-0.36 mm)
Three Leg Armature . . 0.016-0.019 in.
(0.41-0.48 mm)

LUBRICATION. Vertical crankshaft engines are lubricated by an oil slinger wheel driven by the cam gear. On vertical crankshaft engines, the oil slinger wheel, pin and bracket are an integral unit with the bracket being retained by the lower end of the engine camshaft. A spring washer is placed on lower end of camshaft between bracket and oil sump boss. Renew the oil slinger assembly if teeth are worn on slinger gear or gear is loose on bracket. On horizontal crankshaft engines, a splash system (oil dipper on connecting rod) is used for engine lubrication.

Use oils labeled API classification SE or SF. SAE-30, 10W-30 or 10W-40 oil is recommended for temperatures above 40°F, SAE 10W-30 or 10W-40 recommended for temperatures above 40°F, SAE 10W-30 or 10W-40 for temperatures between 40°F and 0°F, or SAE 5W-20 or 5W-30 for below 0°F. Fill crankcase to point of overflowing or to **FULL** mark on dipstick when engine is level.

CRANKCASE BREATHER. The crankcase breather is built into the engine valve cover. The mounting holes are offset so the breather can only be installed one way. Rinse breather in solvent and allow to drain. A vent tube connects the breather to the carburetor air horn on certain model engines for extra protection against dusty conditions.

REPAIRS

NOTE: When checking compression on models with "Easy-Spin" starting, turn engine opposite the direction of normal rotation. See CAMSHAFT paragraph.

CYLINDER HEAD. When removing cylinder head, be sure to note the position from which each of the different length screws were removed. If they are not used in the same holes when installing the head, it will result in screws bottoming in some holes and not enough thread contact in others. Lubricate the cylinder head screws with graphite grease before installation. Do not use sealer on head gasket. When installing cylinder head, tighten all screws lightly and then retighten them in sequence shown in Fig. B106 and Fig. B106A to a torque of 165 in.-lbs. (18.63 N·m) on seven and eight horsepower models. On all other models, torque screws to 140 in.-lbs. (15.81 N·m). Run engine for 2 to 5 minutes to allow it to warm up and retighten the head screws again following the sequence and torque value mentioned above.

CONNECTING ROD. The connecting rod and piston are removed from cylinder head end of block as an assembly. The aluminum alloy connecting rod rides directly on the induction hardened crankpin. The rod should be rejected if the crankpin hole is scored or out-of-round over 0.0007-inch (0.018 mm) or if the piston pin hole is scored or out-of-round over 0.0005-inch (0.013 mm). Wear limit sizes are given in the following chart. Reject the connecting rod if either the crankpin or piston pin hole is worn to or larger than the sizes given in the chart.

NOTE: Piston pins of 0.005-inch (0.13 mm) oversize are available for service. Piston pin hole in rod can be reamed to this size if crankpin hole is O.K.

Torque connecting rod cap screws to 165 in.-lbs. (18.63 N·m) on seven and eight horsepower engines and 100 in.-lbs. (11.29 N·m) on all other engines.

PISTON, PIN AND RINGS. Pistons for use in engines having aluminum bore are not interchangeable with those for use in cylinders having cast-iron sleeve. Pistons may be identified as follows: Those for use in cast-iron sleeve

CONNECTING ROD REJECTION SIZES

Basic Model	Crankpin Hole	*Piston Pin Hole
60000	0.876 in. (22.25 mm)	0.492 in. (12.50 mm)
80000, 90000, 110000 & 130000	1.0013 in. (25.433 mm)	0.492 in. (12.50 mm)
170000	1.0949 in. (27.810 mm)	0.674 in. (17.12 mm)
190000	1.1265 in. (28.613 mm)	0.674 in. (17.12 mm)

*Standard Size

1. Snap ring
2. Washer
3. Ratchet
4. Steel balls
5. Starter clutch
6. Washer
7. Flywheel
8. Breaker cover
9. Breaker point spring
10. Breaker arm & pivot
11. Breaker plunger
12. Condenser clamp
13. Coil spring (primary wire retainer)
14 Condenser
15. Governor air vane & bracket assy.
16. Spark plug wire
17. Armature & coil assy.
18. Air baffle
19. Spark plug grounding switch
20. Cylinder head
21. Header head gasket
22. Cylinder block
23. Crankshaft oil seal
24. Cylinder shield
25. Flywheel key
26. Gasket
27. Breather & tappet chamber cover
28. Breather tube assy.
29. Coil spring
30. Crankshaft
31. Cam gear & shaft
32. Piston rings
33. Piston
34. Connecting rod
35. Rod bolt lock
36. Piston pin retaining rings
37. Piston pin
38. Intake valve
39. Valve springs
40. Valve spring keepers
41. Tappets (cam followers)
42. Exhaust valve
43. Gasket (0.005, 0.009 or 0.015 in.)
44. Oil slinger assy.
45. Oil sump (engine base)
46. Crankshaft oil seal

Fig. B107—Exploded view of typical vertical crankshaft model with air vane (pneumatic) governor. To remove flywheel, remove blower housing and starter unit; then, unscrew starter clutch housing (5). Flywheel can then be pulled from crankshaft.

cylinders have a plain, dull aluminum finish, have an "L" stamped on top and use an oil ring expander. Those for use in aluminum bore cylinders are chrome plated (shiny finish), do not have an identifying letter and do not use an oil ring expander.

Reject pistons showing visible signs of wear, scoring or scuffing. If, after cleaning carbon from top ring groove, a new top ring has a side clearance of 0.007-inch (0.18 mm) or more, reject the piston. Reject piston or hone piston pin hole to 0.005-inch (0.13 mm) oversize if pin hole is 0.0005-inch (0.013 mm) or more out-of-round, or is worn to a diameter of 0.491-inch (12.47 mm) on 60000, 80000, 90000, 110000 or 130000 model engines. On 170000 and 190000 models, reject piston or hone piston pin

hole to 0.005-inch (0.13 mm) oversize if pin hole is 0.0005-inch (0.013 mm) or more out-of-round, or is worn to a diameter of 0.673-inch (17.09 mm).

If piston pin is 0.0005 (0.013 mm) or more out-of-round, or is worn to a diameter of 0.489-inch (12.42 mm) or smaller on 60000, 80000, 90000, 110000 and 130000 models, reject pin. On 170000 and 190000 models, reject piston pin if pin is 0.0005-inch (0.013 mm) or more out-of-round, or is worn to a diameter of 0.671-inch (17.04 mm) or smaller.

Specified piston ring gap for new rings is 0.010-0.025 inch (0.25-0.64 mm) on models with aluminum cylinder bore and 0.010-0.018 inch (0.25-0.46 mm) on models with cast-iron cylinder bore. Reject compression rings having an end

gap of 0.035-inch (0.89 mm) or more and reject oil rings having an end gap of 0.045-inch (1.14 mm) or more.

Pistons and rings are available in 0.010-inch (0.25 mm), 0.020-inch (0.51 mm) and 0.030-inch (0.76 mm) oversizes as well as standard size.

A chrome ring set is available for slightly worn standard bore cylinders. Refer to note in **CYLINDER** paragraph.

CYLINDER. If cylinder bore wear is 0.003-inch (0.08 mm) or more or is 0.0025-inch (0.06 mm) or more out-of-round, cylinder must be rebored to next larger oversize.

Standard bore sizes for each basic model series are given below:

STANDARD CYLINDER BORE SIZES

Basic Model	Standard Cylinder Bore
60000 & 80000	2.374-2.375 in. (60.30-60.33 mm)
90000	2.5615-2.5625 in. (65.062-65.088 mm)
110000	2.7802-2.7812 in. (70.617-70.642 mm)
130000	2.5615-2.5625 in. (65.062-65.088 mm)
170000 & 190000 . .	2.999-3.000 in. (76.17-76.2 mm)

It is recommended that a hone be used for resizing cylinders. Operate hone at 300-700 rpm with an up and down movement that will produce a 45 degree crosshatch pattern. Clean cylinder after honing with oil or soap suds. Always resize to exact 0.010-inch (0.25 mm), 0.020-inch (0.51 mm) or 0.030-inch (0.76 mm) oversize from given dimensions. Approved hones are as follows: For aluminum bore, use Ammco hone 3956 for rough and finishing or Sunnen hone AN200 for rough and Sunnen hone AN500 for finishing. For sleeved bores, use Ammco hone 4324 for rough and finishing or Sunnen hone AN100 for rough and Sunnen hone AN300 for finishing.

NOTE: A chrome piston ring set is available for slightly worn standard bore cylinders. No honing or cylinder deglazing is required for these rings. Cylinder bore can be a maximum of 0.005-inch (0.13 mm) oversize when using chrome rings.

CRANKSHAFT AND MAIN BEARINGS. Except where equipped with ball bearings, main bearings are an integral part of crankcase and cover or sump. Bearings are renewable by reaming out crankcase and cover on sump bearing bores and installing service bushings. Tools for reaming crankcase and cover or sump and for installing service bushings are available from Briggs & Stratton. If bearings are scored, out-of-round 0.0007-inch (0.018 mm) or more, or are worn to or larger than the reject sizes given at bottom of page, ream and install service bushings.

Rejection sizes for crankshaft bearing journals are given in the adjoining chart. Figures given for main bearing journals apply to plain bearing applications only.

Ball bearing mains are a press fit on crankshaft and must be removed by pressing crankshaft out of bearing. Reject ball bearing if worn or rough. Expand new bearing by heating in hot oil (325°F maximum) and install on crankshaft with seal side towards crankpin journal.

Crankshaft end play on all models is 0.002-0.008 inch (0.05-0.20 mm) with at least one 0.015-inch (0.38 mm) cover or sump gasket in place. Additional sump or cover gaskets of 0.005-inch (0.13 mm) and 0.009-inch (0.23 mm) thicknesses are available if end play is less than 0.002-inch (0.05 mm). If end play is over 0.008-inch (0.20 mm), metal shims are available for use on crankshaft between crankshaft gear and cylinder block.

CAMSHAFT. Camshaft and camshaft gear are an integral part which rides in journals at each end of the camshaft. Inspect camshaft assembly for wear on journals, cam lobes and gear teeth. Rejection sizes for journals and cam lobes are given in the chart at the bottom of the page.

On models with "Easy-Spin" starting, intake cam lobe is designed to hold intake valve slightly open on part of the compression stroke. Therefore, to check compression, engine must be turned backwards.

"Easy-Spin" camshafts (cam gears) can be identified by two holes drilled in web of gear. Where part number of an older cam gear and an "Easy-Spin" cam gear are the same (except for an "E" following the "Easy-Spin" part number), the gears are interchangeable.

VALVE SYSTEM. Intake valve tappet clearance is 0.005-0.007 inch (0.13-0.18 mm) and exhaust tappet

21. Exhaust valve
22. Intake valve
23. Valve spring retainers
24. Cylinder block
25. Muffler
26. Gasket
27. Gasket
28. Breather & tappet chamber cover
29. Breather pipe
30. Governor lever
31. Clamping bolt
32. Governor crank

Fig. B109 — Exploded view of typical horizontal crankshaft engine assembly.

1. Crankshaft oil seal
2. Crankcase cover
3. Gasket (0.005, 0.009 or (0.015 in.)
4. Thrust washer
5. Governor assy.
6. Cam gear & shaft
7. Tappets (cam followers)
8. Crankshaft
9. Rod bolt lock
10. Oil dipper
11. Connecting rod
12. Piston
13. Piston rings
14. Cylinder head
15. Spark plug ground switch
16. Air baffle
17. Cylinder head gasket
18. Piston pin retaining rings
19. Piston pin
20. Air baffle

CRANKSHAFT REJECTION SIZES

Basic Model	Magneto Journal	Crankpin Journal	Drive End Journal
60000	0.873 in. (22.17 mm)	0.870 in. (22.10 mm)	0.873 in. (22.17 mm)
80000, 90000 & 1100000	0.873 in. (22.17 mm)	0.996 in. (25.30 mm)	0.873 in. (22.17 mm)
130000	0.873 in. (22.17 mm)	0.996 in. (25.30 mm)	0.998 in. (25.35 mm)
170000	0.9975 in. (25.336 mm)	1.090 in. (27.686 mm)	1.1790 in. (29.947 mm)
190000	0.9975 in. (25.336 mm)	1.122 in. (28.50 mm)	1.1790 in. (29.947 mm)

MAIN BEARING REJECT SIZES

Basic Model	Bearing Magneto	Bearing Drive
60000, 80000, 90000 & 110000	0.878 in. (22.30 mm)	0.878 in. (22.30 mm)
130000	0.878 in. (22.30 mm)	1.003 in. (25.48 mm)
170000 & 190000	1.0036 in. (25.49 mm)	1.185 in. (30.10 mm)

CAMSHAFT REJECTION SIZES

Basic Model	Journal Reject Size	Lobe Reject Size
60000, 80000 & 90000	0.498 in. (12.65 mm)	0.883 in. (22.43 mm)
110000	0.498 in. (12.65 mm)	0.870 in. (22.10 mm)
130000	0.498 in. (12.65 mm)	0.950 in. (24.13 mm)
170000 & 190000	0.4985 in. (12.660 mm)	0.977 in. (24.82 mm)

Fig. B112—Align timing marks on cam gear with mark on crankshaft counterweight on ball bearing equipped models.

Fig. B113—Align timing marks on cam gear and crankshaft gear on plain bearing models.

clearance is 0.009-0.011 inch (0.23-0.28 mm) on all models when engine is cold. Valve seat angle is 45 degrees. Regrind or renew valve seat insert if seat width is 0.078-inch (1.98 mm) or wider. Regrind to a width of 0.047-0.063 inch (1.19-1.60 mm). Obtain specified valve tappet clearance by grinding end of valve stem squarely. Replace valve if margin is 0.063-inch (1.60 mm) or less after refacing.

Valve guides on all engines with aluminum blocks are an integral part of the cylinder block. To renew valve guides, ream out old guide and install a bushing. Reamers and bushings are available from Briggs & Stratton. Part numbers are as follows:

Engine Model	Reamer Part No.	Bushing Part No.
60000, 80000 90000, 110000 & 130000......	19064, 19066 (Driver-10965)	63709
170000 & 190000..........	19183	230655

On 60000, 80000, 90000, 110000 and 130000 models, use reamer 19064 with oil to ream worn guides and ream only

Fig. B110—Exploded view of typical vertical engine with mechanical governor.

1. Snap ring
2. Washer
3. Starter ratchet
4. Steel balls
5. Starter clutch
6. Washer
7. Flywheel
8. Breaker cover
9. Breaker arm spring
10. Breaker arm & pivot
11. Breaker plunger
12. Condenser clamp
13. Primary wire retainer spring
14. Condenser
15. Air baffle
16. Spark plug wire
17. Armature & coil assy.
18. Intake pipe
19. Air baffle
20. Cylinder head
21. Cylinder head gasket
22. Linkage lever
23. Crankshaft oil seal
24. Muffler
25. Cylinder block
26. Gasket
27. Breather & tappet chamber cover
28. Governor link
29. Governor lever
30. Governor crank
31. Flywheel key
32. Piston rings
33. Piston
34. Connecting rod
35. Rod bolt lock
36. Piston pin retaining rings
37. Piston pin
38. Intake valve
39. Valve springs
40. Valve spring retainers
41. Tappets (cam followers)
42. Crankshaft
43. Camshaft & gear
44. Oil slinger assy.
45. Exhaust valve
46. Gasket (0.005, 0.009 & 0.015 in.)
47. Oil sump (engine base)
48. Thrust washer
49. Crankshaft oil seal

Fig. B114—Location of tooth to align with timing mark on cam gear if mark is not visible on crankshaft gear.

Fig. B120—View of Briggs & Stratton rewind starter assembly.

N. Nylon bumpers
OS. Old style spring
R. Starter rope
S. Rewind spring

FOR LONG STUB SHAFT

Fig. B123—Exploded view of early production starter clutch unit; refer to Fig. B126 for view of "long stub shaft". A late type unit (Fig. B125) should be installed when renewing "long" crankshaft with "short" (late production) shaft.

1. Starter rope pulley
2. Rotating screen
3. Snap ring
4. Ratchet cover
5. Starter ratchet
6. Steel balls
7. Clutch housing (flywheel nut)
8. Spring washer

about 1/16-inch (1.6 mm) deeper than length of bushing. Press in bushing with driver 19065 until it is flush with top of guide bore. Finish ream bushing with reamer 19066.

On 170000 and 190000 models, use reamer 19183 to ream worn valve guides and ream only about 1/16-inch (1.6 mm) deeper than top end of flutes on reamer. Press in bushings with soft driver as bushing is finish reamed at factory.

VALVE TIMING. On engines equipped with ball bearing mains, align the timing mark on the cam gear with the timing mark on the crankshaft counterweight as shown in Fig. B112. On engines with plain bearings, align the timing marks on the camshaft gear with timing mark on the crankshaft gear (Fig. B113). If the timing mark is not visible on the crankshaft gear, align the timing mark on the camshaft gear with the second tooth to the left of the crankshaft counterweight parting line as shown in Fig. B114.

Fig. B121—Using square shaft and wrench to wind up the rewind starter spring. Refer to text.
H. Hole in starter pulley
N. Nylon bumpers

Fig. B122—Threading starter rope through guide (G) in blower housing and hole (H) in starter pulley with wire hooked in end of rope. Tie knot in end of rope as shown.

FOR SHORT STUB SHAFT

Fig. B124—View of late production sealed starter clutch unit. Late unit can be used with "short stub shaft" only; refer to Fig. B126. Refer to Fig. B125 for cutaway view of ratchet (5).

1. Starter rope pulley
2. Rotating screen
3. Rubber seal
4. Ratchet cover
5. Starter ratchet
6. Steel balls
7. Clutch housing (flywheel nut)
8. Spring washer

SERVICING BRIGGS & STRATTON ACCESSORIES

REWIND STARTERS

OVERHAUL. To renew broken rewind spring, proceed as follows: Grasp free outer end of spring (S–Fig. B120) and pull broken end from starter housing. With blower housing removed, bend nylon bumpers (N) up and out of the way and remove starter pulley from housing. Untie knot in rope (R) and remove rope and inner end of broken spring from pulley. Apply a small amount of grease on inner face of pulley, thread inner end

of new spring through notch in starter housing, engage inner end of spring in pulley hub (on older models, install retainer in hub with split side of retainer away from spring hook) and place pulley in housing. Renew nylon bumpers if necessary and bend bumpers down to within 1/8-inch (3.2 mm) of the pulley. Insert a 3/4-inch (19 mm) square bar in pulley hub and turn pulley approximately 13 1/2 turns in a counterclockwise direction as shown in Fig. B121. Tie wrench to blower housing with wire to hold pulley so that hole (H) in pulley is aligned with rope guide (G) in housing as shown in Fig. B122. Hook a wire in inner end of rope and thread rope through guide and hole in pulley; then, tie a knot in rope and release the pulley allowing

Fig. B125—Cutaway view showing felt seal and plug in end of late production starter ratchet (5–Fig. B124).

the spring to wind the rope into the pulley groove.

To renew starter rope only, it is not generally necessary to remove starter pulley and spring. Wind up the spring

Fig. B126—Crankshaft with short stub (top view) must be used with late production starter clutch assembly. Early crankshaft (bottom view) can be modified by cutting off stub end to the dimension shown in top view and beveling end of shaft to allow installation of late type clutch unit.

Fig. B127—When installing a late type starter clutch unit as replacement for early type, either install new starter rope pulley or cut hub of old pulley to dimension shown.

Fig. B128—When reinstalling blower housing and starter assembly, turn starter ratchet so that word "TOP" stamped on outer end of ratchet is towards engine cylinder head.

and install new rope as outlined in preceding paragraph.

Two different types of starter clutches have been used; refer to exploded view of early production unit in Fig. B123 and exploded view of late production unit in Fig. B124. The outer end of the late production ratchet (refer to cutaway view in Fig. B125) is sealed with a felt and a retaining plug and a rubber ring is used to seal ratchet to ratchet cover.

To disassemble early type starter clutch unit, refer to Fig. B123 and proceed as follows: Remove snap ring (3) and lift ratchet (5) and cover (4) from starter housing (7) and crankshaft. Be careful not to lose the steel balls (6).

Fig. B202—Exploded view of 12 volt 4-brush starter motor.

1. Cap
2. Roll pin
3. Retainer
4. Pinion spring
5. Spring cup
6. Starter gear
7. Clutch assy.
8. Drive end cap assy.
9. Armature
10. Housing
11. Spring
12. Brush assy.
13. Battery wire terminal
14. Commutator end cap assy.

Fig. B203—View of test connections for 110 volt rectifier. Refer to text for procedure.

Starter housing (7) is also flywheel retaining nut; to remove housing, first remove screen (2) and using Briggs & Stratton flywheel wrench 19114, unscrew housing from crankshaft in counterclockwise direction. When reinstalling housing, be sure spring washer (8) is placed on crankshaft with cup (hollow) side towards flywheel, then install starter housing and tighten securely Reinstall rotating screen. Place ratchet on crankshaft and into housing and insert the steel balls. Reinstall cover and retaining snap ring.

To disassemble late starter clutch unit, refer to Fig. B124 and proceed as follows: Remove rotating screen (2) and starter ratchet cover (4). Lift ratchet (5) from housing and crankshaft and extract the steel balls (6). If necessary to remove housing (7), hold flywheel and unscrew housing in counterclockwise direction using Briggs & Stratton flywheel wrench 19114. When installing housing, be sure spring washer (8) is in place on crankshaft with cup (hollow) side towards flywheel; then, tighten housing securely. Inspect felt seal and plug in outer end of ratchet; renew ratchet if seal or plug are damaged as these parts are not serviced separately. Lubricate the felt with oil and place ratchet on crankshaft. Insert the steel balls and install ratchet cover, rubber seal and rotating screen.

NOTE: Crankshafts used with early and late starter clutches differ; refer to Fig. B126. If renewing early (long) crankshaft

with late (short) shaft, also install late type starter clutch unit. If renewing early starter clutch with late type unit, the crankshaft must be shortened to the dimension shown for short shaft in Fig. B126; also, hub of starter rope pulley must be shortened to ½-inch (12.7 mm) dimension shown in Fig. B127. Bevel end of crankshaft after removing the approximate ⅜-inch (9.5 mm) from shaft.

When installing blower housing and starter assembly, turn starter ratchet so that word "TOP" on ratchet is toward engine cylinder head.

GEAR-DRIVE STARTERS

Two types of gear drive starters may be used, a 110 volt AC starter or a 12 volt DC starter. Refer to Fig. B202 for exploded view of starter motor. A properly grounded receptacle should be used with power cord connected to 110 volt AC starter motor. A 32 ampere hour capacity battery is recommended for use with 12 volt DC starter motor.

To renew a worn or damaged flywheel ring gear, drill out retaining rivets using a 3/16-inch drill. Attach new ring gear using screws provided with new ring gear.

To check for correct operation of starter motor, remove starter motor from engine and place motor in a vise or other holding fixture. Install a 0-5 amp ammeter in power cord to 110 volt AC starter motor. On 12 volt DC motor,

Fig. B204 — Tool shown may be fabricated to hold brushes when installing motor end cap.

Fig. B206 — Stator and rectifier assemblies used on the 4 ampere nonregulated flywheel alternator. Fuse is 7½ amp AGC or 3AG.

Fig. B207 — Install ammeter as shown for output test.

Fig. B208 — Connect a test lamp as shown to test for shorted stator or defective rectifier. Refer to text.

connect a 12 volt battery to motor with a 0-50 amp ammeter in series with positive line from battery to starter motor. Connect a tachometer to drive end of starter. With starter activated on 110 volt motor, starter motor should turn at 5200 rpm minimum with a maximum current draw of 3½ amps. The 12 volt motor should turn at 6200 rpm minimum with a current draw of 16 amps maximum. If starter motor does not operate satisfactorily, check operation of rectifier or starter switch. If rectifier and starter switch are good, disassemble and inspect starter motor.

To check the rectifier used on the 110 volt AC starter motor, remove rectifier unit from starter motor. Solder a 10,000 ohm 1 watt resistor to the DC internal terminals of the rectifier as shown in Fig. B203. Connect a 0-100 range DC voltmeter to resistor leads. Measure the voltage of the AC outlet to be used. With starter switch in "OFF" position, a zero reading should be shown on DC voltmeter. With starter switch in "ON" position, the DC voltmeter should show a reading that is 0-14 volts lower than AC line voltage measured previously. If voltage drop exceeds 14 volts, renew rectifier unit

Disassembly of starter motor is self-evident after inspection of unit and referral to Fig. B202. Note position of bolts during disassembly so that they can be installed in their original positions during reassembly. When reassembling motor, lubricate end cap bearings with #20 oil. Be sure to match the drive cap keyway to the stamped key in the housing when sliding the armature into the motor housing. Brushes may be held in their holders during installation by making a brush spreader tool from a piece of metal as shown in Fig. B204.

FLYWHEEL ALTERNATORS

4 Amp. Non-Regulated Alternator

Some engines are equipped with the 4 ampere non-regulated flywheel alternator shown in Fig. B206. A solid state rectifier and 7½ amp fuse is used with this alternator.

If battery is run down and no output from alternator is suspected, first check the 7½ amp fuse. If fuse is good, clean and tighten all connections. Disconnect charging lead and connect an ammeter as shown in Fig. B207. Start engine and check for alternator output. If ammeter shows no charge, stop engine, remove ammeter and install a test lamp as shown in Fig. B208. Test lamp should not light. If it does light, stator or rectifier is defective. Unplug rectifier plug

Fig. B209 — Use an ohmmeter to check condition of stator. Refer to text.

Fig. B210 — If ohmmeter shows continuity in both directions or in neither direction, rectifier is defective.

19151—Check valve guide bore on Models 170000 and 190000.
19164—Check camshaft bearings on all models.
19166—Check main bearing bore on Models 60000, 80000, 90000, 110000 and 130000.
19178—Check main bearing bore on engine Series 170000 and 190000.

REAMERS

19056—Ream hole to install breaker plunger bushing on all models.
19058—Finish ream breaker plunger bushing on same models as 19056 Reamer.
19064—Ream valve guide bore to install bushing on Models 60000, 80000, 90000, 110000 and 130000.
19066—Finish ream valve guide bushing on same models as listed for 19064 Reamer.
19095—Finish ream main bushings on same models as listed for 19064 Reamer.
19099—Ream counterbore for main bearings on Models 60000, 80000, 90000 and 110000.
19172—Ream counterbore for main bearing on Model 130000.
19173—Finish reamer for main bearing on Model 130000.
19174—Ream counterbore for main bearing on Series 170000 and 190000.
19175—Finish ream main bearing on Series 170000 and 190000.

GUIDE BUSHINGS FOR VALVE GUIDE REAMERS

19191—For Models 60000, 80000, 90000, 110000 and 130000.
19192—For Models 170000 and 190000.

PILOTS

19096—Pilot for main bearing reamer on all models.
19126—Expansion pilot for valve seat counterbore cutter on Models 60000, 80000, 90000, 110000 and 130000.
19127—Expansion pilot for valve seat counterbore cutter on Models 170000 and 190000.

DRIVERS

19057—To install breaker plunger bushing on all models.
19065—To install valve guide bushings on Models 60000, 80000, 90000, 110000 and 130000.
19124—To install main bearing bushings on Models 60000, 80000, 90000, 110000 and 130000.

under blower housing. If test lamp does not go out, stator is shorted.

If shorted stator is indicated, use an ohmmeter and check continuity as follows: Touch one test lead to lead inside of fuse holder as shown in Fig. B209. Touch the other test lead to each of the four pins in rectifier connector. Unless the ohmmeter shows continuity at each of the four pins, stator winding is open and stator must be renewed.

If defective rectifier is indicated, unbolt and remove the flywheel blower housing with rectifier. Connect one ohmmeter test lead to blower housing and other test lead to the single pin connector in rectifier connector. See Fig. B210. Check for continuity, then reverse leads and again test for continuity. If tests show no continuity in either direction or continuity in both directions, rectifier is faulty and must be renewed.

BRIGGS & STATTON SPECIAL TOOLS

The following special tools are available from Briggs & Stratton Central Service Distributors.

TOOL KITS

19158—Main bearing service kit for engine Models 60000, 80000, 90000, 110000 and 130000. Includes tool numbers 19094, 19095, 19096, 19097, 19099, 19100, 19101, 19123, 19124 and 19166.
19184—Main bearing service kit for Series 170000 and 190000. Includes tool numbers 19096, 19168, 19169, 19170, 19171, 19172, 19173, 19174, 19175, 19178, 19179 and 19201.
291661—Dealer service tool kit. Includes tool numbers 19051, 19055, 19056, 19057, 19058, 19061, 19062, 19063, 19064, 19065, 19066, 19068, 19069, 19070, 19114, 19122, 19151, 19165, 19167, 19191 and 19203.

PLUG GAGES

19055—Check breaker plunger hole on all models.
19122—Check valve guide bore on Models 60000, 80000, 90000, 110000 and 130000.

19136—To install valve seat inserts on all models.

19179—Install main bearing on Models 170000 and 190000.

GUIDE BUSHINGS FOR MAIN BEARING REAMERS

19094—For Models 60000, 80000, 90000, 110000 and 130000.

19100—For Models 60000, 80000, 90000 and 110000.

19101—For Models 60000, 80000, 90000, 110000 and 130000.

19168—For Models 130000, 170000 and 190000.

19169—For Models 170000 and 190000.

19170—For Models 130000, 170000 and 190000.

19171—For Models 170000 and 190000.

19186—For Model 130000.

COUNTERBORE CUTTERS

19131—To install intake valve seat on Model 190000.

CRANKCASE SUPPORT JACK

19123—To support crankcase when removing and installing main bearing bushings on all models.

FLYWHEEL PULLERS

19069—For Models 60000, 80000, 90000, 110000 and 130000.

19165—For Models 170000 and 190000.

FLYWHEEL HOLDER

19167—For Models 60000, 80000, 90000, 110000 and 130000.

VALVE SPRING COMPRESSOR

19063—For all models.

PISTON RING COMPRESSOR

19070—For all models.

STARTER WRENCH

19114—All models with rewind starters.

19161—All models with rewind starters.

IGNITION SPARK TESTER

19051—For all models.

VALVE SEAT REPAIR TOOLS

19129—Planer shank-driver for counterbore cutter on all models.

19130—T-handle for planer shank 19129 on all models.

19135—Knockout pin to remove counterbore cutter from planer shank.

19137—T-handle for expansion pilots

19138—Insert puller to remove valve seats on all models (when puller nut 19140, included with 19138, is ground to 1/32-inch (0.8 mm) thick for pulling insert on aluminum alloy models).

19141—Puller nut to remove valve seats for Models 170000 and 190000.

19182—Puller nut to adapt 19138 puller to aluminum alloy models.

CLINTON

**CLINTON ENGINES
CORPORATION
Maquoketa, Iowa**

HP	Crankshaft	Basic Model (Series)	Bore	Stroke	Displacement
3 (2.24 kW)	Horizontal	500-0100-000	2⅛ in. (54 mm)	1⅝ in. (41.3 mm)	5.76 cu. in. (94.39 cc)

Fig. CL5—Exploded view of typical "LMG" series carburetor. "LMV" and "LMB" series are similar.

1. Throttle shaft
2. Choke shaft
3. Spring
4. Throttle disc
5. Spring
6. Carburetor body
7. Idle stop screw
8. Springs
9. Idle fuel needle
10. Spring
11. Choke disc
12. Inlet needle & seat
13. Main nozzle
14. Float
14A. Float pin
15. Gasket
16. Gaskets
17. Float bowl
18. Drain valve
19. Retainer
20. Seal
21. Spring
22. Main fuel needle
23. Lever (optional)

Clinton two-stroke engines are of aluminum alloy die-cast construction with an integral cast-in cast iron cylinder sleeve. Reed type inlet valves are used on all models.

MAINTENANCE

SPARK PLUG. Recommended spark plug is Champion J-12J or equivalent. Set electrode gap to 0.030 inch (0.76 mm). Use graphite on threads when installing spark plug and tighten spark plug to a torque of 275-300 in.-lbs. (31.05-33.88 N·m).

CARBURETOR. Clinton (Walbro designed) "LMB" and "LMG" float type carburetors are used. Refer to Fig. CL5 for exploded view of typical model.

For initial adjustment, open both of the fuel adjustment needles approximatley 1¼ turns. Make final adjustments with engine running at operating temperature. Move speed control to "fast" position and turn main fuel needle in or out to obtain maximum power under load. If load cannot be applied, turn main fuel needle in or out for smoothest engine operation; then, turn needle out (counterclockwise) approximately ⅛ to ¼-turn to provide a richer fuel mixture.

Move engine speed control to "slow" or idle position and adjust idle fuel needle and stop screw for best performance and correct idle speed. Check acceleration from slow to fast idle and open idle needle approximately ⅛-turn (counterclockwise) if necessary for proper acceleration.

When overhauling "LMB" and "LMG"

Fig. CL6—When original main fuel nozzle is removed from "LM" series carburetor, it must be discarded and service type nozzle shown must be installed.

carburetors and main fuel nozzle is removed, it must be discarded and a service type nozzle installed (See Fig. CL6). Do not reinstall old nozzle.

Float setting on "LMB" and "LMG" carburetors should be 5/32-inch (4.0 mm) clearance between outer rim of carburetor casting and top of free side of float. Bend tabs on float hinge to adjust float setting and to limit float travel to approximately 3/16-inch (4.8 mm) at free side of float.

GOVERNOR. Speed control is maintained by an air-vane type governor. Renew bent or worn governor vane or linkage and be sure that linkage does not bind in any position when moved through fulll range of travel.

Renew or re-tension governor spring to limit maximum speed to 3600 rpm. Be sure that blower housing is clean and free of dents that would cause binding of air vane.

MAGNETO AND TIMING. Ignition timing is 27 degrees BTDC and is nonadjustable. Specified armature air gap is 0.007-0.017 inch (0.18-0.43 mm). Adjust breaker contact gap to 0.018-0.021 inch (0.46-0.53 mm).

Fig. CL16—Magneto can be considered in satisfactory condition if it will fire an 18 mm spark plug with electrode gap set at 0.156-0.187 inch (3.96-4.75 mm).

Magneto may be considered satisfactory if it will fire an 18 mm spark plug with gap set at 0.156-0.187 inch (3.96-4.75 mm). Refer to Fig. CL16.

LUBRICATION. Use a high-quality outboard motor or two-stroke engine oil, SAE 30 weight. There are no precise API ratings for two-stroke engine oils; consequently, the safest course is to use oil identified by the refiner as designed for two-cycle or outboard motor use. Because of the high level of additives used in four-stroke (automotive) oils, their use should be avoided. Never use oils marked ML (light duty), DG (diesel) or SA (light duty). If an improper oil is used to meet an emergency, change to correct two-stroke oil as soon as possible and discard the improper fuel-oil mix.

Oil to gasoline mixing ratio is determined by type of bearings installed in a particular two-stroke engine. Plain sleeve main and connecting rod bearings require ¾-pint of oil for each gallon of gasoline. Engines equipped with needle bearings call for a mixing ratio of ½-pint of oil per gallon of gasoline. During break-in (first five hours of operation) a 50% increase of oil portion is advisable, especially if engine will be operated at or near maximum load or rpm.

CARBON. Power loss on two-stroke engines can often be corrected by cleaning the exhaust ports and muffler. To clean the exhaust ports, remove the muffler and turn engine until piston is below ports. Use a dull tool to scrape carbon from the ports; take care not to damage top of piston or cylinder walls.

REPAIRS

NOTE: Graphite should be applied to the threads of all screws which thread into die cast parts.

TIGHTENING TORQUES. Engine tightening torques are as follows:

Bearing plate to block .....75-95 in.-lbs.
(8.47-10.73 N·m)

Blower housing ....65-70 in.-lbs.
(7.34-7.90 N·m)
Carburetor mounting .....60-65 in.-lbs.
(6.77-7.90 N·m)
Connecting rod ....35-45 in.-lbs.
(3.95-5.08 N·m)
Engine base..........125-150 in.-lbs.
(14.11-16.94 N·m)
Flywheel.............375-400 in.lbs.
(42.34-45.17 N·m)
Muffler ....40-60 in.-lbs.
(2.46-6.75 N·m)
Spark plug...........275-300 in.-lbs.
(31.05-33.87 N·m)
Stator to bearing plate ....50-60 in.-lbs.
(5.65-7.90 N·m)

BEARING PLATE. Because of the pressure and vacuum pulsations in crankcase, bearing plate and gasket must form an air-tight seal when installed. Make sure gasket surfaces are not cracked, nicked or warped, that oil passages in crankcase, gasket and plate are aligned and that correct number and thickness of thrust washers are used. Also check to be sure the right cap screws are installed when engine is reassembled.

CAUTION: Cap screws (1 – Fig. C17) may bottom in threaded holes (2) if incorrect screws are used. When long screws are tightened, damage to cylinder walls can result.

CONNECTING ROD. Connecting rod and piston unit can be removed after removing the reed plate and crankshaft.

An aluminum connecting rod with bronze bearing surfaces is used. Recommended clearances are as follows:
Connecting rod to
crankshaft ....0.0026-0.004 in.
(0.635-0.10 mm)
Renew rod and/or crankshaft if
clearance exceeds ....0.0055 in.
(0.140 mm)
Connecting rod to
piston pin ....0.0004-0.0011 in.
(0.010-0.028 mm)
Renew rod and/or piston pin
if clearance exceeds ....0.002 in.
(0.05 mm)

Reinstall cap to connecting rod with embossments (A – Fig. CL18) aligned and carefully tighten screws to recommended torque value; bend the locking tabs against screw heads as shown in Fig. CL19.

PISTON, PIN AND RINGS. Pistons may be equipped with either two or three compression rings. On three-ring pistons, a locking wire is fitted in a small groove behind each piston ring to prevent ring rotation on the piston. To install the three locking wires, refer to Fig. CL20 and proceed as follows: Hold piston with top up and intake side of piston to right. Install top and bottom locking wires with locking tab (end of wire ring bent outward) to right of locating hole in ring groove and install center locking wire with locking tab to left of locating hole.

Piston and rings are available in oversizes of 0.010-inch (0.25 mm) and 0.020-inch (0.51 mm) as well as standard size. Piston pin is available in standard size only.

When installing pistons with ring locating pins or locking wires, be sure that end gaps of rings are properly located over the pins or the locking tabs and install piston using a ring compressor. Refer to Fig. CL20.

Be sure to reinstall piston and rod assembly with exhaust side of piston (long sloping side of piston dome) towards exhaust ports in cylinder.

Check piston, pin and rings against the following specifications:

Two-Ring Piston
Ring End Gap:
Desired ....0.007-0.017 in.
(0.18-0.43 mm)
Max. Allowable ....0.025 in.
(0.64 mm)

Ring Side Clearance:
Desired ....0.0015-0.004 in.
(0.038-0.10 mm)
Max. Allowable ....0.006 in.
(0.15 mm)

(See Next Page)

Fig. CL17—If cap screws (1) which thread into holes (2) are too long, they may bottom and damage cylinder walls.

OIL ACCESS OPENINGS

Fig. CL18—Be sure that embossments (A) are aligned when assembling cap to connecting rod.

BEND LOCKS UP

Fig. CL19—Bend connecting rod cap retaining screw locks up as shown.

Fig. CL20—View showing method of installing ring locking wires on 3-ring pistons and placement of rings on two and three-ring pistons. Some two-ring pistons do not have ring locking pins.

Skirt Clearance:
  Desired . . . . 0.005-0.007 in.
  (0.13-0.18 mm)
  Max. Allowable . . . . 0.008 in.
  (0.20 mm)

Three-Ring Piston
  Ring End Gap:
  Desired . . . . 0.010-0.015 in.
  (0.25-0.38 mm)
  Max. Allowable . . . . 0.017 in.
  (0.43 mm)
  Ring Side Clearance:
  Desired . . . . 0.002-0.004 in.
  (0.05-0.10 mm)
  Max. Allowable . . . . 0.0055 in.
  (0.140 mm)
  Skirt Clearance:
  Desired . . . . 0.0045-0.005 in.
  (0.114-0.13 mm)
  Max. Allowable . . . . 0.007 in.
  (0.18 mm)

All Models
Piston pin diameter . . . 0.4999-0.5001 in.
  (12.697-12.702 mm)
Pin bore in piston . . . . . 0.5000-0.5003 in.
  (12.700-12.708 mm)
Piston pin-to-rod clearance:
  Desired . . . . 0.0004-0.0011 in.
  (0.010-0.028 mm)
  Max. Allowable . . . . 0.002 in.
  (0.05 mm)

CYLINDER AND CRANKCASE.
The one-piece aluminum alloy cylinder and crankcase unit is integrally die-cast around a cast iron sleeve (cylinder liner).

Fig. CL22—Details of two-petal reed inlet valve used on some models.

Cylinder can be honed to 0.010-inch (0.25 mm) or 0.020-inch (0.51 mm) oversize for oversize piston and rings. Standard cylinder bore size is 2.125-2.126 inches (53.98-54.00 mm).

CRANKSHAFT. To remove crankshaft, proceed as follows: Remove blower housing and nut retaining flywheel to crankshaft. Thread an impact nut to within 1/8-inch (3.20 mm) of flywheel, pull on flywheel and tap impact nut with hammer. After flywheel is removed, remove magneto assembly. Remove the engine base and inlet reed valve plate from crankcase and detach connecting rod from crankshaft. Push connecting rod and piston unit up against top of cylinder. On models with ball bearing main on output end of crankshaft, remove the snap ring retaining ball bearing in crankcase. Remove the magneto stator plate and withdraw crankshaft from engine taking care not to damage connecting rod.

Fig. CL24 — Exploded view of typical 500-0100-000 series engine.

1. Muffler	10. Air cleaner	19. Piston	28. Breaker points
2. Gas tank assy.	11. Gasket	20. Wrist pin	29. Condenser
3. Fuel shut-off valve	12. Carburetor	21. Rings	30. Gasket
4. Block	13. Gasket	22. Link	31. Cover
5. Gasket	14. Reed valve plate	23. Bushing	32. Flywheel
6. Seal	15. Gasket	24. Bearing plate	33. Screen
7. Bushing	16. Gasket	25. Coil	34. Pulley
8. Reed valve	17. Crankshaft	26. Seal	35. Recoil starter
9. Reed valve stop	18. Rod	27. Bushing	36. Blower housing

On crankshafts used with plain bushing mains and/or cast-in crankpin bearing, check crankshaft against the following values:

Crankpin diameter . . . 0.7788-0.7795 in. (19.782-19.799 mm)
Main journal diameter, flywheel end . . . . 0.7495-0.7502 in. (19.037-19.055 mm)
Main journal diameter, output end . . . . 0.8745-0.8752 in. (22.212-22.230 mm)
or . . . . 0.995-1.002 in. (25.387-25.405 mm)
Rod, crankpin end I.D . 0.7829-0.7827 in. (19.860-19.881 mm)
Main bearing bushing I.D., flywheel end . . . . 0.7517-0.7525 in. (19.093-19.114 mm)
Main bearing bushing I.D., output end . . . . 0.8770-0.8780 in. (22.276-22.301 mm)
or . . . . 1.0020-1.0030 in. (25.451-25.476 mm)
Main bearing clearance, desired . . . . 0.0015-0.0030 in. (0.038-0.076 mm)
Max. allowable clearance . . . 0.0055 in. (0.140 mm)

Renew crankshaft if either main bearing journal or crankpin journal is out-of-round 0.0015-inch (0.038 mm) or more.

Main bearing bushings, bushing remover and driver, reamers and reamer alignment plate are available through Clinton parts sources for renewing bushings in crankcase and bearing plate. On vertical crankshaft engines having two bushings in crankcase, the outer bushing must be removed towards outside of crankcase and the inner bushing towards inside of crankcase. Bushings must be recessed 0.031-inch (0.79 mm) from insider surface of bearing plate or crankcase except when thrust washer is used between crankcase or plate and thrust surface of crankshaft.

Renew ball bearing type mains if bearing is rough or is worn. Renew needle type main bearings if one or more needles show any defect or if needles can be separated the width of one roller.

When reinstalling crankshaft with bushing or needle roller mains, crankshaft end play should be 0.005-0.020 inch (0.13-0.51 mm). The gasket used between bearing (stator) plate and crankcase is available in thicknesses of 0.025-inch (0.64 mm), 0.030-inch (0.76 mm) and 0.035-inch (0.90 mm) for adjusting crankshaft end play. It may also be necessary to renew crankshaft thrust washer.

There is no specification covering end play where ball type main bearing is used, however, crankshaft should turn freely after installation.

CRANKSHAFT OIL SEALS. As on all two-stroke engines, crankshaft oil seals must be maintained in good condition to hold crankcase compression on the downward stroke of the piston. It is usually good service procedure, therefore, to renew seals when overhauling an engine. apply a small amount of gasket sealer to outer rim of seal and install with lip towards inside of crankcase. Outer surface of seal should be flush with outer face of crankcase or bearing plate.

REED VALVE. The 3 degree setting of the dual reed shown in Fig. CL22 is the design of the reed as stamped in the manufacturing process. The 3 degree bend should be towards the reed seating surface. Reed stop should be adjusted to approximately 0.280-inch (7.11 mm) from tip of stop to reed seating surface.

Renew reed if any petal is cracked, rusted or does not lay flat against the reed plate. Renew reed plate if rusted, pitted or shows any signs of wear.

CLINTON SERVICE TOOLS

(500 SERIES ENGINES)

Bearing Tools

951-18 and 951-39 BEARING DRIVER. Used to remove and reinstall bearings in engine block.
951-48 REAMER GUIDE. Three bushings included with the following inside diameters: 0.878-inch (22.301 mm), 1.0003-inch (25.408 mm) and 1.030-inch (26.162 mm). Used to line ream bearing in engine block.
951-29 REAMER. Diameter, 0.877-inch (22.283 mm). Used to ream bearing in engine block.
951-30 REAMER. Diameter, 0.7518-0.7523 inch (19.096-19.108 mm). Used to ream bearing in bearing plates.

Flywheel and Crankshaft Tools

IMPACT NUTS. Impact or knock-off nuts are available for removing flywheels as follows:
951-23, for crankshafts having 7/16-inch threads.
951-36, for crankshafts having 7/8-inch threads.
951-66, for crankshafts having 1/2-inch threads.
951-133 FLYWHEEL PULLER
951-42 FLYWHEEL HOLDER
951-45 HAND CRANK. Used for turning engine when adjusting breaker point gap, checking timing etc.
951-64 CRANKSHAFT RUNOUT GAGE. Used for checking for bent crankshafts.

Oil Seal Pullers and Drivers

951-62 OIL SEAL DRIVER. Inside diameter, 0.760-inch (19.30 mm): outside diameter, 1-inch (25.40 mm).

Piston Ring Tools

951-153 SLEEVE FOR 2.125-inch (53.975 mm) BORE. Used for installing standard size and 0.020-inch (0.51 mm) oversize piston assemblies.

CLINTON

HP	Crankshaft	Basic Model (Series)	Bore	Stroke	Displacement
4½ (3.36 kW)	Horizontal	498-0301-000	2 15/32 in. 62.7 mm	2⅛ in. 54 mm	10.2 cu. in. 167 cc

MAINTENANCE

SPARK PLUG. All models use a 14 mm, ⅜-inch reach spark plug. Recommended plug is a Champion J-8 or equivalent. Set electrode gap to

Fig. CL46—Exploded view of typical "LMG" series carburetor. "LMV" and "LMB" series are similar.

1. Throttle shaft	13. Main nozzle
2. Choke shaft	14. Float
3. Spring	14A. Float pin
4. Throttle disc	15. Gasket
5. Spring	16. Gaskets
6. Carburetor body	17. Float bowl
7. Idle stop screw	18. Drain valve
8. Springs	19. Retainer
9. Idle fuel needle	20. Seal
10. Spring	21. Spring
11. Choke disc	22. Main fuel needle
12. Inlet needle & seat	23. Lever (optional)

0.025-0.028 inch (0.64-071 mm). When installing, apply graphite to threads and tighten to a torque of 275-300 in.-lbs. (31.05-33.88 N·m).

CARBURETOR. Several different carburetors, both suction lift and float type, have been used on this series of Clinton engines. Refer to the following paragraphs for information on each carburetor model.

NOTE: The throttle shaft on some carburetors may have several holes in which the throttle link and governor backlash spring (if used) may be installed. On these carburetors, be sure to mark the holes in which spring and linkage were installed so that they may be reinstalled correctly.

CLINTON FLOAT CARBURETORS. Several different Clinton "LMG" and "LMV" series float type carburetors have been used. To identify a particular carburetor, look for the identification number on carburetor body as shown in Fig. CL47.

Refer to the exploded view shown in Fig. CL46 for typical "LM" series carburetor. When overhauling or cleaning carburetor, do not remove main fuel nozzle (13) unless necessary. If nozzle is removed, it must be discarded and a service type nozzle (Fig. CL48) installed.

Install choke plate (11–Fig. CL46) with the "W" or part number to the outside. Install throttle plate with the side marked "W" facing towards mounting flange and with part number toward idle needle side of carburetor bore when plate by gently tapping with a small ing throttle plate, back idle speed adjustment screw out, turn plate and throttle shaft to closed position and seat plate by gently tapping with a small screwdriver before tightening plate retaining screws.

If either float or seat is damaged, install a new matched valve and seat assembly (12) and tighten seat to a torque of 40-50 in.-lbs. (4.52-5.65 N·m).

Fig. CL47—View showing locations of identification numbers on "LMB", "LMG" and "LMV" carburetors. Identification number must be used when ordering service parts.

When carburetor body (6) and float (14) assembly are inverted, there should be 5/32-inch (4.0 mm) clearance between body casting and free side of float.

Adjust float level by bending tab that contacts float valve. When carburetor body and float assembly are returned to normal position, float should not drop more than 3/16-inch (4.8 mm) at free side. Adjust by bending tab that contacts carburetor body.

Reassemble carburetor using new gaskets.

Initial adjustment for both idle needle and high speed is 1¼ turns open. Make final adjustment with engine at operating temperature. If engine does not accelerate properly, open high speed adjustment needle slightly.

CARTER FLOAT TYPE CARBURETORS. Refer to Fig. CL49 for exploded view typical of the Carter "N" series carburetors used on this group of Clinton engines. Some carburetors may differ as to shape of float and bowl.

Refer to the following chart for float setting and for initial adjustment (turns open) of idle and high speed fuel adjustment needles:

Carburetor Model	Float Setting	Initial Mixture Setting	
		Idle	High Speed
N-705S	13/64 in. (5.16 mm)	1½	1½
N-707S, SA	13/64 in. (5.16 mm)	1½	1½

(See Next Page)

Fig. CL48—When original main fuel nozzle is removed from "LM" series carburetor, it must be discarded and service type nozzle shown installed.

Fig. CL49—Exploded view of typical Carter Model "N" carburetor. Design of float and float bowl may vary from that shown.

1. Idle fuel needle	9. Inlet valve seat
2. Idle stop screw	10. Inlet needle
3. Throttle shaft	11. Float pin
4. Main fuel needle	12. Float bowl
5. Carburetor body	13. Retainer
6. Choke shaft	14. Float
7. Choke disc	15. Main nozzle
8. Detent ball	16. Throttle disc
8A. Spring	

Carburetor Model	Float Setting	Initial Mixture, Setting Idle	High Speed
N-2020S	11/64 in. (4.37 mm)	1½	1½
N-2147S	11/64 in. (4.37 mm)	1½	1½
N-2236S	11/64 in. (4.37 mm)	1	2
N-2246S	11/64 in. (4.37 mm)	1	1½
N-2399S	11/64 in. (4.37 mm)	1½	2

Carburetor Model	Float Setting	Initial Mixture, Setting Idle	High Speed
N-2449S	13/64 in. (5.16 mm)	1½	1½
N-2456S	13/64 in. (5.16 mm)	1½	1½
N-2459S	11/64 in. (4.37 mm)	1	1½
N-2466S	11/64 in. (4.37 mm)	1½	2

Float setting is measured by inverting carburetor casting and float assembly and gaging distance between casting and free side of float. Adjust by bending tab that contacts float valve.

Make final idle and high speed fuel mixture adjustments after engine is at operating temperature.

TILLOTSON FLOAT CARBURETOR. Some early models were equipped with Tillotson "ML" series carburetors. Float setting on ML carburetors is 1 5/64-1 3/32 inch (27.4-27.8 mm) from edge of carburetor casting to farthest side of float when carburetor body and float assembly is held in inverted position.

Initial adjustment for idle fuel adjustment needle is 1 turn open; initial adjustment for high speed needle is 1½ turns open. Make final adjustment with engine running at operating temperature.

ZENITH FLOAT TYPE CARBURETORS. Zenith float type carburetors 10390, 10658 and 10665 were used on some early model engines:

The 10390 model carburetor has only one fuel mixture adjustment needle. Adjust mixture screw so maximum high idle speed is obtained then set fuel mixture ¼-turn rich (counterclockwise). On Models 10658 and 10665, turning idle fuel mixture needle clockwise will enrichen the fuel mixture and turning the main fuel needle clockwise will lean the fuel mixture. Float setting is nonadjustable on this series of Zenith carburetors.

GOVERNOR. The mechanical governor is shown in the exploded view in Fig. CL56.

NOTE: The carburetor throttle shaft, governor arm and speed control devices may have several different holes in which springs and linkage can be installed. Before removing carburetor, governor arm, springs, linkage or controls, be sure to mark location of holes in which springs and linkage were installed so that they may be reassembled correctly.

Fig. CL49A—Magneto can be considered in satisfactory condition if it will fire an 18 mm spark plug with electrode gap set at 0.156-0.187 inch (3.96-4.75 mm).

TIMING. Condenser, breaker points and armature coil are located under flywheel on all models. Condenser capacity is 0.15-0.19 mfd. Adjust breaker point gap to 0.018-0.021 inch (0.46-0.53 mm). Specified armature air gap is 0.007-0.017 inch (0.18-0.43 mm). Timing is fixed and nonadjustable at 21 degrees BTDC.

Ignition system can be assumed to be in satisfactory condition if it will fire an 18 mm spark plug with the electrode gap set at 0.156-0.187 inch (3.96-4.75 mm). See Fig. CL49A.

LUBRICATION. Oil of "SE" or "SF" grade should be used. Use SAE 30 above 32°F (0°C), SAE 10W from −10°F (−23°C) and SAE 5W below −10°F (1−23°C)

Use SAE 30 oil in reduction gearbox if so equipped.

CRANKCASE BREATHER. Crankcase breather assembly (37A– Fig. CL56) should be removed and cleaned if difficulty is experienced with oil loss through hole in valve cover or whenever engine is being overhauled. Be sure that breather is correctly reassembled and reinstalled.

MECHANICAL GOVERNOR. The governor weight unit (26–Fig. CL56) is driven by the cam gear and is retained to the gear by a pin (27A) driven into the gear. Governor collar (27) has a notch in the inner flange of the collar which fits around weight unit retaining pin. Governor shaft (38A) is fitted with a square crosssection weight that contacts outer flange of governor collar and shaft is supported in a renewable bushing.

It is very important that travel of governor and carburetor throttle be synchronized. With engine not running,

Fig. CL52—When assembling cap to connecting rod, be sure that embossments on rod and cap are aligned as shown.

Fig. CL54—On early models, connecting rod bearing was lubricated by oil spray from hole in oil line as shown. Be sure the squared-off end of the oil line fits into the recess in oil pump adapter when reassembling engine.

move governor throttle arm (38) so that governor shaft holds governor weight unit in the fully closed position. At this time, there should be 1/32-1/16 inch (0.8-1.6 mm) clearance between high speed stop on carburetor throttle arm and carburetor casting. To obtain this adjustment, loosen adjustment screw (38B) and reposition arm (38) on adjuster (38C) and tighten adjustment screw (38B).

Adjust desired maximum speed (do not exceed 3600 rpm) by adjusting tension of govern spring (39).

CAUTION: Do not use any spring other than correct Clinton part specified for a particular engine as spring must be balanced to governor weight unit for proper speed control.

On most models, a backlash spring is used to hold any free play out of governor to carburetor linkage and thereby reduce any tendency for engine to surge.

REPAIRS

TIGHTENING TORQUES. Recommended torque values are as follows:
Adapter flange . . . . .120-150 in.lbs.
            (13.55-16.94 N·m)
Base bolts . . . . .325-375 in.lbs.
            (36.70-42.34 N·m)
Carburetor to manifold . . . .35-50 in.lbs.
            (3.95-4.17 N·m)
Carburetor (or manifold) to
    block . . . . .60-65 in.lbs.
            (6.78-7.34 N·m)
Connecting rod . . . . .70-80 in.lbs.
            (7.90-9.03 N·m)
Cylinder head . . . . .200-220 in.lbs.
            (22.58-24.84 N·m)
End cover . . . . .120-150 in.lbs.
            (13.55-16.94 N·m)
Flywheel . . . . .400-450 in.lbs.
            (45.17-50.81 N·m)*
Spark plug . . . . .275-300 in.lbs.
            (31.05-33.88 N·m)
Stator plate . . . . .50-60 in.lbs.
            (4.17-6.78 N·m)
*350 in.lbs. (39.52 N·m) maximum on 7/16-inch (11.1 mm) crankshaft.

CONNECTING ROD. Rod and piston assembly can be removed from engine after cylinder head and crankshaft rear cover are removed.

Recommended clearances are as follows:
Connecting rod to
    crankshaft . . . . .0.0018-0.0035 in.
            (0.046-0.089 mm)
    Maximum allowable . . . . . . .0.0045 in.
            (0.114 mm)
Connecting rod to piston
    pin . . . . .0.0004-0.0011 in.
            (0.010-0.028 mm)
    Maximum allowable . . . . .0.002 in.
            (0.05 mm)
Rod side play . . . . .0.005-0.020 in.
            (0.13-0.51 mm)
Connecting rod is available in standard size only. When reassembling, be sure that embossments on connecting rod and cap are aligned as shown in Fig. CL52. Oil hole or oil access slot in connecting rod should face flywheel side of engine. On some models, the connecting rod has a "clearance side" which must be towards the camshaft. Be sure that rod locks and oil distributor (on horizontal crankshaft models) clears the camshaft after assembly.

PISTON, PIN AND RINGS. Piston is fitted with two compression rings and one oil control ring. Recommended piston ring end gap is 0.007-0.017 inch (0.18-0.43 mm). Renew rings if end gap of top ring is 0.025 inch (0.64 mm) or more. Specified ring side clearance in groove is 0.002-0.005 inch (0.05-0.13 mm). Maximum allowable side clearance is 0.006 inch (0.15 mm). Rings are available in oversizes of 0.010 inch (0.25 mm) and 0.020 inch (0.51 mm) as well as standard size.

Piston pin is retained in piston with a snap ring at each end of pin. Piston pin is available in standard size only and should be a "hand push fit" in piston. Specifications are as follows:

Piston pin diameter . . .0.5624-0.5626 in.
            (14.285-14.290 mm)
Pin bore in piston . . . . .0.5625-0.5628 in.
            (14.287-14.295 mm)

Pin bore in rod . . . . . . .0.5630-0.5635 in.
            (14.300-14.313 mm)
Max. pin to rod clearance . . . . .0.002 in.
            (0.05 mm)

Specified piston skirt clearance is 0.005-0.007 inch (0.13-0.18 mm). Maximum skirt clearance for all models is 0.008 inch (0.20 mm). Piston is available in oversizes of 0.010 inch (0.25 mm) and 0.020 inch (0.51 mm) as well as standard size.

CYLINDER. Standard cylinder bore diameter is 2.4685-2.4695 inches (62.700-62.725 mm).

If piston skirt clearance is 0.008 inch (0.20 mm) or more with new piston or ring gap is 0.025 inch (0.64 mm) or more with new rings, cylinder must be rebored or honed and oversize piston and rings installed or cylinder and crankcase assembly must be renewed. Piston and rings are available in oversizes of 0.010 inch (0.25 mm) and 0.020 inch (0.51 mm) as well as standard size.

CRANKSHAFT. Specified connecting rod to crankpin clearance is 0.0018-0.0035 inch (0.046-0.089 mm). Renew rod and/or crankshaft if clearance exceeds 0.0045 inch (0.114 mm). Standard crankpin diameter is either 0.8745-0.8752 inch (22.212-22.230 mm) or 0.9114-0.9120 inch (23.150-23.165 mm). Specified maximum out-of-round is 0.001 inch (0.03 mm). Renew crankshaft if crankpin is out-of-round 0.0015 inch (0.038 mm). Connecting rod is available in standard size only.

Specified main bearing clearance is 0.0018-0.0035 inch (0.046-0.089 mm) on all plain bushing models. Renew crankshaft and/or bushings if clearance exceeds 0.005 inch (0.13 mm). Flywheel end journal diameter is 0.8745-0.8752 inch (22.212-22.230 mm). Pto end journal diameter is either 0.8745-0.8752 inch (22.212-22.230 mm) or 0.9995-1.0002 inch (25.387-25.405 mm). Bushings are available in standard size only and must be reamed after installation for proper size. Bushing driving tools, reamers and reamer alignment plates are available through Clinton parts sources.

Inspect tapered roller main bearings and renew bearing cones and cups if roller or cup is scored or rough.

Specified crankshaft end play is 0.001-0.006 inch (0.03-0.15 mm) with a maximum allowable end play of 0.008 inch (0.20 mm). Bearing plate gaskets are available in thicknesses of 0.005 inch (0.13 mm), 0.010 inch (0.25 mm), 0.015 inch (0.38 mm) and 0.020 inch (0.51 mm) for adjustment of end play.

CAMSHAFT AND GEAR. The hollow camshaft and cam gear unit rotates on an axle that is pressed into the engine crankcase. Camshaft can be removed after removing engine crankshaft and pressing camshaft axle from crankcase. On models with mechanical governor, governor weight unit is attached to cam gear by a pin that is pressed into the gear.

Specified operating clearance between camshaft axle and camshaft is 0.001-0.003 inch (0.03-0.08 mm). Renew axle and/or camshaft if clearance exceeds 0.005 inch (0.13 mm).

Specified camshaft end play is 0.003-0.010 inch (0.08-0.25 mm). Maximum allowable camshaft end play is 0.015 inch (0.38 mm).

VALVE SYSTEM. Recommended valve tappet gap for both intake and exhaust valves is 0.009-0.011 inch (0.23-0.28 mm). Adjust clearance by grinding end of valve stem. A 45 degree bevel should be maintained on ends of stems. Specified valve face angle is 45 degrees and valve seat angle is between 43½ and 44½ degrees. Specified seat width is 0.030-0.045 inch (0.76-1.14 mm). Recut seat width with combination tool 951-37 which has cutters of 44 and 30 degrees. Do not allow seat width to exceed 0.060 inch (1.52 mm).

Valve head margin for a new valve is 1/32-inch (0.8 mm). When margin is reduced by regrinding and wear to 1/64-inch (0.4 mm), valve should be renewed.

Recommended valve stem-to-guide clearance is 0.002-0.0045 inch (0.05-0.114 mm). If clearance is 0.006 inch (0.15 mm) or more, guides may be reamed to 0.260 inch (6.60 mm) or 0.2812 inch (7.142 mm) for valves with 0.010 inch (0.25 mm) or 0.031 inch (0.79 mm) oversize stem. Also, valve guide may be knurled and reamed to 0.250 inch (6.35 mm) for standard size stem.

Stellite exhaust valves and seats are available; also, stellite exhaust valves with roto-caps are available for service. Install regular exhaust valve in place of intake valve if installing a stellite exhaust valve with seat. Stellite valves are available with standard and 0.010 inch (0.25 mm) oversize stems only.

Intake and exhaust valves are actuated by mushroom type tappets that ride directly in unbushed bores in engine crankcase. Tappet stem diameter is 0.2475-0.2485 inch (6.287-6.312 mm). Tappet guide bore diameter is 0.2495-0.2510 inch (6.337-6.375 mm). Tappets are available in standard size only. If guides are worn excessively, they may be knurled and reamed with same tools as used to knurl and ream

valve guides. Tappets may be removed from engine block after removing camshaft.

CAUTION: If ends of valve stems or ends of tappet stems have become enlarged or burred, do not force stems through bores in block. Remove burrs with emery cloth before attempting to remove valves and tappets.

Valve seat inserts are available for service; also, tools for cutting counterbore and installing valve seat inserts are available through Clinton parts sources.

Fig. CL56 — Exploded view of Model 498-0000-000 series engine.

1. Cylinder head
2. Head gasket
3. Oil filler cap
4. Block
5. Rings
6. Piston
7. Wrist pin
8. Retainer
9. Rod
10. Bearing
11. Bearing race
12. Gasket
13. Woodruff key
14. Seal
15. Bearing plate
16. Fuel shut-off valve
17. Oil dipper
18. Lock tab
19. Coil
20. Contacts
21. Cover & gasket
22. Condenser
23. Camshaft axle
24. Tappets
25. Camshaft
26. Weight assy.
27. Collar
27A. Pin
28. Valve keeper
29. Retainer
30. Spring
31. Intake valve
32. Exhaust valve
33. Valve seat
34. Muffler
35. Seal
36. Gasket
37. Valve cover
37A. Breather
38. Governor lever
38A. A governor shaft
38B. Screw
38C. Adjuster
39. Governor spring
40. Adjustable link
41. Base
42. Intake manifold
43. Gasket
44. Gasket
45. Carburetor
46. Air cleaner
47. Blower housing
48. Flywheel
49. Screen
50. Starter pulley
51. Adapter
52. Recoil starter

Fig. CL102—Exploded view of late production Clinton rewind starter.

7. Actuator spring
8. Pulley
9. Pan head screw
10. Housing
11. Handle
12. Rope
13. Nut & washer assy.
14. Spring

1. Starter cup
2. Snap ring
3. Actuator
4. Snap ring
5. Washer
6. Pawl & pin assy.

Fig. CL119—Exploded view of polyurethane air cleaner.

1. Gasket
2. Body
3. Retainer
4. Element
5. Cover
6. Screws

SERVICING CLINTON ACCESSORIES

REWIND STARTERS

Exploded view of rewind starter currently used on most Clinton engines is shown in Fig. CL102. Care should be taken when reassembling all starters to be sure the recoil spring is not wound too tightly. The spring should be wound tight enough to rewind the rope, but so the spring will not be fully wound when the rope is pulled out to full length. Coat spring and all internal parts with Lubriplate or equivalent grease when reassembling. Be sure that spring, pulley and related parts are assembled for correct rotation.

MAINTENANCE

POLYURETHANE AIR CLEANER. Some Clinton models are equipped with a polyurethane air filter element. After each 10 hours of use, the element should be removed and washed in solvent or kerosene. (Element may be washed in detergent soap and water.) Re-oil the element with 10 weight or 10-30 weight motor oil and wring out to remove excess oil. Insert the element evenly into air cleaner housing and snap cover in place. See Fig. CL119 for exploded view of this type air cleaner.

CLINTON SERVICE TOOLS

(498 SERIES ENGINES)

Oil Seal Loaders (Installation Sleeves)

951-12, 951-57, 951-145. Diameter, 0.750-inch (19.050 mm) OD. For installing oil seals over shafts.

Flywheel and Crankshaft Tools

IMPACT NUTS. Impact or knock-off nuts are available for removing flywheels as follows:
951-23, for crankshafts having 7/16-inch threads.
951-36, for crankshafts having 7/8-inch threads.
951-66, for crankshafts having 1/2-inch threads.

951-133 FLYWHEEL PULLER

951-42 FLYWHEEL HOLDER

951-45 HAND CRANK. Used for turning engine when adjusting breaker point gap, checking timing etc.

951-64 CRANKSHAFT RUNOUT GAGE. Used for checking for bent crankshafts.

Valve Tools

951-22 VALVE GUIDE REAMER. Diameter, 0.281-inch (7.14 mm). Used to enlarge valve guide holes so oversize stemmed valves can be used.

951-58 VALVE GUIDE PILOT ASSEMBLY. Used in conjunction with 951-37 valve seat cutter and 951-41 & 951-61 counter cutters.

951-37 VALVE SEAT CUTTER. Used to reface valve seats.

951-53 ROLLING TOOL. Used to peen or roll metal around outside diameter of valve seat insert after installation.

Camshaft Tool

951-46 CAMSHAFT AXLE DRIVER. Used to drive camshaft axle from block.

KOHLER

KOHLER COMPANY
Kohler, Wisconsin 53044

HP	Crankshaft	Basic Model (Series)	Bore	Stroke	Displacement
4	Horizontal	K91	2³/₈-in.	2 in.	8.86 in.
(2.98 kW)			(60.3 mm)	(50.8 mm)	(145 cc)

MAINTENANCE

SPARK PLUG. Recommended plug is Champion J-8, AC-C45, Autolite A7 or Prestolite 14-7. Electrode gap is 0.025-inch (0.64 mm).

CARBURETOR. Engines are equipped with the Kohler carburetor shown in Fig. KO2.

For initial adjustment, open idle fuel needle 1½ turns and open main fuel needle 2 turns. Make final adjustment with engine warm and running. Place engine under load and adjust main fuel needle for leanest setting that will allow satisfactory acceleration and steady governor operation. Adjust idle speed stop screw to maintain an idle speed of 1000 rpm, then adjust idle needle for smoothest idle operation. As adjustments affect each other, the adjustment sequence may have to be repeated.

To check float level, invert carburetor casting and float assembly. There should be 13/64-inch (5.2 mm) between free side of float and machined surface of body casting. If not, carefully bend float lever tang that contacts inlet valve as necessary to provide correct measurement.

GOVERNOR. A mechanical flyball type governor with external adjustments is used. The governor flyball unit is attached to and rotates with the camshaft gear. Refer to Fig. KO4 for exploded view of governor flyball unit. Engine speed is controlled by tension on governor spring (B – Fig. KO5).

NOTE: Maximum (no load) engine speed is 4000 rpm.

Before attempting to adjust governed speed, synchronize linkage as follows: Loosen clamp bolt nut (N) and using a pair of pliers, turn shaft (H) counterclockwise as far as possible. Pull arm (L) completely to the left (away

from carburetor) and tighten clamp bolt nut. To increase or decrease maximum engine speed, vary tension of governor spring (B). On engine with remote throttle control, this is accomplished by moving bracket (F) up or down; on engines without remote throttle control, by rotating disc (D) after loosening bushing (C).

MAGNETO AND TIMING. Bendix Scintilla K1-300 or Phelon Model F2100 (now called Repco) is used. Recommended spark timing is 20 degrees BTDC.

A timing port is provided in left side of bearing plate and there are two timing marks on the flywheel. (See Fig. KO6.) Satisfactory timing is obtained by adjusting breaker contact gap to 0.020 inch (0.51 mm). For precision timing, use timing light and adjust breaker gap until the first or "SP" timing mark is centered in timing port, engine running.

On Bendix-Scintilla (Fig. KO7) equipped engines, a wave washer is installed on crankshaft between magneto rotor and flywheel; on Phelon (Fig. KO6) equipped engines, the wave washer is omitted.

LUBRICATION. Crankcase capacity is approximately 1½ pints. Use SAE 30 oil when operating in temperatures above 30°F (−1°C), SAE 10W-30 in temperatures between 0°F (−18°C) and 30°F (−1°C) and SAE 5W-20 in

Fig. KO2 – Exploded view of Kohler carburetor used on late production engines.

1. Main fuel needle
2. Spring
3. Carburetor body assy.
4. Spring
5. Idle speed stop screw
6. Spring
7. Idle fuel needle
8. Sealing washer
9. Inlet valve seat
10. Inlet valve
11. Float pin
12. Float
13. Gasket
14. Float bowl
15. Sealing washer
16. Bowl retainer

Fig. KO4 – Exploded view of camshaft and flyball governor assembly.

1. Snap ring
2. Thrust cone
3. Steel balls
4. Flyball retainer
5. Camshaft
6. Camshaft pin

Fig. KO5 – Points of adjustment of governor.

temperatures below 0°F (−18°C). Use high quality motor oil having API classification SE or SF. An oil dipper which is attached to the connecting rod cap provides for splash type lubrication. On engines with reduction gear power take-off, use same grade oil in reduction gear housing as used in crankcase.

CRANKCASE BREATHER. The crankcase breather, which serves to eliminate oil leaks at crankcase seals, is attached to valve cover plate. There should be 1/64-1/32 inch (0.4-0.8 mm) clearance between flapper valve and its seat. If a slight amount of crankcase vacuum is not present, breather valve is faulty or engine has excessive blow-by past rings and/or valves.

AIR CLEANER. Engines may be equipped with either an oil bath type air cleaner shown in Fig. KO8 or a dry element type shown in Fig. KO9.

Oil bath air cleaner should be serviced every 25 hours of operation or more often if operating in extremely dusty conditions. To service the oil bath type, remove complete cleaner assembly from engine. Remove cover and element from

FILL TO LEVEL MARK
WITH SAME OIL AS ENGINE

Fig. KO8 — View of oil bath type air cleaner.

USE GENUINE KOHLER ELEMENT

Fig. KO9 — Exploded view of dry element type air cleaner.

bowl. Empty used oil from bowl, then clean cover and bowl in solvent. Clean element in solvent and allow to drip dry. Lightly re-oil element. Fill bowl to oil level marked on bowl using same grade and weight oil as used in engine crankcase. Renew gaskets as necessary when reassembling and reinstalling unit.

Dry element type air cleaner should be cleaned every 100 hours of operation or more frequently if operating in dusty conditions. Remove dry element and tap element lightly on a flat surface to remove surface dirt. Do not wash ele-

ment or attempt to clean element with compressed air. Renew element if extremely dirty or if it is bent, crushed or otherwise damaged. Make certain the sealing surfaces of element seal effectively against the back plate and cover.

REPAIRS

TIGHTENING TORQUES. Specified tightening torques are as follows:
Spark plug . . . . 325 in.-lbs.
(36.70 N·m)
Connecting rod cap screws *140 in.-lbs.
(15.81 N·m)
Cylinder head cap screws . . 200 in.-lbs.*
(22.58 N·m)
Flywheel retaining nut . . . . . 540 in.-lbs.
(60.98 N·m)
*With threads lubricated.

CONNECTING ROD. Connecting rod assembly is removed from above after removing cylinder head and oil pan (engine base). The aluminum alloy connecting rod rides directly on the crankpin. A connecting rod with 0.010-inch (0.25 mm) undersize crankpin bore is available for reground crankshaft. Oversize piston pins are also available. Desired running clearances are as follows:
Connecting rod to
crankpin . . . . 0.001-0.0025 in.
(0.3-0.064 mm)
Connecting rod to
piston pin . . . . 0.0005-0.001 in.
(0.013-0.3 mm)
Connecting rod side
play on crankpin . . . . . . 0.005-0.016 in.
(0.13-0.41 mm)

Fig. KO6 — Phelon (Repco) magneto installation.
A. Magnets
B. Timing marks
C. Coil
D. Condenser

Fig. KO7 — Bendix-Scintilla magneto installation. Rotating magnet (E) is pressed on crankshaft.
A. Ground button
B. Bearing plate
C. Magneto coil
D. Pole shoes
E. Rotating magnet
F. Condenser

Fig. KO10 — Tighten cylinder head cap screws to a torque of 200 in.-lbs. in sequence shown.

Standard crankpin diameter is 0.9355-0.936 inch (23.762-23.77 mm). Standard piston pin diameter is 0.563-inch (14.27 mm).

When reinstalling connecting rod and piston assembly, piston can be installed either way on rod, but make certain the match marks on connecting rod and cap are aligned and are towards flywheel side of engine. Tighten connecting rod cap screws to a torque of 140 in.-lbs. (15.81 N·m) (with threads lubricated).

PISTON, PIN AND RINGS. The aluminum alloy piston is fitted with two 0.093-inch (2.34 mm) wide compression rings and one 0.187-inch (4.75 mm) wide oil control ring. Renew piston if scored or if side clearance of new ring in piston top groove exceeds 0.005-inch (0.13 mm). Pistons and rings are available in oversizes of 0.010-inch (0.25 mm), 0.020-inch (0.51 mm) and 0.030-inch (0.76 mm) as well as standard. Piston pin fit in piston bore should be from 0.0002-inch (0.005 mm) interference to 0.0002-inch (0.005 mm) loose. Piston pins are available in oversizes of 0.005-inch (0.13 mm) and 0.010-inch (0.25 mm). Always renew piston pin retaining rings.

Recommended piston-to-cylinder bore clearance (measured at thrust face of piston) is 0.003-0.004 inch (0.08-0.10 mm).

Piston ring specifications are as follows:

Ring end gap . . . . .0.007-0.017 inch
(0.18-0.43 mm)

Ring side clearance:
Compression rings . .0.003-0.004 inch
(0.08-0.10 mm)
Oil control ring. . . .0.0015-0.0035 inch
(0.04-0.09 mm)

If compression ring has a groove or bevel on outside surface, install ring with groove or bevel down. If groove or bevel is on inside surface of compression ring, install ring or bevel up. Oil control ring can be installed either side up.

CYLINDER HEAD. Always use a new head gasket when installing cylinder head. Tighten cylinder head cap screws evenly and in steps using the sequence shown in Fig. KO10 until a tightening torque of 200 in.-lbs. (22.58 N·m) is reached.

CYLINDER BLOCK. If cylinder wall is scored or bore is tapered or out-of-round more than 0.005 inch (0.13 mm), hone cylinder to nearest suitable oversize of either 0.010-inch (0.25 mm), 0.020-inch (0.51 mm) or 0.030-inch (0.76 mm). Standard cylinder bore diameter is 2.375 inches (60.33 mm).

CAMSHAFT. The hollow camshaft

Fig. KO11 — Exploded view of typical engine. Breaker points (55) are actuated by cam on right end of camshaft (27) through push rod (56).

1. Spark plug	29. Steel balls	43. Breather reed
2. Air baffle	30. Thrust cone	44. Breather plate
3. Cylinder head	31. Snap ring	45. Gaskets
4. Head gasket	32. Spring retainer	46. Governor shaft
5. Cylinder block	33. Valve spring	47. Bracket
6. Piston rings	34. Valve tappets	48. Link
7. Piston	35. Exhaust valve	49. Speed disc
8. Piston pin	36. Intake valve	50. Bushing
9. Retaining rings	37. Muffler	51. Governor spring
10. Connecting rod	38. Carburetor	52. Governor lever
11. Rod cap	39. Air cleaner assy.	53. Breaker cover
12. Rod bolt lock	40. Valve cover	54. Gasket
13. Oil seal	41. Filter	55. Breaker points
14. Ball bearing	42. Breather seal	56. Push rod
15. Crankshaft		
16. Gasket		
17. Bearing plate		
18. Magneto		
19. Flywheel		
20. Pulley		
21. Shroud		
22. Screen retainer		
23. Screen		
24. Oil pan		
25. Gasket		
26. Camshaft pin		
27. Camshaft		
28. Flyball retainer		

and integral cam gear (27 – Fig. KO11) rotate on a pin (26). To remove camshaft, first remove bearing plate (17) and crankshaft, then drive pin out towards bearing plate side of crankcase. Camshaft pin is a press fit in closed (pto) side of crankcase and a slip fit in bearing plate side. Specified slip fit clearance of camshaft pin in bearing plate side is 0.0005-0.0012 inch (0.013-0.030 mm). Specified camshaft-to-camshaft pin clearance is 0.001-0.0025 inch (0.03-0.064 mm). Desired camshaft end play is 0.005-0.020 inch (0.13-0.51 mm) and is adjusted by installing shim washers between camshaft and bearing plate side of crankcase. Shim washers are available in thicknesses of 0.005-inch (0.13 mm) and 0.010-inch (0.25 mm). Flyball retainer (28), flyballs (29), thrust cone (30) and snap ring (31) are attached to and rotate with camshaft assembly.

CRANKSHAFT. The crankshaft is

supported in two ball bearing mains. Renew ball bearings (14 – Fig. KO11) if excessively loose or rough. Desired crankshaft end play of 0.0038-0.0228 inch (0.096-0.579 mm) is controlled by thickness of bearing plate gaskets (16). Gaskets in thicknesses of 0.010-inch (0.25 mm) and 0.020-inch (0.51 mm) are available.

Standard crankpin journal diameter is 0.9355-0.9360 inch (23.762-23.774 mm). Specified connecting rod to crankpin journal running clearance is 0.001-0.0025 inch (0.03-0.064 mm). Crankpin journal may be ground to 0.010-inch (0.25 mm) undersize for use of undersize connecting rod if journal is scored or out-of-round.

When installing crankshaft, align timing marks on crankshaft gear and camshaft gear. Install seals (13) in crankcase and bearing plate after crankshaft and bearing plate are installed. Carefully work seals over crankshaft with lips to inside and drive seals into place with hollow driver that contacts outer edge of seals.

VALVE SYSTEM. Valve tappet gap (cold) is 0.005-0.009 inch (0.13-0.23 mm) for intake valve and 0.011-0.015 inch (0.28-0.38 mm) for exhaust valve. Correct tappet gap is obtained by grinding end of valve stems squarely. Be sure to remove all burrs from end of stem after grinding.

The exhaust valve seats on a renewable seat insert and intake valve seats directly on machined seat in cylinder block. Intake and exhaust valve seats are available for service. Valve face and seat angle is 45 degrees. Desired seat width is 0.037-0.045 inch (0.94-1.14 mm).

Specified valve stem clearance in guide is 0.0005-0.002 inch (0.013-0.05 mm) for intake valve and 0.002-0.0035 inch (0.01-0.089 mm) for exhaust valve. Valve guides are not renewable. Excessive valve stem-to-guide clearance is corrected by reaming guides and installing new valves with 0.005-inch (0.13 mm) oversize stems. Standard valve stem diameter is 0.248-0.2485 inch (6.30-6.312 mm) for intake valve and 0.246-0.2465 inch (6.25-6.261 mm) for exhaust valve.

KOHLER

HP	Crankshaft	Basic Model (Series)	Bore	Stroke	Displacement
6.25 (4.66 kW)	Horizontal	K-141	2.94 in. (74.7 mm)	2.50 in. (63.5 mm)	16.9 cu. in. (276.9 cc)
7 (5.22 kW)	Horizontal	K-161	2.94 in. (74.7 mm)	2.50 in. (63.5 mm)	16.9 cu. in. (276.9 cc)
8 (5.97 kW)	Horizontal	K-181	2.94 in. (74.7 mm)	2.75 in. (69.8 mm)	18.6 cu. in. (304.8 cc)
10 (7.46 kW)	Horizontal	K-241	3.25 in. (82.5 mm)	2.88 in. (73 mm)	23.9 cu. in. (391.6 cc)

Model K-141 engine has a ball bearing main at pto end of crankshaft, a bushing type main bearing at flywheel end of crankshaft and is equipped with an up-draft carburetor. All other engines of this series have ball bearing mains at each end of crankshaft and are equipped with a side draft carburetor.

All models are horizontal crankshaft engines and are splash lubricated.

MAINTENANCE

SPARK PLUG. Recommended plug for Model K-241 engine is Champion H-10; all other standard engines in series use a Champion J-8 spark plug. For renewal of radio shielded spark plugs, use Champion EH-10 in Model K-241 engine and Champion EJ-8 in other models. Set electrode gap to 0.020 inch (0.51 mm) on radio shielded plug and to 0.025 inch (0.635 mm) on standard plug.

CARBURETOR. Model K-141 engines are equipped with a Tillotson "E" series updraft carburetor. Models K-161, K-181 and K-241 engines are equipped with Kohler side draft carburetors. Refer to appropriate following paragraph for carburetor service information.

Fig. KO12 — Exploded view of Kohler carburetor used on Models K-161, K-181 and K-241.

1. Main fuel needle
2. Spring
3. Carburetor body assy.
4. Spring
5. Idle speed stop screw
6. Spring
7. Idle fuel needle
8. Sealing washer
9. Inlet valve seat
10. Inlet valve
11. Float pin
12. Float
13. Gasket
14. Float bowl
15. Sealing washer
16. Bowl retainer

Fig. KO13 — Exploded view of Tillotson "E" series carburetor used on Model K-141 engine. Refer to Fig. KO14 for method checking float level.

1. Float bowl cover
2. Gasket
3. Gasket
4. Inlet valve assy.
5. Float
6. Gasket
7. Carburetor body
8. Choke shaft
9. Spring
10. Idle speed stop screw
11. Packing
12. Washer
13. Spring
14. Main fuel needle
15. Screw plug
16. Choke disc
17. Idle fuel needle
18. Spring
19. Throttle shaft
20. Spring
21. Choke shaft detent
22. Plug
23. Throttle disc
24. Float pin

KOHLER CARBURETOR. Refer to Fig. KO12 for exploded view of Kohler carburetor. For initial adjustment, open main fuel needle 2 turns and open idle fuel needle 1¼ turns. Make final adjustment with engine warm and running. Place engine under load and adjust main fuel needle (1) to the leanest mixture that will allow satisfactory acceleration and steady governor operation. If engine misses and backfires under load,

mixture is too lean. If engine shows a sooty exhaust and is sluggish under load, mixture is too rich.

Adjust idle speed stop screw (5) to maintain an idle speed of 1000 rpm.

Then, adjust idle fuel needle (7) for smoothest idle operation.

Since main fuel and idle fuel adjustments have some effect on each other, recheck engine operation and readjust fuel needles as necessary for smoothest operation.

To check float level, invert carburetor body and float assembly. There should be 11/64-inch (4.4 mm) clearance between machined surface of body casting and free end of float. Adjust as necessary by bending float lever tang that contacts inlet valve.

Fig. KO14—Check float setting on Tillotson carburetor by inverting float bowl cover and float assembly and measuring distance from free end of float to edge of cover as shown. Float setting is correct if distance is 1 5/64 inches (27.4 mm).

Fig. KO18—On Models K-141, K-161 and K-181, loosen bushing nut (C—Fig. KO17) and move throttle bracket as shown to change governed speed of engine.

TILLOTSON CARBURETOR. Refer to Fig. KO13 for exploded view of Tillotson E series carburetor similar to that used on Model K-141 engine. The design of choke shaft lever will differ from that shown in the exploded view.

For initial adjustment, open the idle fuel needle (17) about ¾-turn and open main fuel needle (14) one turn. Make final adjustment with engine running at operating temperature. Adjust main fuel needle so that engine will accelerate smoothly without misfiring or smoky exhaust. Then, adjust idle fuel needle for smoothest idle performance. Recheck for smooth acceleration and readjust main fuel needle, if necessary.

Check float level as shown in Fig. KO14. If measurement is not 1 5/64 inches (27.4 mm) as shown, remove float and carefully bend float lever tang as necessary to provide correct level measurement.

Fig. KO15—View showing "Thermostatic" automatic choke used on some engines equipped with Kohler carburetors.

AUTOMATIC CHOKE. Some models equipped with Kohler carburetors are also equipped with an automatic choke. The "Thermostatic" type shown in Fig. KO15 is used on manual start models.

Fig. KO17—Drawing showing governor lever and related parts on Models K-141, K-161 and K-181.

A. Drive pin
B. Governor spring
C. Bushing nut
D. Speed control disc
E. Throttle bracket
F. Governor shaft
G. Governor lever

Fig. KO20—View showing governor adjusting points on K-241. Governor sensitivity is adjusted by moving governor spring to alternate holes.

THERMOSTATIC TYPE. To adjust the "Thermostatic" type, loosen lock screw (Fig. KO15) and rotate adjustment bracket as necessary to obtain correct amount of choking. Tighten lock screw. In cold temperature, choke should be closed. At a temperature of 70°-75° F (21°-24° C), choke should be partially open and choke lever should be in vertical position. Start engine and allow it to run until normal operating temperature is obtained. Choke should be fully open when engine is at normal operating temperature.

GOVERNOR. All models are equipped with a gear driven flyweight governor that is located inside engine crankcase. Maximum recommended governed engine speed is 3600 rpm on all engines. Recommended idle speed of 1000 rpm is controlled by adjustment of throttle stop screw on carburetor.

Before attempting to adjust engine governed speed, synchronize the governor linkage on all models as follows: On Models K-141, K-161 and K-181, loosen the bolt clamping governor arm (G—Fig. KO17) to governor cross shaft (F) and turn governor cross shaft counterclockwise as far as possible. While holding cross shaft in this position, move governor arm away from carburetor to limit of linkage travel and tighten clamping bolt.

On Model K-241 refer to Fig. KO20 and loosen governor arm hex nut. Rotate governor cross shaft counterclockwise as far as possible, move governor arm away from carburetor to limit of linkage travel, then tighten hex nut on arm.

To adjust the maximum governed speed on Model K-241, adjust position of stop so that speed control lever contacts stop at desired engine speed. On Models K-141, K-161 and K-181, loosen governor shaft bushing nut (C—Fig. KO17) and move throttle bracket (E) to increase or decrease governed speed. See Fig. KO18 for direction of movement.

On Model K-241, governor sensitivity is adjusted by moving governor spring to alternate holes in governor arm and speed lever.

Governor unit is accessible after removing engine crankshaft and camshaft. The governor gear and flyweight assembly turns on a stub shaft pressed into engine crankcase. Renew gear and weight assembly if gear teeth or any part of assembly is excessively worn. Desired clearance of governor gear to stud shaft is 0.0025-0.0055 inch (0.064-0.140 mm) for Models K-141, K-161 and K-181 and 0.0005-0.002 inch (0.013-0.05 mm) for Model K-241.

MAGNETO IGNITION. The breaker points are located externally on engine crankcase as shown in Fig. KO21. The breaker points are actuated by a cam through a push rod.

Models K-141, K-161, K-181 and K-241 engines are equipped with an automatic compression release (see CAMSHAFT paragraph) and do not have an automatic timing advance; ignition occurs at 20 degrees BTDC at all engine speeds.

Nominal breaker point gap on all models is 0.020 inch (0.51 mm); however, breaker point gap should be varied to obtain exact ignition timing as follows:

With a static timing light, disconnect coil and condenser leads from breaker point terminal and attach one timing light lead to terminal and ground the other lead. Remove button plug from timing sight hole and turn engine so that piston has just completed its compression stroke and the "DC" mark (models with automatic timing advance) or "SP" mark (models with automatic compression release) on flywheel appears in the sight hole. Loosen breaker point adjustment screw and adjust points to closed position (timing light will be on); then, slowly move breaker point base towards engine until timing light goes out. Tighten the adjustment screw and check

Fig. KO22 – Typical wiring diagram of magneto ignition system used on manual start engines.

point setting by turning engine in normal direction of rotation until timing light goes on. Then, continue to turn engine very slowly until timing light goes out. The "DC" mark (models with automatic time advance) or "SP" mark (models with automatic compression release) should now be in register with the sight hole. Disconnect timing light leads, connect leads from coil and condenser to breaker point terminal and install breaker cover.

If a power timing light is available, more accurate timing can be obtained by adjusting the points with engine running. Breaker point gap should be adjusted so that the light flash causes the "SP" timing mark (20 degrees BTDC) to appear in the sight hole. Engine should be running above 1500 rpm when checking breaker point setting with a power timing light on models with automatic timing advance.

A typical wiring diagram of a magneto ignition system is shown in Fig. KO22.

LUBRICATION. All models are splash lubricated. Maintain crankcase oil level at full mark on dipstick, but do not overfill. High quality detergent oil having API classification SE or SF is recommended.

Use SAE 30 oil in temperatures above 32° F (0° C), SAE 10W-30 oil in temperatures between 32° F (0° C) and 0° F (−18°C). Use SAE 5W-20 oil in subzero temperatures.

Fig. KO21 – Ignition breaker points are located externally on engine crankcase on all models equipped with magneto or battery ignition systems.

Fig. KO23 – Exploded view of crankcase breather assembly used on Models K-141, K-161 and K-181.

Fig. KO24—Exploded view of crankcase breather assembly used on Model K-241.

FILL TO LEVEL MARK WITH SAME OIL AS ENGINE

Fig. KO25—View of oil bath type air cleaner.

USE GENUINE KOHLER ELEMENT

Fig. KO26—Exploded view of dry element type air cleaner.

CRANKCASE BREATHER. Refer to Figs. KO23 and KO24. A reed valve assembly is located in the valve spring compartment to maintain a partial vacuum in the crankcase and thus reduce leakage of oil at bearing seals. If a slight amount of crankcase vacuum (5-10 inches water or ½-1 inch mercury) is not present, the reed valve is faulty or the engine has excessive blow-by past rings and/or valves or worn oil seals.

AIR CLEANER. Engines may be equipped with either an oil bath type air cleaner shown in Fig. KO25 or a dry element type shown in Fig. KO26.

Oil bath air cleaner should be serviced every 25 hours of operation or more often if operating in extremely dusty conditions. To service oil bath type, remove complete cleaner assembly from engine. Remove cover and element from bowl. Empty used oil from bowl, then clean cover and bowl in solvent. Clean element in solvent and allow to drip dry. Lightly re-oil element. Fill bowl to oil level marked on bowl using same grade and weight oil as used in engine crankcase. Renew gaskets as necessary when reassembling and reinstalling unit.

Dry element type air cleaner should be cleaned every 100 hours of operation or more frequently if operating in dusty conditions. Remove dry element and tap element lightly on a flat surface to remove surface dirt. Do not wash element or attempt to clean element with compressed air. Renew element if extremely dirty or if it is bent, crushed or otherwise damaged. Make certain the sealing surfaces of element seal effectively against back plate and cover.

REPAIRS

TIGHTENING TORQUES. Recommended tightening torques are as follows:

Spark plug . . . . .22 ft.-lbs.
(29.81 N·m)

Connecting rod cap screws,
K-141, K-161 and
K-181 . . . . .200 in.-lbs.*
(22.58 N·m)
K-241 . . . . .300 in.-lbs.*
(33.88 N·m)
Cylinder head cap screws,
K141-K-161 and
K-181 . . . . .240 in.-lbs.*
(27.10 N·m)
K-241 . . . . .360 in.-lbs.*
(40.65 N·m)
Flywheel retaining nut,
Models with ⅝-inch
nut . . . . .60 ft.-lbs.
(81.30 N·m)
Models with ¾-inch
nut . . . . .100 ft.-lbs.
(135.50 N·m)

*With threads lubricated.

CONNECTING ROD. Connecting rod and piston unit is removed after removing oil pan and cylinder head. The aluminum alloy connecting rod rides directly on the crankpin. Connecting rod with 0.010-inch (0.25 mm) undersize crankpin bore is available for reground crankshaft. Oversize piston pins are available on some models. Desired running clearances are as follows:
Connecting rod to crank-
pin . . . . .0.001-0.002 in.
(0.03-0.05 mm)
Connecting rod to piston pin,
K-141, K-161 &
K-181 . . . . .0.0006-0.0011 in.
(0.015-0.028 m)
K-241 . . . . .0-0003-0.008 in.
(0.008-0.020 mm)
Rod side play on crankpin,
K-141, K-161 and
K-181 . . . . .0.005-0.016 in.
(0.13-0.41 mm)
K-241 . . . . .0.007-0.016 mm
(0.18-0.041 mm)
Standard crankpin diameter is 1.1855-1.1860 inches (30.112-30.124 mm) on Models K-141, K-161 and K-181 and 1.4995-1.5000 (38.087-38.100 mm) on Model K-241.

When reinstalling connecting rod and piston assembly, piston can be installed either way on rod, but make certain the match marks (Fig. KO27) on rod and cap are aligned and are towards flywheel side of engine. Kohler recommends that connecting rod cap screws be tightened, then loosened and retightened to prevent the possibility of screws tightening in threads instead of tightening cap to rod. Tighten connecting rod cap screws to a torque of 200 in.-lbs. (22.58 N·m) on Models K-141, K-161 and K-181. On Model K-241, tighten cap screws to 300 in.-lbs. (33.86 N·m).

NOTE: Torque values for connecting rod cap screws are with lubricated threads.

PISTON, PIN AND RINGS. The aluminum alloy piston is fitted with two 0.093-inch (2.36 mm) wide compression rings and one 0.187-inch (4.75 mm) wide oil control ring. Renew piston if scored or if side clearance of new ring in piston top groove exceeds 0.006-inch (0.15 mm). Pistons and rings are available in oversizes of 0.010-inch (0.25 mm), 0.020-inch (0.51 mm) and 0.030-inch (0.76 mm) as well as standard size. Specified piston pin fit in piston bore is 0.0001-inch (0.003 mm) interference to

INSTALL WITH MARKS TOWARD BEARING PLATE

Fig. KO27—When installing connecting rod and piston unit, be sure that marks on rod and cap are aligned and are facing toward flywheel side of engine.

Fig. KO28 — On Models K-141, K-161 and K-181 tighten cylinder head cap screws evenly, in sequence shown, to a torque of 240 in.lbs. (27.10 N·m).

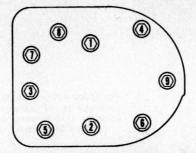

Fig. KO29 — On Model K-241, tighten cylinder head cap screws evenly, in sequence shown, to a torque of 360 in.lbs. (40.65 N·m).

Fig. KO30 — When installing crankshaft, make certain that timing mark (A) on crankshaft is aligned with timing mark (B) on camshaft gear.

0.0003-inch (0.008 mm) loose on Models K-141, K-161 and K-181. On Model K-241, specified clearance between piston pin and piston bore should be no more than 0.0002-0.0003 inch (0.005-0.008 mm). Standard piston pin diameter is 0.6248-inch (15.870 mm) on Models K-141, K-161 and K-181. On Model K-241, piston pin diameter is 0.8592-inch (21.824 mm).

Piston pins are available in oversize of 0.005-inch (0.13 mm) on some models. Always renew piston pin retaining rings.

Recommended piston-to-cylinder bore clearances are as follows:

K-141, K-161, and
K-181 ....0.0045-0.007 in.*
                  (0.114-0.18mm)
K-241 ....0.003-0.004 in.*
                  (0.08-0.10 mm)
K-141, K-161 and
K-181 ....0.006-0.008 in.**
                  (0.15-0.20 mm)
K-241 ....0.0075-0.0085 in.**
                  (0.191-0.216 mm)

*Measure at **bottom** of piston skirt on thrust side.

Measure just **below oil ring on thrust side.

Kohler recommends that rings be renewed whenever pistons are removed. Piston ring specifications are as follows:

Ring end gap –
K-141, K-161 &
K-181 ....0.007-0.017 in.
                  (0.18-0.43 mm)
K-241 ....0.010-0.020 in.
                  (0.25-0.51 mm)

Ring side clearance (comp. rings) –
K-141, K-161 &
K-181 ....0.0025-0.004 in.
                  (0.064-0.102 mm)
K-241 ....0.002-0.004 in.
                  (0.05-0.10 mm)

Ring side clearance (oil control ring) –
K-141, K-161 &
K-181 ....0.001-0.0025 in.
                  (0.03-0.064 mm)
K-241 ....0.001-0.003 in.
                  (0.03-0.08 mm)

If compression ring has a groove or bevel on outside surface, install ring with groove or bevel down. If groove or bevel is on inside surface of compression ring, install ring with groove or bevel up. Oil control ring can be installed either side up.

CYLINDER BLOCK. Rebore cylinder to nearest suitable oversize of 0.010-inch (0.25 mm), 0.020-inch (0.51 mm) or 0.030-inch (0.76 mm) if bore is: (1) out-of-round more than 0.005-inch (0.13 mm); (2) cylinder wall is scored or bore is tapered more than 0.0025-inch (0.064 mm) on Models K-141, K-161 and K-181 or 0.0015-inch (0.038 mm) on Model K-241. Standard cylinder bore is 2.9375 inches (74.610 mm) on Models K-141, K-161 and K-181. On Model K-241, standard cylinder bore is 3.251 inches (82.58 mm).

CYLINDER HEAD. Always use a new head gasket when installing cylinder head. Tighten cylinder head cap screws evenly and in steps using correct sequence shown in Fig. KO28 or KO29.

CRANKSHAFT. Crankshaft on standard K-141 engine is supported by a ball bearing in crankcase at pto end of shaft and a bushing type bearing in bearing plate at flywheel end.

Crankshaft on all other models is supported in two ball bearings.

On Model K-141 engine with bushing type main bearing, renew crankshaft and/or bearing plate if crankshaft journal and bearing are excessively worn or scored. Recommended crankshaft journal-to-bushing running clearance is 0.001-0.0025 inch (0.03-0.064 mm).

On all models, renew ball bearing type main bearings if excessively loose or rough. Specified crankshaft end play is 0.003-0.020 inch (0.08-0.051 mm) on Model K-241 and 0.002-0.023 inch (0.05-0.58 mm) on other models. End play is controlled by thickness of bearing plate gaskets. Gaskets are available in thicknesses of 0.010-inch (0.25 mm) and 0.020-inch (0.51 mm). Install ball bearing mains with sealed side toward crankpin.

Crankpin journal may be reground to 0.010-inch (0.25 mm) undersize for use

of undersize connecting rod if journal is scored or out-of-round. Standard crankpin diameter is 1.1855-1.1860 inches (30.112-30.124 mm) on Models K-141, K-161 and K-181. On Model K-241, standard crankpin diameter is 1.4995-1.500 inches (38.087-38.100 mm).

When installing crankshaft, align timing marks on crankshaft and camshaft gear as shown in Fig. KO30. On Model K-241 equipped with dynamic balancer, refer to DYNAMIC BALANCER para-

Fig. KO31 — Views showing operation of camshaft with automatic compression release. In view 1, spring (C) has moved control lever (D) which moves cam lever (B) upward so that tang (T) is above exhaust cam lobe. This tang holds exhaust valve open slightly on a portion of the compression stroke to relieve compression while cranking engine. At engine speeds of 650 rpm or more, centrifugal force moves control lever (D) outward allowing tang (T) to move below lobe surface as shown in view 2.

TOP BALANCE GEAR

CRANKSHAFT

BOTTOM BALANCE GEAR

CAMSHAFT

Fig. KO32 — View showing components of dynamic balancer system used on some K-241 models

PRIMARY TIMING MARK (BALANCE GEAR)

STANDARD TIMING MARK (CRANKSHAFT)

SECONDARY MARK (BALANCE GEAR)

SECONDARY TIMING MARK (CRANKSHAFT)

Fig. KO33 — View showing timing marks for installing dynamic balance gears.

graph for installation and timing of balancer gears. On all models, Kohler recommends that crankshaft seals be installed in crankcase and bearing plate after crankshaft and bearing plate are installed. Carefully work oil seals over crankshaft and drive seals into place with hollow driver that contacts outer edge of seals.

CAMSHAFT. The hollow camshaft and integral camshaft gear turn on a pin that is slip fit in flywheel side of crankcase and a drive fit in closed side of crankcase. Remove and install pin from open side (bearing plate side) of crankcase. Desired camshaft to pin running clearance is 0.0005-0.003 inch (0.013-0.08 mm) on Models K-141, K-161 and K-181. On Model K-241, desired clearance is 0.001-0.0035 inch (0.03-0.089 mm). Desired camshaft end play of 0.005-0.010 inch (0.13-0.25 mm) is controlled by use of 0.005 inch (0.13 mm) and 0.010 inch (0.25 mm) thick spacer washers between camshaft and cylinder block at bearing plate side of crankcase.

Fig. KO34 — Exploded view of Model K-181 basic engine assembly. Models K-141, and K-161 are similar. Standard Model K-141 engine is equipped with a bushing type main bearing in bearing plate (18).

1. Spark plug
2. Cylinder head
3. Head gasket
4. Exhaust valve seat
5. Valve guide
6. Cylinder block
7. Piston rings
8. Piston
9. Piston pin
10. Retaining rings
11. Connecting rod
12. Rod cap
13. Rod bolt lock
14. Oil seal
15. Ball bearing
16. Crankshaft
17. Gasket
18. Bearing plate
19. Magneto
20. Condenser
21. Magneto rotor
22. Wave washer
23. Flywheel
24. Pulley
25. Shroud
26. Screen retainer
27. Screen
28. Oil pan
29. Gasket
30. Camshaft pin
31. Shim washer
32. Camshaft
33. Spring retainer
34. Valve spring
35. Valve tappet
36. Intake valve
37. Exhaust valve
38. Governor gear & weight assy.
39. Needle bearing
40. Governor shaft
41. Bracket
42. Speed disc
43. Bushing
44. Governor spring
45. Governor lever
46. Link
47. Muffler
48. Carburetor
49. Air cleaner assy.
50. Breaker cover
51. Gasket
52. Breaker points
53. Push rod
54. Gaskets
55. Filter
56. Valve cover
57. Breather seal
58. Reed plate
59. Fuel pump

Camshafts are equipped with an automatic compression release mechanism shown in Fig. KO31. The automatic compression release mechanism holds the exhaust valve slightly open during the first part of compression stroke, reducing compression pressure and allowing easier cranking of engine. Refer to Fig. KO31 for operational details. At speeds above 650 engine rpm, compression release mechanism is inactive. Service procedures remain the same as for early production camshaft units, except for the difference in timing advance and compression release mechanisms.

To check compression on engine equipped with automatic compression release, engine must be cranked at 650 rpm or higher to overcome compression release action. A reading can also be obtained by rotating flywheel in reverse direction with throttle wide open. Compression reading should be 110-120 psi on an engine in top mechanical condition. When compression reading falls below 100 psi, it indicates leaking rings or valves.

VALVE SYSTEM. Valve tappet gap (cold) is as follows:

Models K-141, K-161 and K-181
Intake . . . . .0.006-0.008 in.
(0.15-0.20 mm)
Exhaust . . . . .0.015-0.017 in.
(0.38-0.43 mm)

Model K-241
Intake . . . . .0.008-0.010 in.
(0.20-0.25 mm)
Exhaust . . . . .0.017-0.020 in.
(0.43-0.51 mm)

Correct valve tappet gap is obtained by grinding ends of valve stems on Models K-141, K-161 and K-181. Be sure to grind end square and remove all burrs from end of stem after grinding. Model K-241 has adjustable tappets.

Exhaust valve seats are renewable and intake valve seats are machined in cylinder block on most models. Valve face and seat angle is 45 degrees. Desired seat width is 1/32-1/16 inch (0.8-1.6 mm).

Fig. KO35 — Exploded view of Model K-241 basic engine assembly.

1. Spark plug	21. Screen	41. Governor shaft	49. Push rod
2. Cylinder head	22. Oil pan	42. Needle bearing	50. Valve cover
3. Head gasket	23. Gasket	43. Governor spring	51. Breather seal
4. Valve seat insert	24. Fuel pump	44. Speed lever	52. Gasket
5. Valve guide	25. Camshaft pin	45. Governor gear &	53. Filter
6. Piston rings	26. Valve tappets	weight unit	54. Baffle
7. Piston	27. Shim washer	46. Breaker cover	55. Reed
8. Retaining rings	28. Camshaft	47. Gasket	56. Gasket
9. Piston pin	29. Valve rotator	48. Breaker point assy.	57. Breather plate
10. Connecting rod	30. Valve spring		
11. Rod cap	31. Spring retainer		
12. Oil seal	32. Exhaust valve		
13. Ball bearing	33. Intake valve		
14. Crankshaft	34. Cylinder block		
15. Gasket	35. Camshaft cover		
16. Bearing plate	36. Carburetor		
17. Flywheel	37. Muffler		
18. Pulley	38. Air cleaner assy.		
19. Shroud	39. Governor lever		
20. Screen retainer	40. Bushing		

Valve guides are renewable on all models. Specified intake valve stem-to-guide clearance is 0.001-0.0025 inch (0.03-0.064 mm) and specified exhaust valve-to-guide clearance is 0.0025-0.004 inch (0.064-0.10 mm) on all models. Ream valve guides, after installation, to obtain correct inside diameter of 0.312-0.313 inch (7.93-7.95 mm).

DYNAMIC BALANCER. Refer to Fig. KO32 for view of dynamic balancer system used on some K-241 engines. The two balance gears, equipped with needle bearings, rotate on two stub shafts which are pressed into bosses on pto side of crankcase. Snap rings secure gears on stub shafts and shim spacers are used to control gear end play. Balance gears are driven by crankshaft in opposite direction of crankshaft rotation. Use the following procedure to install and time dynamic balancer components.

To install new stub shafts, press shafts into special bosses in crankcase until they protrude 0.691-inch (17.55 mm) above thrust surface of bosses.

To install top balance gear-bearing assembly, first place one 0.010-inch (0.25 mm) thick shim spacer on stub shaft, then slide top gear assembly on shaft. Timing marks must face flywheel side of crankcase. Install one 0.005-inch (0.13 mm), one 0.010-inch (0.25 mm) and one 0.020-inch (0.51 mm) thick shim spacers in this order, then install snap ring. Using a feeler gage, check gear end play. Proper end play of balance gear is 0.005-0.010 inch (0.13-0.25 mm). Add or remove 0.005-inch (0.13 mm) thick spacers as necessary to obtain correct end play.

NOTE: Always install the 0.020-inch (0.51 mm) thick spacer next to snap ring.

Refer to Fig. KO33 and install crankshaft in crankcase. Align primary timing mark on top balance gear with standard timing mark on crankshaft. With primary timing marks aligned, engage crankshaft gear 1/16-inch (1.6 mm) into narrow section of top balance gear, then rotate crankshaft to align timing marks on camshaft gear and crankshaft as shown in Fig. KO30. Press crankshaft into crankcase until it is seated firmly into ball bearing main. Rotate crankshaft until crankpin is approximately 15 degrees past bottom dead center. Install one 0.010-inch (0.25 mm) thick shim spacer on stub shaft. Align secondary timing mark on bottom balance gear with secondary timing mark on crankshaft. Slide gear assembly into position on stub shaft. If properly timed, secondary timing mark on bottom balance gear will be aligned with standard timing mark on crankshaft after gear is fully on stub shaft. Install one 0.005-inch (0.13 mm) thick and one 0.020-inch (0.51 mm) thick shim spacer, then install snap ring. Check bottom balance gear end play and add or remove 0.005-inch (0.13 mm) thick spacers as required to obtain proper end play of 0.005-0.010 inch (0.13-0.25 mm). Make certain 0.020-inch (0.51 mm) spacer is used against snap ring.

KOHLER

SERVICING KOHLER ACCESSORIES

RETRACTABLE STARTERS

Fairbanks-Morse or Eaton retractable starters are used on some Kohler engines. When servicing the starters, refer to appropriate following paragraphs.

Fairbanks-Morse

OVERHAUL. To disassemble the starter, remove retainer ring, retainer washer, brake spring, friction washer, friction shoe assembly and second friction washer as shown in Fig. KO100. Hold the rope handle in one hand and the cover in the other and allow rotor to rotate to unwind the recoil spring preload. Lift rotor from cover, shaft and recoil spring. Check the winding direction of recoil spring and rope for aid in reassembly. Remove recoil spring from cover and unwind rope from rotor.

When reassembling the unit, lubricate recoil spring, cover shaft and its bore in rotor with Lubriplate or equivalent. Install the rope on rotor and the rotor to the shaft and engage the recoil spring inner end hook. Preload the recoil spring four turns and install middle flange and mounting flange. Check friction shoe sharp ends and renew if necessary. Install friction washers, friction shoe assembly, brake spring, retainer washer and retainer ring. Make certain that friction shoe assembly is installed properly for correct starter rotation. If properly installed, sharp ends of friction shoe plates will extend when rope is pulled.

Starter operation can be reversed by winding rope and recoil spring in opposite direction and turning the friction shoe assembly upside down. See Fig. KO101 for counterclockwise assembly.

Eaton

OVERHAUL. To disassemble the starter, first release tension of rewind spring as follows: Hold starter assembly with pulley facing up. Pull starter rope until notch in pulley is aligned with rope hole in cover. Use thumb pressure to prevent pulley from rotating. Engage rope in notch of pulley and slowly release thumb pressure to allow spring to unwind until all tension is released.

After securing the pulley assembly in housing, align notch in pulley with rope bushing in housing. Engage rope in notch and rotate pulley at least two full turns in same direction it is pulled, to properly preload starter spring. Pull rope to fully extended position. Release

Fig. KO100 – Fairbanks-Morse retractable starter with friction shoe assembly removed.

Fig. KO101 – View showing recoil spring and rope installed for counterclockwise starter operation.

handle and if spring is properly preloaded, the rope will fully rewind.

Before installing starter on engine, check teeth in starter driven hub (165 – Fig. KO103) for wear and renew hub if necessary.

Fig. KO102 – Exploded view of Eaton retractable starter assembly.

1. Retainer screw	5. Pawl	9. Pulley hub
2. Brake washer	6. Spring	10. Pulley	13. Rope
3. Spacer	7. Brake	11. Screw	14. Handle
4. Retainer	8. Thrust washer	12. Recoil spring	15. Starter housing

Fig. KO103—View showing retractable starter and starter hub.

165. Starter hub
166. Screen
170. Bracket
171. Air director
203. Retractable starter assy.

Fig. KO105—Exploded view of 2-brush compact gear drive starting motor.

A. Frame & field coil assy.
B. Armature
C. Spacer
D. Thrust washer
E. Bendix drive assy.
F. Drive end plate & mounting bracket
G. Lockwasher
H. Through-bolt
J. Commutator end plate
K. Ground brush
L. Terminal nuts
M. Lockwashers
N. Flat washer
O. Insulating washer
P. Field brush

12-VOLT GEAR DRIVE STARTERS

TWO BRUSH COMPACT TYPE. To disassemble starting motor, clamp mounting bracket in a vise. Remove through-bolts (H–Fig. KO105) and slide commutator end plate (J) and frame assembly (A) off the armature. Then, clamp steel armature core in vise and remove Bendix drive retaining nut. Remove Bendix drive (E), drive end plate (F), thrust washer (D) and spacer (C) from armature (B).

Renew brushes if unevenly worn or worn to a length of 5/16-inch (7.9 mm) or less. To renew ground brush (K), drill out rivet, then rivet new brush lead to end plate. Field brush (P) is soldered to field coil lead.

Reassemble by reversing disassembly procedure. Lubricate bushings with a light coat of SAE 10 oil. Inspect Bendix drive pinion and splined sleeve for damage. If Bendix is in good condition, wipe clean and install completely dry. Tighten Bendix drive retaining nut to a torque of 130-150 in.-lbs. (14.68-16.94 N·m). Tighten through-bolts (H) to a torque of 40-55 in.-lbs. (4.52-6.21 N·m).

TECUMSEH

TECUMSEH PRODUCTS COMPANY
Grafton, Wisconsin 53024

LIGHT FRAME MODELS

HP	Crankshaft	Bore	Stroke	Displacement
3	Horizontal	2.3 in.	1.81 in.	7.61 cu. in.
(2.24 kW)		(58.7 mm)	(46.04 mm)	(124.71 cc)
3	Horizontal	2.3 in.	1.84 in.	7.75 cu. in.
(2.24 kW)		(58.7 mm)	(46.74 mm)	(126.00 cc)
3.5	Horizontal	2.5 in.	1.81 in.	8.90 cu. in.
(2.61 kW)		(63.5 mm)	(46.04 mm)	(145.84 cc)
3.5	Horizontal	2.5 in.	1.84 in.	9.06 cu. in.
(2.61 kW)		(63.5 mm)	(46.74 mm)	(148.47 cc)
4	Horizontal	2.6 in.	1.94 in.	10.50 cu. in.
(2.98 kW)		(66.7 mm)	(49.21 mm)	172.06 cc
5	Horizontal	2.8 in.	1.94 in.	12.00 cu. in.
(3.73 kW)		(71.4 mm)	(49.21 mm)	(196.64 cc)

MEDIUM FRAME MODELS

HP	Crankshaft	Bore	Stroke	Displacement
4	Horizontal	2.5 in.	2.25 in.	11.04 cu. in.
(2.98 kW)		(63.5 mm)	(57.15 mm)	(180.91 cc)
5	Horizontal	2.4 in.	2.25 in.	12.18 cu. in.
(3.73 kW)		(66.7 mm)	(57.15 mm)	(199.53 cc)
6	Horizontal	2.4 in.	2.50 in.	13.53 cu. in.
(4.47 kW)		(66.7 mm)	(63.50 mm)	(221.72 cc)
7	Horizontal	2.9 in.	2.53 in.	17.16 cu. in.
(5.22 kW)		(74.6 mm)	(64.29 mm)	(281.20 cc)
8	Horizontal	3.1 in.	2.53 in.	19.41 cu. in.
(5.97 kW)		(79.38 mm)	(64.29 mm)	(318.07 cc)

Engines must be identified by the complete model number, including the specification number in order to obtain correct repair parts. These numbers are located on the name plate and/or tags that are positioned as shown in Fig. T1. It is important to transfer identification tags from the original engine to replacement short block assemblies so that unit can be identified when servicing later.

MAINTENANCE

SPARK PLUG. Recommended spark plug is Champion J-8 or equivalent. Set electrode gap to 0.030 inch (0.762 mm). Spark plug should be removed, cleaned and adjusted periodically. Renew plug if electrodes are burned and pitted or if porcelain is cracked. If frequent plug fouling is experienced, check for following conditions:

 a. Carburetor setting too rich
 b. Partially closed choke
 c. Clogged air filter
 d. Incorrect spark plug
 e. Poor grade of gasoline
 f. Too much oil or crankcase breather clogged

CARBURETOR. Several different carburetors are used on these engines. Refer to the appropriate following paragraph for service and adjustment.

TECUMSEH DIAPHRAGM CARBURETOR. Idle mixture is adjusted at needle (10 – Fig. T2). High speed mixture is adjusted at main fuel needle (14). Initial setting is 1 turn open for both needles and clockwise rotation will lean the mixture. Make final mixture adjustment with engine warm and operating with the normal amount of load. Adjust the main fuel needle (14) for smoothest operation at governed speed, then adjust idle needle (10) for smoothest operation at idle (slow) speed. Idle speed is adjusted at stop screw (9) and should be approximately 1800 rpm.

Observe the following when overhauling Tecumseh diaphragm carburetors: The carburetor model number is stamped on the mounting flange. The fuel strainer in the fuel inlet fitting can be cleaned by reverse flushing with compressed air after the inlet needle and

Fig. T1 – Tags and plates used to identify model will most often be located in a position shown.

Fig. T2 — Exploded view of typical Tecumseh diaphragm carburetor.

1. Throttle shaft
2. Return spring
3. Choke shaft
4. Choke stop spring.
5. Return spring
6. Carburetor body
7. Choke plate
8. Throttle plate
9. Idle speed screw
10. Idle mixture needle
11. Washers
12. "O" rings
13. Welch plug
14. Main fuel needle
15. Cup plug
16. Welch plug
17. Inlet needle spring
18. Gasket
19. Inlet needle & seat assy.
20. Gasket
21. Diaphragm
22. Cover

Fig. T4 — Exploded view of standard Tecumseh float type carburetor.

1. Idle speed screw
2. Throttle plate
3. Return spring
4. Throttle shaft
5. Choke stop spring
6. Choke shaft
7. Return spring
8. Fuel inlet fitting
9. Carburetor body
10. Choke plate
11. Welch plug
12. Idle mixture needle
13. Spring
14. Washer
15. "O" ring
16. Ball plug
17. Welch plug
18. Pin
19. Cup plugs
20. Bowl gasket
21. Inlet needle seat
22. Inlet needle
23. Clip
24. Float shaft
25. Float
26. Drain stem
27. Gasket
28. Bowl
29. Gasket
30. Bowl retainer
31. "O" ring
32. Washer
33. Spring
34. Main fuel needle

toward the fuel inlet fitting side of carburetor. Mark on choke plate should be parallel to shaft and should face INWARD when choke is closed. Diaphragm (21–Fig. T2) should be installed with rounded head of center rivet up toward the inlet needle (19), regardless of size or placement of washers around the rivet. On carburetor Models 0234-252, 265, 266, 269, 270, 271, 282, 293, 303, 322, 327, 333, 334, 344, 345, 348, 349, 350, 351, 352, 356, 368, 371, 374, 378, 379, 380, 404 and 405, gasket (20) must be installed between diaphragm (21) and cover (22). All other models are assembled as shown, with gasket between diaphragm and carburetor body.

TECUMSEH STANDARD FLOAT CARBURETOR. Idle mixture is adjusted at needle (12–Fig. T4) and high speed mixture at main fuel needle (34). Initial setting is 1 turn open for both needles and clockwise rotation will lean the mixture. Make final mixture adjustment with engine warm and operating with the normal amount of load. Adjust the main fuel needle (34) for smoothest operation at governed speed, then adjust idle needle (12) for smoothest operation at idle (slow) speed. Idle speed is adjusted at stop screw (1) and should be approximately 1800 rpm.

Observe the following when overhauling: Disassemble the carburetor before attempting to clean. Most commercial cleaners will damage neoprene and Viton rubber parts. Do not attempt to reuse any expansion plugs. Install new plugs if any are removed for cleaning. The fuel inlet needle valve closes against a neoprene or Viton seat which must be removed before cleaning in most commercial solvents.

Fig. T5 — View of float and fuel inlet valve needle. The valve needle shown is equipped with resilient tip and a clip. Bend tab shown to adjust float height.

Three types of fuel inlet valves are used. Some carburetors are equipped with a resilient tip on the fuel inlet needle (Fig. T5). The soft tip contacts the seating surface machined into the carburetor body to shut off the fuel. Do not attempt to remove the inlet valve seat. Some carburetors are equipped with a Viton seat (21–Fig. T4) that is located in bore of carburetor body. The rubber seat can be removed by blowing compressed air in from the fuel inlet fitting

Fig. T6 — The Viton seat used on some Tecumseh carburetors must be installed correctly to operate properly. All metal needle is used with seat shown.

seat (19–Fig. T2) are removed. The inlet needle seat fitting is metal with a neoprene seat, so the fitting (and enclosed seat) should be removed before carburetor is cleaned with a commercial solvent. The stamped line on carburetor throttle plate should be toward top of carburetor, parallel with throttle shaft and facing OUTWARD as shown in Fig. T3. Flat side of choke plate should be

Fig. T3 — The mark (M) on throttle plate should be parallel to the throttle shaft and outward as shown. Some models may also have mark at 3 o'clock position.

Fig. T7 — A 10-24 or 10-32 tap is used to pull the brass seat fitting and fuel inlet valve seat from some carburetors. Use a close fitting flat punch to install new seat and fitting.

Fig. T8 — Float height can be measured on some models by using a drill as shown. Refer to text for correct setting height.

Fig. T9 — Flat part of float bowl should be located under the fuel inlet fitting.

Fig. T10 — The bowl retainer contains a drilled fuel passage which is different for carburetors with external and internal fuel bowl vent.

or by using a hooked wire. The grooved face of valve seat should be IN toward bottom of bore and the valve needle should seat on smooth side of the Viton seat. Refer to Fig. T6. On some carburetors, the Viton seat is contained in a brass seat fitting. Use a 10-24 or 10-32 tap to pull the seat and fitting from carburetor bore as shown in Fig. T7. Use a flat, close fitting punch to install new seat and fitting.

Install the throttle plate (2 – Fig. T4) with the two stamped marks and at 12 and 3 o'clock positions. The 12 o'clock line should be parallel with the throttle shaft and toward top of carburetor. Install choke plate (10) with flat side down toward bottom of carburetor. Float setting should be 0.200-0.220 inch (5.08-5.59 mm) and can be measured with a No. 4 drill as shown in Fig. T8. Remove float and bend tab at float hinge to change float setting. The fuel inlet fitting (8 – Fig. T4) is pressed into body on some models. Start fitting, then apply a light coat of "Loctite" (grade A) to shank and press fitting into position. The flat on fuel bowl should be under the fuel inlet fitting. Refer to Fig. T9.

Be sure to use correct parts when servicing the carburetor. Some gaskets used as (20 – Fig. T4) are square section, while others are round. The bowl retainer (39) contains a drilled passage for fuel to the high speed metering needle (34). A diagonal port through one side the bowl retainer is used on carburetors with external vent. The port is through both sides on models with internal vent. Refer to Fig. T10.

WALBRO. On Walbro carburetors, clockwise rotation of both the low idle mixture needle (9 – Fig. T18) and the main fuel adjusting needle (33) leans the mixture. Initial setting for both needles is 1 turn open. Make final adjustment with engine warm and running. Adjust main fuel needle until engine runs smoothly at normal operating speed. Back out idle speed screw (7), hold throttle to slowest engine speed possible without stalling and adjust idle mixture needle for smoothest operation. Read-

Fig. T18 — Exploded view of Walbro LMG carburetor.

1. Choke shaft	17. Spring
2. Throttle shaft	18. Inlet valve
3. Throttle return spring	19. Main nozzle
4. Choke return spring	20. Float
5. Choke stop spring	21. Float shaft
6. Throttle plate	22. Spring
7. Idle speed stop screw	23. Gasket
	24. Bowl
8. Spring	25. Drain stem
9. Idle mixture needle	26. Gasket
10. Spring	27. Spring
11. Baffle	28. Retainer
12. Carburetor body	29. Gasket
13. Choke plate	30. Bowl retainer
14. Bowl gasket	31. Spring
15. Gasket	32. "O" ring
16. Inlet valve seat	33. Main fuel adjusting needle

just idle speed screw so engine idles at 1800 rpm.

To check float setting, hold carburetor body and float assembly in inverted position. A clearance of ⅛-inch (3.2 mm) should exist between free end of float and machined surface of carburetor body. Refer to Fig. T19. Bend tab on float as necessary to provide correct measurement.

NOTE: If carburetor has been disassembled and main nozzle (19 – Fig. T18) removed, do not reinstall the original equipment nozzle; obtain and install a new service nozzle. Refer to Fig. T20 for differences between original and service nozzles.

MECHANICAL GOVERNOR. Most engines are equipped with a mechanical

(flyweight) type governor. To adjust the governor linkage, refer to Fig. T28 and loosen governor lever screw. Twist protruding end of governor shaft clockwise as far as possible on horizontal crankshaft engines. On all models, move the governor lever until carburetor throttle shaft is in wide open position, then tighten governor lever clamp screw.

Binding or worn governor linkage will result in hunting or unsteady engine operation. An improperly adjusted carburetor will also cause a surging or hunting condition.

Refer to Figs. T29, T30, T31, T32, T35, T36, T37, T39 and T40 for views of typical mechanical governor speed con-

Fig. T31 — Mechanical governor linkage.
1. Governor lever
2. Throttle control link
3. Carburetor throttle lever
4. Governor spring
5. Governor spring linkage
7. Speed control lever
8. Choke lever
10. Stop switch
16. Idle speed stop screw
18. High speed stop screw

Fig. T19 — Float height (H) should be measured as shown on Walbro float carburetors. Bend the adjusting tab to adjust height.

Fig. T29 — View of mechanical governor with one type of constant speed control. Refer also to Fig. T30 through T43 for other mechanical governor installations.
1. Governor lever
2. Throttle control
3. Carburetor throttle lever
4. Governor spring
8. Choke lever
16. Idle speed stop screw

Fig. T32 — Mechanical governor linkage. Refer to Fig. T31 for legend. Bellcrank is shown at (6).

Fig. T30 — Mechanical governor linkage. Refer to Fig. T29 for legend except the following.
6. Bellcrank
7. Speed control lever
18. High speed stop screw

Fig. T35 — Mechanical governor linkage. Governed speed of engine is increased by closing loop in linkage (5); decrease speed by spreading loop.
1. Governor lever
2. Throttle control link
3. Throttle lever
5. Governor spring linkage
6. Bellcrank
7. Speed control lever
8. Choke lever
10. Stop switch

Fig. T28 — Views showing location of mechanical governor lever and direction to turn when adjusting position on governor shaft.

trol linkage installations. The governor gear shaft must be pressed into bore in cover until the correct amount of the shaft protrudes (A – Fig. T44). The correct distance (B) is 1-5/16 inches (33.3 mm) for all light frame engines. Governor shaft protrusion (D) for 4, 5 and 6 hp engines should be 1-17/64 inches (32.1 mm). Governor shaft protrusion (D) for 7 and 8 hp engines should be 1-15/64 inches (31.4 mm).

Fig. T36 — Mechanical governor linkage.
1. Governor lever
2. Throttle control link
3. Throttle lever
4. Governor spring
5. Governor spring linkage
6. Bellcrank
7. Speed control lever
8. Choke lever
9. Choke control link
10. Stop switch
16. Idle speed stop screw
18. High speed stop screw

Fig. T37 — View of control linkage used on some engines. To increase governed engine speed, close loop (5); to decrease speed, spread loop (5). Refer to Fig. T36 for legend.

Fig. T39 — Linkage for mechanical governor. Refer to Fig. T36 for legend. Bellcrank is shown at (6).

MAGNETO AND TIMING. Breaker point gap at maximum opening should be 0.020 inch (0.5 mm) for all models. Marks are usually located on stator and mounting post to facilitate timing. Ignition timing can be checked and adjusted to occur when piston is at specific location (BTDC) if marks are missing. Refer to the following specifications for recommended timing.

Models (Displacement)	Piston Position Inch (mm) BTDC
7.75 Cu. In. (126.00 cc)	0.060-0.070 (1.524-1.778)
8.90 Cu. In. (145.84 cc)	0.050-0.060 (1.270-1.524)
9.06 Cu. In. (148.47 cc)	0.035 (0.889)
10.50 Cu. In. (172.06 cc)	0.035 (0.889)
17.16 Cu. In. (281.20 cc)	0.085-0.095 (2.159-2.413)
19.41 Cu. In. (318.07 cc)	0.085-0.095 (2.159-2.413)
All Other Light Frame Models	0.060-0.070 (1.524-1.778)
All Other Medium Frame Models	0.050 (1.270)

Fig. T40 — Mechanical governor linkage.
1. Governor lever
2. Throttle control link
4. Governor spring
5. Governor spring linkage

Fig. T44 — The governor gear shaft must be pressed into bore until the correct amount of shaft protrudes (A). Refer also to illustrations for correct assembly of governor gear and associated parts. See text for protrusion dimension (B or D).

SOLID-STATE IGNITION. The Tecumseh solid-state ignition system does not use ignition breaker points. The only moving part of the system is the rotating flywheel with the charging magnets. As the flywheel magnet passes position (1A – Fig. T46), a low voltage AC current is induced into input coil (2). Current passes through rectifier (3) converting this current to DC. It then travels to capacitor (4) where it is stored. The flywheel rotates approximately 180 degrees to position (1B). As it passes trigger coil (5), it induces a very small electric charge into the coil. This charge passes through resistor (6) and turns on the SCR (silicon controlled rectifier) switch (7). With the SCR switch closed, low voltage current stored in capacitor (4) travels to pulse transformer (8). Voltage is stepped up instantaneously and current is discharged across the electrodes of spark plug (9), producing a spark before top dead center.

Some units are equipped with a second trigger coil and resistor set to turn the

Fig. T45 — Align timing marks as shown on magneto ignition engines.

Tecumseh

SCR switch on at a lower rpm. This second trigger pin is closer to the flywheel and produces a spark at TDC for easier starting. As engine rpm increases, the first (shorter) trigger pin picks up the small electric charge and turns the SCR switch on, firing the spark plug BTDC.

If system fails to produce a spark to the spark plug, first check high tension lead (Fig. T47). If condition of high tension lead is questionable, renew pulse transformer and high tension lead assembly. Check low tension lead and renew if insulation is faulty. The magneto charging coil, electronic triggering system and mounting plate are available only as an assembly. If necessary to renew this assembly, place unit in position on engine. Start retaining screws, turn mounting, plate counterclockwise as far as possible, then tighten retaining screws to a torque of 5-7 ft.-lbs. (6.775-9.485 N·m).

LUBRICATION. Engines may be equipped with a gear driven rotor type pump or a dipper type oil slinger attached to the connecting rod.

On engines equipped with gear driven rotor oil pump, check drive gear and rotor for excessive wear or other damage. End clearance of rotor in pump body should be within limits of 0.006-0.007 inch (0.152-0.178 mm) and is controlled by cover gasket. Gaskets are available in thicknesses of 0.005 inch (0.127 mm) and 0.010 inch (0.254 mm).

On all models with oil pump, be sure to prime during assembly to assure immediate lubrication of engine. On all models, use SAE 30 or SAE 10W-30 oil when operating in temperatures above 30°F and SAE 5W-30 or SAE 10W oil in temperatures 32°F and below.

ROTARY TILLER

REPAIRS

TIGHTENING TORQUES. Recommended tightening torques are as follows:
Cylinder Head
  7 HP & 8 HP models......170 in.-lbs.
        (19.20 N·m)
  All other models .....160-200 in.-lbs.
        (18.07-22.58 N·m)
Connecting Rod Nuts
(Except Durlok Type)
  3 HP & 3.5 HP ....65-75 in.-lbs.
        (7.34-8.47 N·m)
  4 HP & 5 HP Light
    frame models ....80-95 in.-lbs.
        (9.03-10.73 N·m)
  5 HP Medium frame ...86-110 in.-lbs.
        (9.71-12.42 N·m)
Connecting Rod Bolts
(Durlock Type)
  5 HP Light
    frame model ....110-130 in.-lbs.
        (12.42-14.68 N·m)
  5 HP Medium frame
    & 6 HP model........130-150 in.-lbs.
        (14.68-16.94 N·m)
  7 HP & 8 HP models......120 in.-lbs.
        (13.55 N·m)
Crankcase Cover
  All models ....65-110 in.-lbs.
        (7.34-12.42 N·m)
Ball Bearing Retaining Nut
  7 HP & 8 HP models ....15-22 in.-lbs.
        (1.69-2.48 N·m)
Flywheel
  Light frame models ...360-400 in.-lbs.
        (40.65-45.17 N·m)
  Medium frame models .430-480 in.-lbs.
        (48.55-54.20 N·m)
Spark Plug ....250-300 in.-lbs.
        (28.23-33.88 N·m)
Magneto Stator.........40-90 in.-lbs.
        (4.52-10.16 N·m)

Fig. T46—Diagram of solid state ignition system used on some engines.

Fig. T47—Diagram of solid state ignition system used on some engines.

Fig. T49—Disassembled view of typical gear driven rotor type oil pump.

Fig. T50—Match marks on connecting rod and cap should be aligned and should be toward pto end of crankshaft.

Mounting Flange . . . . 75-110 in.-lbs.
(8.47-12.42 N·m)
Carburetor to
Intake Pipe . . . . 48-72 in.-lbs.
(5.42-8.13 N·m)
Intake Pipe to Cylinder . . . 72-96 in.-lbs.
(8.13-10.84 N·m)
Breather Screws . . . . 20-26 in.-lbs.
(2.26-2.94 N·m)

CONNECTING ROD. Piston and rod assembly is removed from cylinder head end of engine. The aluminum alloy connecting rod rides directly on crankshaft. Crankpin journal diameter is 0.9995-1.000 inch (25.387-25.400 mm) for 10.5 cu. in. (172.06 cc) and 12.0 cu. in. (196.64 cc) displacement Light

Frame engines: 0.8610-0.8615 inch (21.869-21.882 mm) for other Light frame engines; 1.0615-1.0620 inch (26.962-26.975 mm) for Medium Frame engines. Specified inside diameter of connecting rod crankpin bearing is 1.0005-1.0010 inches (25.413-25.425 mm) for 10.5 cu. in. (172.06 cc) and 12.0 cu. in. (196.64 cc) displacement Light Frame engines; 0.8620-0.8625 inch (21.895-21.9075 mm) for other Light Frame engines; 1.0630-1.0635 inches (27.000-27.013 mm) for Medium Frame engines. Crankpin journal diameter is 1.1865-1.1870 inches (30.137-30.150 mm) for 17.16 cu. in. (281.20 cc) and 19.41 cu. in. (318.07 cc) displacement engines. Align match marks on connecting rod and cap as shown in Fig. T50. On some models, piston pin hole is offset in piston and arrow on top of piston should point toward valves. On all engines, match marks on rod and cap must be installed toward power take off (pto) end of crankshaft. Renew lock plates, if so equipped, for connecting rod cap retaining screws each time cap is removed.

PISTON, PIN, RINGS AND CYLINDER. Aluminum alloy pistons are equipped with two compression rings and one oil control ring. Specified ring end gap for all models is 0.007-0.020 inch (0.18-0.51 mm). Specified piston skirt clearance in cylinder (measured at thrust side of piston just below oil ring) is as follows:

7.61 cu. in.
(124.71 cc) . . . . 0.005-0.0065 in.
(0.127-0.165 mm)
7.75 cu. in.
(126.0 cc) . . . . 0.0025-0.0040 in.
(0.064-0.102 mm)
11.04 cu. in.
(180.91 cc) . . . . 0.0055-0.0070 in.
(0.14-0.178 mm)

Fig. T52—The camshaft and crankshaft must be correctly timed to assure that valves open at correct time. Different types of marks have been used, but marks should be aligned when assembling.

8.90 cu. in.
(145.84 cc)
9.06 cu. in.
(148.47 cc)
10.50 cu. in.
(172.06 cc)
12.00 cu. in.
(196.64 cc) . . . . 0.0045-0.0060 in.
(0.114-0.152 mm)
12.18 cu. in.
(199.53 cc)
13.53 cu. in.
(221.72 cc) . . . . 0.0035-0.0050 in.
(0.089-0.127 mm)
17.16 cu. in.
(281.20 cc)
19.41 cu. in.
(318.07 cc) . . . . 0.004-0.006 in.
(0.10-0.15 mm)

Fig. T51—View of insta-matic Ezee-Start compression release camshaft.

Fig. T53—View of light frame engine with horizontal crankshaft. Air vane (V) type governor and rotor type oil pump (R) are used on model shown.

Fig. T54—View of light frame horizontal crankshaft engine with mechanical governor and splash lubrication. Governor centrifugal weights are shown at (C) and lubrication dipper at (D).

Pistons and rings are available in standard, 0.010-inch (0.25 mm) and 0.020-inch (0.51 mm) oversizes. On light frame 12.0 cu. in. (196.64 cc) displacement models, arrow on top of piston should point towards valves and match marks on connecting rod and cap should point toward pto end of crankshaft (Fig. T50).

Bore and hone cylinder and fit with next suitable oversize piston and rings if cylinder is scored, tapered or out-of-round more than 0.005-inch (0.13 mm). Standard cylinder bore is as follows:

7.61 cu. in.
(124.71 cc)
7.75 cu. in.
(126.0 cc)........2.3125-2.3135 in.
　　　　　　　　(58.738-58.763 mm)
8.90 cu. in.
(145.84 cc)
9.06 cu. in.
(148.47 cc)
11.04 cu. in.
(180.91 cc)..........2.500-2.501 in.
　　　　　　　　(63.50-63.53 mm)
10.50 cu. in.
(172.06 cc)
12.18 cu. in.
(199.53 cc)
13.53 cu. in.
(221.72 cc).........2.625-2.626 in.
　　　　　　　　(66.68-66.70 mm)
17.16 cu. in.
(281.20 cc).........2.9375-2.9385 in.
　　　　　　　　(74.613-74.638 mm)
19.41 cu. in.
(318.07 cc)..........3.125-3.126 in.
　　　　　　　　(79.38-79.40 mm)

CRANKSHAFT AND MAIN BEARINGS. Crankshaft main bearing journals are 0.8735-0.8740 inch (22.187-22.200 mm), 0.9985-0.9990 inch (25.362-25.375 mm), 1.124-1.125 inch (28.55-28.58 mm) or 1.1870-1.1875 inch (30.150-30.163 mm) in diameter when new. On some engines, main bearing journals ride directly in the aluminum alloy bores in cylinder block and crankcase cover (mounting flange). A special tool kit is available from Tecumseh to ream cylinder block and cover so renewable main bearing bushings may be installed. Other engines are originally equipped with renewable steel backed bronze bushings and some are originally equipped with a ball type main bearing at pto end of crankshaft.

All bushing type main bearings for 0.8735-0.8740 inch (22.187-22.200 mm) diameter journals have a specified clearance of 0.0010-0.0025 inch (0.025-0.064 mm). Specified clearance between bushing bore and all larger diameter journals is 0.0015-0.0025 inch (0.038-0.064 mm). Specified crankshaft end play is 0.005-0.027 inch (0.13-0.69 mm) for all models.

Connecting rod crankpin diameter is 0.9995-1.000 inch (25.387-25.400 mm) for 10.50 cu.in. (172.06 cc), 11.04 cu.in. (180.91 cc) and 12.00 cu. in. (196.64 cc) displacement light frame engines. Crankpin diameter is 0.8610-0.8615 inch (21.869-21.882 mm) for all smaller displacement Light Frame engines. Crankpin diameter is 1.0615-1.0620 inches (26.962-26.975 mm) for four, five and six horsepower Medium Frame engines. Crankpin diameter is 1.1865-1.1870 inches (30.137-30.150 mm) for seven and eight horsepower Medium Frame engines. Specified connecting rod-to-crankpin bearing clearance is 0.0005-0.0015 inch (0.013-0.038 mm) for all Light Frame engines and 0.0010-0.0020 inch (0.025-0.051 mm) for all Medium Frame engines.

CAMSHAFT. The camshaft and camshaft gear are an integral part which rides on journals at each end of camshaft. Renew camshaft if gear teeth are worn or if bearing surfaces or cam lobes are worn or scored.

Specified cam lobe diameter is as follows:

10.50 cu. in.
(172.06 cc)
12.00 cu. in.
(196.64 cc) ...Intake—1.2939-1.2959 in.
　　　　　　　　(32.865-32.916 mm)
　　　　　　Exhaust—0.9775-0.9795 in.
　　　　　　　　(24.829-24.879 mm)

Fig. T55—View of medium frame horizontal crankshaft engine with mechanical governor (C). An oil dipper for splash lubrication may be cast onto the connecting rod cap instead of using the rotor type oil pump (R).

Other light frame
 engines . . . . . Intake – 0.9775-0.9795 in.
 (24.829-24.879 mm)
 Exhaust – 0.9775-0.9795 in.
 (24.829-24.879 mm)
Other medium frame
 engines . . . . Intake – 1.258-1.262 in.
 (31.95-32.06 mm)
 Exhaust – 1.258-1.262 in.
 (31.95-32.06 mm)
17.16 cu. in.
 (281.20 cc) . . . . . Intake – 1.263-1.267 in.
 (32.08-32.18 mm)
 Exhaust – 1.263-1.267 in.
 (32.08-32.18 mm)
19.41 cu. in.
 (318.07 cc) . . . Intake – 1.3045-1.3085 in.
 (33.134-33.236 mm)
 Exhaust – 1.3045-1.3085 in.
 (33.134-33.236 mm)

Fig. T56 – View of light frame horizontal crankshaft engine with mechanical governor and splash lubrication.

Cam followers (lifters) are identical for most engines; however, parts should not be interchanged once they have been used. Exhaust valve cam follower is longer than intake valve follower on some 10.50 cu. in. (172.06 cc) displacement and larger light frame engines.

On engines equipped with Instamatic Ezee-Start compression release type camshaft (Fig. T51), check compression release parts for binding, excessive wear or other damage. If any parts are damaged or excessively worn, renew complete camshaft assembly. Component parts are not serviced separately for the compression release.

When installing the camshaft, align timing marks on camshaft gear and crankshaft gear (Fig. T52) on all models.

VALVE SYSTEM. Intake and exhaust valve tappet gap should be 0.010 inch (0.25 mm) (cold). Correct tappet gap is obtained by grinding end of stems squarely. Intake and exhaust valve seats
are nonrenewable. Valve seat angle is 46 degrees. Valve seat width should be 3/64-inch (1.2 mm).

Valve stem guides are cast into cylinder block and are nonrenewable. If excessive clearance exists between valve stem and valve guide, ream guide and install a new valve with oversize stem.

Valve timing is correct when timing mark on camshaft gear is aligned with timing mark on crankshaft gear.

SERVICING TECUMSEH ACCESSORIES

REWIND STARTERS

FRICTION SHOE TYPE. To disassemble the starter, refer to Fig. TE17 and proceed as follows: Hold starter rotor (12) securely with thumb and remove the four screws securing flanges (1 and 2) to cover (15). Remove flanges and release thumb pressure enough to allow spring to rotate pulley until spring (13) is unwound. Remove retaining ring (3), washer (4), spring (5), slotted washer (6) and fiber washer (7). Lift out friction shoe assembly (8,9,10 and 11), then remove second fiber washer and slotted washer. Withdraw rotor (12) with rope from cover and spring. Remove rewind spring from cover and unwind rope from rotor.

When reassembling, lubricate rewind spring, cover shaft and center bore in rotor with a light coat of "Lubriplate" or

Fig. TE17 – Exploded view of typical friction shoe rewind starter.

1. Mounting flange
2. Flange
3. Retaining ring
4. Washer
5. Spring
6. Slotted washer
7. Fiber washer
8. Spring retainer
9. Spring
10. Friction shoe
11. Actuating lever
12. Rotor
13. Rewind spring
14. Centering pin
15. Cover
16. Rope
17. Roller

equivalent. Install rewind spring so that windings are in same direction as removed spring. Install rope on rotor, then place rotor on cover shaft. Make certain that inner and outer ends of spring are correctly hooked on cover and rotor. Preload the rewind spring by rotating the rotor two full turns. Hold rotor in preload position and install flanges (1 and 2). Check sharp end of friction shoes (10) and sharpen or renew
as necessary. Install washers (6 and 7), friction shoe assembly, spring (5), washer (4) and retaining spring (3). Make certain that friction shoe assembly is installed properly for correct starter rotation. If properly installed, sharp ends of friction shoes will extend when rope is pulled.

Remove brass centering pin (14) from cover shaft, straighten pin if necessary, then reinsert pin 1/3 of its length into cover shaft. When installing starter on engine, centering pin will align starter with center hole in end of crankshaft.

DOG TYPE. To disassemble the dog type starter, refer to Fig. TE18 and release preload tension of rewind spring as follows: Pull starter rope until notch in pulley half (5) is aligned with rope hole in cover (1). Use thumb pressure to prevent pulley from rotating. Engage rope in notch of pulley and slowly release thumb pressure to allow spring to unwind. Remove retainer screw (11), retainer (10) and spring (6). Remove brake screw (9), brake (8) and starter dog (7). Carefully remove pulley assembly with rope from spring and cover. Note direction of spring winding and carefully remove spring from cover. Unbolt and separate pulley halves (4 and 5) and remove rope.

To reassemble, reverse the disassembly procedure. Then, preload rewind spring as follows: Align notch in

Fig. TE18 — Exploded view of typical dog type rewind starter assembly. Some units of similar construction use three starter dogs (7).

1. Cover
2. Rope
3. Rewind spring
4. Pulley half
5. Pulley half & hub
6. Retainer spring
7. Starter dog
8. Brake
9. Brake screw
10. Retainer
11. Retainer screw
12. Hub & screen assy.

pulley with rope hole in cover. Engage rope in notch and rotate pulley two full turns to properly preload the spring.

Pull rope to full extended position. Release handle and if spring is properly preloaded, the rope will fully rewind.

WISCONSIN ROBIN

TELEDYNE WISCONSIN MOTOR
Milwaukee, Wisconsin 53246

HP	Crankshaft	Model	Bore	Stroke	Displacement
4.6	Horizontal	EY18W	2 9/16 in.	2 5/32 in.	11.14 cu. in.
(3.43 kW)			65.1 mm	54.8 mm	182.55 cc

MAINTENANCE

SPARK PLUG. Recommended spark plug is Champion L86, AC 44F, NGK B6HS or equivalent. Electrode gap is 0.020-0.025 inch (0.51-0.635 mm). Tighten spark plug to a torque of 24-27 ft.-lbs. (32.5-36.6 N.m).

CARBURETOR. Mikuni Model BV18H carburetor is used on Model EY18W engine. Refer to Fig. WR1 for exploded view. To adjust idle fuel mixture, gently seat the idle mixture needle (1), then back needle out (counterclockwise) 1½ turns. Main fuel is metered through main jet (19) and is nonadjustable. With engine operating, adjust idle speed stop screw (3) to obtain an idle speed of 1250 rpm. Make final adjustments on idle mixture needle and idle speed stop screw with engine running at normal operating temperature.

To check and adjust float setting, remove jet holder (20) and fuel bowl (17). Place carburetor body on end (on manifold flange) so that float pin is in vertical position. Move float to close inlet needle valve.

NOTE: Needle valve is spring loaded.

Float tab should just contact needle valve pin but should not compress the spring. Using a depth gage, measure distance between body flange and free end of float as shown in Fig. WR2. Distance should be 0.710-0.790 inch (18.03-20.07 mm). If not, bend tab on float lever to obtain correct setting.

GOVERNOR. The mechanical flyweight governor is mounted to and operated by the camshaft gear. See Fig.

Fig. WR3—Exploded view of mechanical governor and linkage.

1. Governor lever shaft
2. Yoke
3. Link spring
4. Carburetor link
5. Thrust sleeve
6. Governor plate
7. Camshaft assy.
8. Flyweights (3 used)
9. Wing nut
10. Stop plate
11. Wave washer
12. Control lever
13. Speed stop screw
14. Governor spring
15. Governor lever
16. Clamp nut
17. Retaining ring

Fig. WR1—Exploded view of Mikuni model BV18H carburetor used on Model EY18W engine.

1. Idle mixture needle
2. Spring
3. Idle speed stop screw
4. Spring
5. Idle jet
6. Carburetor body
7. Throttle plate
8. Throttle shaft
9. Float pin
10. Nozzle
11. Bowl gasket
12. Gasket
13. Inlet needle & seat
14. Choke plate
15. Choke shaft
16. Float
17. Bowl
18. Washer
19. Main jet
20. Jet holder

Fig. WR2—With fuel bowl removed, stand carburetor on manifold flange and measure float setting as shown.

FLOAT HINGE PIN

FLOAT

TAB JUST CONTACTING NEEDLE VALVE

0.710 – 0.790

WR3. Engine speed is controlled by the tension on governor spring (14).

Before attempting to adjust governed speed, synchronize governor linkage as follows: Loosen clamp nut (16) and turn governor lever (15) counterclockwise until carburetor throttle plate is in wide open position. Then, insert screwdriver in slot in end of governor lever shaft (1) and rotate shaft counterclockwise as far as possible. Tighten governor clamp nut.

To adjust for a particular loaded rpm, hook governor spring (14) to control lever (12) and governor lever (15). Start engine, loosen wing nut (9), move control lever (12) counterclockwise and adjust stop screw (13) until the required no-load speed is obtained. If engine is to operate at a fixed speed, tighten wing nut (9). For variable speed operation, do not tighten wing nut.

For the following loaded engine speeds, adjust governor to the following no-load speeds:

Loaded RPM	No Load RPM
1800	2370
2000	2515
2200	2665
2400	2815
2600	2975
2800	3140
3000	3310
3200	3485
3400	3670
3600	3855

MAGNETO AND TIMING. Flywheel type magneto is used and breaker points and condenser are located under flywheel. Initial point gap is 0.014 inch (0.36 mm) See Fig. WR4. To check and adjust engine timing, disconnect lead wire from shut-off switch. Connect a continuity light lead to lead wire and ground other lead to engine. Slowly rotate flywheel in normal direction until light goes out. Immediately stop turning flywheel and check location of timing marks. Timing marks should be aligned as shown in Fig. WR5. If timing mark (M) on flywheel is below timing mark (D), breaker point gap is too large. If mark (M) is above mark (D), breaker point gap is too small. Carefully measure the distance necessary to align the two marks, then remove flywheel and breaker point cover. Changing point gap 0.001 (0.03 mm) will change timing mark (M) position ⅛-inch (3.2 mm). Reassemble and tighten flywheel retaining nut to a torque of 47 ft.-lbs. (63.685 N·m).

LUBRICATION. Crankcase capacity is 1¼ pints. Use SAE 30 oil when operating in temperatures above 40° F, SAE 20 oil in temperatures between 15° F and 40° F and SAE 10W-30 in temperatures below 15° F. Recommended motor oil is API classification SE or SF. An oil dipper attached to the connecting rod cap provides for splash type lubrication.

CRANKCASE BREATHER. A floating poppet type breaker valve is located in the breather plate behind the valve cover plate. A breather tube connects breather into air cleaner. Restricted or faulty breather is indicated when oil seeps from gasket surfaces and oil seals.

REPAIRS

TIGHTENING TORQUES. Recommended tightening torques are as follows:
Spark plug . . . . .27 ft.-lbs. (36.58 N·m)
Connecting rod cap screws . . .14 ft.-lbs. (18.97 N·m)
Cylinder head nuts . . . . .22 ft.-lbs. (29.81 N·m)
Flywheel nut . . . . .47 ft.lbs. (63.69 N·m)
Gear cover cap screws . . . . . . .13 ft.-lbs. (17.62 N·m)

CYLINDER HEAD. Always use a new head gasket when installing cylinder head. Tighten cylinder head nuts evenly in three stages; first to 12 ft.-lbs. (16.26 N·m), then 18 ft.-lbs. (24.39 N·m) and finally 22 ft.-lbs. (29.81 N·m).

CONNECTING ROD. Connecting rod and piston assembly is removed from above after cylinder head and gear cover are removed. Specified connecting rod to crankpin clearance is 0.0021-0.0031 inch (0.053-0.079 mm) with a maximum clearance of 0.005-inch (0.13 mm). Specified rod side clearance is 0.008-0.0235 inch (0.20-0.597 mm) with maximum clearance of 0.039-inch (0.99 mm). Specified connecting rod-to-piston pin clearance is 0.0004-0.0012 inch (0.010-0.030 mm) with a maximum clearance of 0.0032-inch (0.081 mm).

When installing connecting rod and piston assembly, make certain match marks (cast ribs) on connecting rod and cap are together as shown in Fig. WR6. Install oil dipper with offset toward gear cover end of engine if engine is to be operated on a tilt toward take-off end. Mount dipper with offset toward flywheel end if operated on a tilt in that direction or with no tilt operation. Use a new lock plate and tighten connecting rod cap screws to a torque of 14 ft.lbs. (18.97 N·m).

PISTON, PIN AND RINGS. Piston is equipped with one compression ring, one scraper ring and one oil control ring. Install rings as shown in Fig. WR7.

Fig. WR4 — View showing flywheel magneto. Flywheel and breaker cover are removed.

Fig. WR5 — 23 degrees BTDC timing mark (M) on flywheel aligned with timing mark (D) on crankcase.

CONNECTING ROD

CAST RIBS

CAP

LOCK PLATE TAB

OIL DIPPER (toward flywheel end)
Mount toward gear cover if operating
tilt is toward take-off end.

Fig. WR6—Connecting rod and cap must be installed with cast ribs together.

Specified ring end gap is 0.002-0.010 inch (0.05-0.25 mm). Specified piston ring side clearance in piston grooves is 0.0004-0.003 inch (0.010-0.08 mm). Stagger ring end gaps 90 degrees apart around piston.

Recommended piston-to-cylinder bore clearance (measured at thrust face of piston) is 0.0016-0.0032 inch (0.041-0.081 mm). Standard piston diameter at skirt thrust face is 2.5567-2.5575 inch (64.940-64.961 mm).

Pistons and piston rings are available in standard size as well as oversizes of 0.010 inch (0.25 mm) and 0.020 inch (0.51 mm).

Standard piston pin diameter is 0.5509-0.5512 inch (13.993-14.000 mm). Piston pin-to-piston fit is 0.00035-inch (0.0090 mm) tight to 0.00039-inch (0.0100mm) loose with a maximum clearance of 0.0023-inch (0.058 mm) loose. Specified piston pin-to-connecting rod clearance is 0.0004-0.0012 inch (0.010-0.030 mm) with a maximum clearance of 0.0032 inch (0.081 mm).

CYLINDER BLOCK. If cylinder wall is scored, out-of-round more than 0.003-inch (0.08 mm) or tapered more than 0.006-inch (0.15 mm), bore and/or hone cylinder to nearest suitable oversize of 0.010-inch (0.25 mm) or 0.020-inch (0.51 mm). Standard cylinder bore is 2.5519-2.5599 inch (64.818-65.021 mm).

CAMSHAFT. Camshaft rides in bores in crankcase and gear cover. When removing camshaft assembly, lay engine on side to prevent tappets from falling out. If valve tappets are removed, identify them so they can be reinstalled in their original position. Valve tappets have an operating clearance in crankcase bores of

0.001-0.0024 inch (0.03-0.061 mm) with a maximum clearance of 0.004-inch (0.10 mm). Camshaft journal diameter is 0.5889-0.5893 inch (14.958-14.968 mm).

When reinstalling camshaft, install governor thrust sleeve (5–Fig. WR3) on governor flyweights, then slide cam-

Fig. WR7—Install piston rings as shown.

COMPRESSION RING

SCRAPER RING

OIL RING

Fig. WR8—Crankshaft end play is controlled by adjusting collar. Refer to text for procedure to determine the length of collar.

B

CRANKSHAFT

MAIN BEARING

ADJUSTING COLLAR

CRANK GEAR

C

A

shaft into position. Make certain that the marked tooth on crankshaft gear is between the two marked teeth on camshaft gear.

CRANKSHAFT. Crankshaft is supported in two ball bearings. Renew bearings if any indication of roughness, noise or excessive wear is found. Crankshaft end play of 0.001-0.009 inch (0.03-0.23 mm) is controlled by the adjusting collar located between crankshaft gear and gear cover main bearing. See Fig. WR8. Three different lengths of adjusting collars are available: 0.701-0.709 inch (17.81-18.01 mm), 0.709-0.717 inch (17.81-18.21 mm) and 0.717-0.725 inch (17.81-18.42 mm). To determine correct length of adjusting collar with gear cover removed, proceed as follows: Measure distance (A–Fig. WR8) between machined surface of crankcase face and end of crankshaft gear. Measure distance (B) between machined surface of gear cover and end of main bearing. Compressed thickness of gear cover gasket (C) is 0.007-inch (0.18 mm). Select adjusting collar that is 0.001-0.009 inch (0.03-0.23 mm) less in length than the total of A, B and C.

After reassembly, check crankshaft end play with a dial indicator.

Standard crankpin diameter is 1.0210-1.0215 inch (25.933-25.946 mm). Specified connecting rod to crankpin clearance is 0.0021-0.0031 inch (0.053-0.079 mm) with a maximum clearance of 0.005-inch (0.13 mm). Replace crankshaft if rod clearance is excessive or if crankpin is out-of-round or tapered more than 0.0002-inch (0.005 mm).

When reassembling engine, make certain that marked tooth on crankshaft gear is between the two marked teeth on camshaft gear. When renewing crankshaft oil seals, install seals with lips toward ball bearings.

VALVE SYSTEM. Valve tappet gap (cold) is 0.006-0.008 inch (0.15-0.20 mm). Valve face and seat angle is 45 degrees. Desired seat width is 0.047-0.059 inch (1.19-1.50 mm). Specified valve spring

free length is 1.4173-inch (35.999 mm) with a minimum length of 1.3582-inch (34.498 mm). Stem diameter of intake and exhaust valves is 0.273-0.274 inch (6.93-6.96 mm). Specified valve stem-to-guide clearance is 0.0016-0.0039 inch (0.041-0.099 mm) with a maximum clearance of 0.006-inch (0.15 mm). Inside diameter of new guides is 0.2756-0.2769 inch (7.000-7.033 mm). If stem-to-guide clearance is excessive, renew guides and/or valves.

SERVICING WISCONSIN ROBIN ACCESSORIES

REWIND STARTER

OVERHAUL. To disassemble the rewind starter, refer to Fig. WR9 and release spring tension by pulling rope handle until about 18 inches (45.7 cm) of rope extends from unit. Use thumb pressure against ratchet retainer to prevent reel from rewinding and place rope in notch in outer rim of reel. Release thumb pressure slightly and allow spring mechanism to slowly unwind. Twist loop of return spring and slip loop through slot in ratchet retainer. Refer to Fig. WR10 and remove nut, lock-

washer, plain washer and ratchet retainer. Reel will completely unwind as these parts are removed. Remove compression spring, three ratchets and spring retainer washer. Slip fingers into two of the cavity openings in reel hub (Fig. WR11) and carefully lift reel from support shaft in housing.

CAUTION: Take extreme care that power spring remains in recess of housing. Do not remove spring unless new spring is to be installed.

If power spring escapes from housing, form a 4½ inch (114 mm) I.D. wire ring and twist the ends together securely. Starting with the outside loop, wind spring inside the ring in a counterclockwise direction.

NOTE: New power springs are secured in a similar wire ring for ease in assembly.

Place spring assembly over recess in housing so that hook in outer loop of spring is over the tension tab in housing. Carefully press spring from wire ring and into recess of housing.

Using a new rope of same length and diameter as original, place rope in handle and tie a figure eight knot about 1½ inches (38 mm) from the end. Pull knot into top of handle. Install other end of rope through guide bushing of housing and through hole in reel groove. Pull rope out through cavity opening and tie a slip knot about 2½ inches (64 mm) from end. Place slip knot around center

bushing as shown in Fig. WR12 and pull knot tight. Stuff end of rope into reel cavity. Spread a film of light grease on power spring and support shaft. Wind rope ¼-turn clockwise in reel and place rope in notch on reel. Install reel on support shaft and rotate reel counterclockwise until tang on reel engages hook on inner loop of power spring. Place outer flange of housing in a vise and use finger pressure to keep reel in housing. Then, by means of rope hooked in the reel notch, preload power spring by turning reel 7 full turns counterclockwise.

Fig. WR11—Use fingers in reel hub cavities to lift reel from support shaft.

Fig. WR12—Install rope through guide bushing and hole in reel groove, then tie slip knot around center bushing.

Fig. WR9—View showing method of releasing spring tension on rewind starter assembly.

Fig. WR10—Exploded view of rewind starter assembly used on Wisconsin Robin engines.

Remove rope from notch and allow reel to slowly turn clockwise as rope winds on pulley and handle returns to guide bushing on housing.

Install spring retaining washer (Fig. WR10), cup side up, and place compression spring into cupped washer. Install return spring with bent end hooked into hole of reel hub. Place the three ratchets in position so that they fit the contour of the recesses. Mount ratchet retainer so that loop end of return spring extends through slot. Rotate retainer slightly clockwise until ends of slots just begin to engage the three ratchets. Press down on retainer, install flat washer, lockwasher and nut, then tighten nut securely.

THIS BOOK WAS

PURCHASED

BY

GOLDEN PLAINS

LIBRARY

FEDERATION